AMERICAN DAREDEVIL

AMERICAN DAREDEVIL

THE EXTRAORDINARY LIFE OF RICHARD HALLIBURTON, THE WORLD'S FIRST CELEBRITY TRAVEL WRITER

Cathryn J. Prince

CHICAGO
REVIEW
PRESS

Published by Chicago Review Press Incorporated
814 North Franklin Street
Chicago, Illinois 60610
ISBN 978-1-61373-159-8

Library of Congress Cataloging-in-Publication Data
Names: Prince, Cathryn J., 1969– author.
Title: The extraordinary life of Richard Halliburton, the world's first
    celebrity travel writer / Cathryn J. Prince.
Description: Chicago, Illinois : American Daredevil, [2016] | Includes
    bibliographical references and index.
Identifiers: LCCN 2016006134 (print) | LCCN 2016012295 (ebook) | ISBN
    9781613731598 | ISBN 9781613731611 (PDF edition) | ISBN 9781613731628
    (EPUB edition) | ISBN 9781613731604 (Kindle edition)
Subjects: LCSH: Halliburton, Richard, 1900–1939. | Travel writers—United
    States—Biography. | Travelers—United States—Biography. | Voyages and
    travels.
Classification: LCC G226.H3 P75 2016 (print) | LCC G226.H3 (ebook) | DDC
    910.4092—dc23
LC record available at http://lccn.loc.gov/2016006134

Interior design: Nord Compo
Map design: Chris Erichsen
Printed in the United States of America
5 4 3 2 1

For Pierre and Nathan and Zoë

Contents

1

Wanderlust

T HE FAIR-HAIRED YOUNG MAN shivered against the cold, despite wearing three sweaters and two pairs of pants. The sky, no longer ashen, stretched a deep blue above the North Sea. The explosion of icy sprays that had drenched the deck of the steel cargo boat for the better part of the transatlantic crossing had finally stopped. "Our portholes are fifteen feet above the water, yet only for the last two days they have been open, as the waves have smacked against them unceasingly," wrote twenty-one-year-old Richard Halliburton from aboard the *Ipswich* in July 1921.[1]

The smell of grease and grime seeped through the *Ipswich*. It permeated everyone's clothes with a mechanical stench. Halliburton didn't mind; there was no place he would rather be. Standing watch on the bridge, he hoped to be the first to sight land.

Thousands of miles away in Memphis, Tennessee, in Halliburton's boyhood room, stacks of geography and adventure books filled the bookcases. For years, the stories like those recounted in his well-thumbed *Stories of Adventure* transported him far from Tennessee. He had tilted at windmills alongside Don Quixote and slain dragons alongside St. George. With his light blue bound geography book as his magic carpet, he had virtually visited every country in Europe and most in Asia.[2]

Reading about author Harry Franck's 1913 adventures as a Panama Canal Zone policeman thrilled him, but it also sparked a competitive streak. Halliburton vowed he wouldn't just visit the canal someday, he would swim its length. Reading about Mount Fuji, he swore to scale its peak. Now he stood not just on the bridge of the *Ipswich* but also on the verge of living his dreams. He felt an obligation to his own curiosity, and travel was how he could fulfill that.

Meanwhile, his parents, Wesley and Nelle, waited anxiously for word from their son. Their unease weighed on Richard, and ever mindful of their apprehension, he continued to write home often. On the ship, he clambered down the metal stairs to his cabin and settled his lanky frame on his bunk. He meticulously chronicled everything he experienced, smelled, and saw. He wrote home about his impressions of people and places, and confided his angst and excitement. Halliburton stuffed the unfinished letter into his canvas knapsack, which held maps, a compass, a few changes of clothing, paper, and pens. He would post the letter as soon as the ship reached its port of call in Hamburg, Germany. He liked picturing his parents sitting in their living room and slicing open another one of his envelopes.

On July 19, 1898, Wesley Halliburton, twenty-eight, took Nelle Nance, twenty-nine, as his wife in a small ceremony at the Methodist Church in Brownsville, Tennessee, just fifty miles north of Memphis. They would enjoy fifty-three years of marriage. However, by Wesley's account, he wasn't desperately in love with Nelle when he walked her down the aisle. They balanced each other and grew to depend on one another. Time burnished their feelings to a deep admiration and love.[3]

Two years later, on January 9, 1900, Richard Halliburton was born in an old redbrick house. When Richard was still an infant, his parents moved to Memphis, a segregated city, where cotton was king and juke joints lined Beale Street. Wesley hoped to make money buying and selling land in east Arkansas, but the land didn't sell. Then, just when Wesley and Nelle decided to pack it in and move back to Brownsville, some timber on the property sold. It was a fine reversal of fortune.[4] The three then moved into the Parkview, a ten-story apartment building on Poplar Avenue. Now a retirement home, the same copper awning still juts forth, aged to a mint-green patina, and large floor-to-ceiling windows line the first floor. Just steps from leafy Overton Park, the building perfectly suited the young couple with baby in tow.

Intellectually curious, the couple adored traveling and infused their son with a quest for knowledge. They were an upper middle-class couple, both coming from solid families.[5] Wesley Halliburton Sr. was of Scottish ancestry. The name Halliburton traced to an ancestor named Burton who built a chapel for his village in Scotland, and thereafter became known as "Holy Burton," which eventually evolved into Halliburton. An avid outdoorsman, Wesley had a penchant for hiking. In 1891 he graduated from Vanderbilt University with a degree in civil engineering.

French Huguenot and Scottish blood ran through Nelle Nance. She had graduated from the Cincinnati College of Music and taught music at a women's college in Memphis. Always active in her community, be it sitting on a committee or chaperoning a clutch of girls to a symphony or a trip to Europe, Nelle served as the Memphis chapter's president of the Nineteenth Century Club, a philanthropic and cultural women's club. Many notable people passed through the double doors of this classic redbrick building with fluted columns. A gracious lady, as Halliburton's friends described her, Nelle appreciated social standing and the importance of connecting with people, traits her son would share. Wesley Halliburton, too, displayed the "stuff of which his illustrious son was made," his own curiosity about the world that was reflected in his oldest son.[6]

Halliburton had no living grandparents. The closest he had to extended family was Mary Grimes Hutchison, dean of the all-girls day school he attended. Indeed, Richard Halliburton was the only boy ever admitted to the college preparatory school. While his parents called Mary "Hutchie," Halliburton nicknamed her Ammudder—his way of saying "another mother"—when he was small. Throughout his life, he frequently wrote to her. She remained a constant and nurturing presence. Acting the doting grandmother, Hutchison often tucked money into her letters, always asking after him, spoiling him.

On May 31, 1903, Wesley and Nelle welcomed Wesley Jr., and the small family was now complete. With their fair hair, brown eyes, and lanky limbs, the brothers thoroughly resembled each other in looks, if not temperament. Whereas Richard was a mediocre violinist and a keen golfer, his brother favored baseball. Whereas Richard was outgoing, his younger brother was more reserved.

Brothers Richard and Wesley Jr. were three years apart. *Princeton University Library*

Throughout his early childhood, Halliburton's most trusted companions were a pony called Roxy and his dog Teddy. Teddy padded behind Halliburton on his way to track, baseball, and football—and often outdoors to explore.

Loving parents, Wesley and Nelle encouraged their boys to be interested and interesting. The family of four often traveled, and young Richard saw a world beyond the borders of the southern city. One of his most exciting moments was his first trip to Washington, DC, when he was fifteen. "Woodrow Wilson was then President, and to my vast delight, as a special favor, I was taken to the White House, right into the President's office, and introduced to him. My fingers trembled a little when we shook hands . . . to me he was the greatest man in the world. He was the *President.*"[7] Richard also especially relished time spent at the Biltmore Hotel in Asheville, North Carolina, where nearby he and his father hiked the low rolling hills and rambled along trails in the Pisgah National Forest. Richard Halliburton desperately wanted to strengthen his slight frame.

Unexplained health problems beset Halliburton from a very young age but came into full force when he was about fifteen. He tended to get breathless and fatigued. He tried to ignore his racing heartbeat. He frequently watched his friends from the sidelines. His malady perplexed and worried his parents. They often reminded their elder son to take it easy, and at one point the adolescent spent four months in bed. Still his health showed no improvement.

The thought of living a cautious life vexed young Halliburton, who, though quiet on the surface, fancied danger. When he was just five years old, a runaway pony dragged him several yards. Nelle recalled feeling petrified her little boy would die. But afterward the little boy was not only calm, he acted as if being dragged by a pony was as normal as being pulled along in a little red wagon. "After that wild ride his life was one escapade after another. Even in play, only the dangerous things appealed to him," she recalled.[8]

The Halliburton family doctor recommended that the sick teenager seek treatment at the famous Battle Creek Sanitarium, so the Halliburtons drove their son to Michigan. There, doctors treated him for probable tachycardia and an overactive thyroid.

Dr. John Harvey Kellogg and his brother William Keith Kellogg had opened the Battle Creek Sanitarium in 1866. The institution's treatments included low-fat, low-protein diets, exercise, cold-air cures, and hydrotherapy. The Kellogg brothers modeled their new sanitarium after European spas with their water cures and mineral baths. In time, the sprawling complex in America's heartland was a place to which the rich and famous retreated to get well. Celebrated American figures including Mary Todd Lincoln, Amelia Earhart, President Warren Harding, and Henry Ford all spent time at the facility for various ailments, physical and mental. Years after Halliburton's successful stay there, his parents returned to the sanitarium to rest and diet on and off for thirty-seven years.[9]

The exercise—including swimming, calisthenics, and gymnastics, coupled with rest—seemed to help Halliburton. And being away from home for the first time did nothing to curb his taste for independence; instead, his stay at Battle Creek whetted his appetite for adventure. Lying awake on his thin mattress each night, Halliburton fantasized about floating down the Mekong River in Indochina and living as Robinson Crusoe on a deserted island. In his dreams, he was Joseph Conrad penetrating the Heart of Darkness or the poet Rupert Brooke writing of war, youth, and longing.

He pondered his future and realized he wanted a different life from his father. Rather than enroll in nearby Memphis University School and then matriculate at Vanderbilt University, as his parents expected and as two generations of Halliburtons had before him, Richard yearned to attend Princeton University. He begged his parents to let him go to New Jersey and enroll in Lawrenceville Academy, an all-boys boarding school. This would increase his chances of being accepted to nearby Princeton. He had met other young teens at Battle Creek who attended Lawrenceville, and their love and loyalty to the school impressed him. He had to attend, he told his parents. He craved that sense of brotherhood, so with his parents' blessing Richard enrolled in 1916.[10]

Lawrenceville Academy may not have been Halliburton's idea of a wonderland—it had rules, after all—but nevertheless, he delighted in his newly won independence and earned excellent grades. During his years there, he became editor-in-chief of the school's newspaper, the *Lawrence*, and was chosen to write the words and music for the class ode. He made fast friends with Irvine "Mike" Hockaday, John Henry "Heinie" Leh, and James Penfield Seiberling of Akron, Ohio, who was the son of F. A. Seiberling, founder of the Goodyear Tire and Rubber Company. Everyone called Seiberling "Shorty," and Edward L. Keyes, the son of a New York physician, became "Larry." Channing Sweet was "Chan" and Halliburton became "Dick" to his friends. These were lifelong friendships in the making.

Each year about fifty Lawrenceville students went on to Princeton University. In the fall of 1917 Halliburton and his friends were admitted to the prestigious institution and moved six miles down the road into a large suite inside the stately dormitory at 41 Patton Hall. During their first year, the friends resolved to write an annual Christmas letter as a way to reflect on the year past and look forward to the next. They maintained the tradition well into the 1960s.[11]

"As young men in the prime of health, we were energetic, robust, zestful individuals, but otherwise quite dissimilar with respect to talents and tastes," Seiberling recalled many years later. "For the most part we each engaged in developing our own special aptitudes and in pursuing our own particular interests."[12] Of the six of them, Halliburton was undoubtedly the most exceptional, Seiberling said. He had a fine intelligence and active mind. He was alert, inquiring, imaginative, and inventive.[13]

Halliburton had started writing at Lawrenceville—short stories, poems, and essays—and continued at Princeton. He worked on the *Daily Princetonian* newspaper and the *Princeton Pictorial Magazine*, a.k.a. the *Pic*, a publication featuring student essays and photographs. A quote from Oscar Wilde's *The Picture of Dorian Gray* inspired him: "Realize your youth while you have it. . . . Don't squander the gold of your days." For the young Halliburton, following a corporate path would be to squander the gold of his days. The notion itself was stultifying. An idea germinated in Halliburton's mind: perhaps his future lay in writing.

When Halliburton left for Princeton, his younger brother, Wesley Jr., took his spot at Lawrenceville. Three years younger, Wesley Jr. was the quintessential kid brother. He idolized Richard and bounded after him with exuberance. Devoted to baseball, Wesley Jr. always kept his well-oiled mitt buckled to his belt. Richard was proud of his brother, and the family of four delighted in each other's company.

Then in November 1917 their world irrevocably fractured. Wesley Jr. fell ill. A few weeks before the long winter recess, he complained of a sore throat. Soon a fever, cough, and chest pains wracked his young body. After a few days in the Lawrenceville boarding school infirmary, he was taken to Mercer Hospital. Two weeks later his parents raced to bring him home to Memphis. The brick Tudor house with its large front door and portico became an infirmary. Nelle cared for Wesley Jr. as best she could; he was showing signs of rheumatic fever.

The boy grew weaker daily. Without access to the antibiotics that would someday effectively treat the illness, complications ensued. His heart valves thickened and scarred. Constant and intense pain seized the boy.[14] Nelle and Wesley Sr. called for Richard, who hurried home from Princeton. For several days, the family huddled around young Wesley. Though the windows and doors were closed against the Memphis chill, death, uninvited, found its way inside, as death will do.

Less than five weeks after his parents picked him up from Lawrenceville and tucked him into his childhood bed, fifteen-year-old Wesley Jr. died in his father's arms. And so was plucked a thread of the close-knit family. It was dawn on January 1, 1918.

Devastated, Richard returned to Princeton in January just before the second semester got underway. He clipped his brother's obituary from the pages of Lawrenceville's newspaper and neatly pasted it in his black leather-bound scrapbook.[15] Shortly before the anniversary of his brother's death, Halliburton would return to Lawrenceville for a look at the dormitory room his brother had called home for only two months.[16]

He wrote his suffering parents at least once a week, and his father responded every Sunday, to "aid him in building up an ambition plan for his life."[17] Richard was always pleased when he saw one of the envelopes bearing his parents' familiar handwriting.[18] The letters tethered Halliburton as he set about navigating his way through grief. "Dear Mother: —I've thought of nothing else but my last week home. I try to think of something else, but it's no use. I've tried to read, but I forget to read. . . . I know just how lonesome and sad you are—I know it is much worse now than before I left," Halliburton wrote. "I never in my life hated absence from home as I do now. Someway the longer time elapses from New Year's dawn, the more terrible and unjust it seems. I know I did not comprehend that Wesley was *gone, actually*, but the more I think about it the more realistic it grows, and I, too, have that 'sinking feeling.'"[19]

Richard knew his schoolwork and his friends would eventually distract him from his grief, but he felt for his parents, who were living in a house amid recollections of their second born. The Halliburtons wrapped their grief around them like a shawl. In time they entered the world again, attending lectures and touring Europe and the Middle East. However uneasy they might have been at the thought of their surviving son living far away, they would offer him their full support. Still, whenever someone knocked on the door of the Halliburtons' Memphis home or delivered a telegram, the two parents sometimes feared it was the worst sort of news—that their firstborn son was dead.

If Wesley Jr.'s death compelled the Halliburtons to clasp their surviving son ever closer, it had the opposite effect on Richard. His brother's death impressed upon Halliburton that life could end in an instant, and the only way to quell his growing "inner turmoil" was to run toward the future. He often wrote home of wanting to fight in World War I, or what he called "the Big Show."[20] Many of his older classmates had already traded the campus's Revolutionary War–scarred Nassau Hall for the newly scarred battlefields of Europe. He and Hockaday decided the

US Navy offered the surest route to a life of high adventure, and so he enrolled in Princeton University's naval courses in ordnance, gunnery, navigation, and seamanship.

At eighteen, he was old enough to fight.[21] Alas, there was to be no action for the young Halliburton. In October 1918, to his exasperation, the university's president announced that only students enlisted in the army would receive commissions. "If I had joined the Army instead of the Navy I would be packing up for a camp and have my leather putts all picked out. It was the last straw when I heard that," he wrote. Halliburton tried to stuff his feelings of frustration away, but the pace of navy classes and drills maddened him. "We are too inactive here, too much leisure time, not enough drill," he wrote.[22] He and Hockaday bought uniforms, attended a school-organized training camp, and prayed nightly for their chance to ship out. Armistice came before he and his eager classmates could taste combat. Feeling caged, he inked zigzag lines over a map of Europe, creating a spiderweb of places he planned to visit.

That Halliburton didn't fight in World War I spared him in ways he didn't realize. Fortunate not to have had mustard gas blister his lungs, nor to have seen close friends fall in the sucking mud of the trenches, he escaped the disillusionment and cynicism that befell other writers of his generation. And so he chased a different type of adventure: adventure writing.

Romancing the road was not what the Halliburtons envisioned for their son while he was still a student. Wesley wanted Richard to live a straightforward, uncomplicated life. Nevertheless, Richard decided to test the waters, and so in the summer of 1919 he ran away from school to New Orleans and boarded the freight ship *Octorara*. During the passage to England he took to the manual labor, scraping paint, cleaning brushes, and lifting and stacking sugar barrels. Mingling with the tattooed and wrinkled sailors aboard, he grew addicted to their stories. He particularly relished an open-cockpit flight across the English Channel in a Handley

Page aircraft. Though he resumed his studies in September 1920, the trip only inflamed his passion for travel; Richard had been able to see many historical haunts in London and France.

"When impulse and spontaneity fail to make my way as uneven as possible then shall I set up nights inventing means of making life as conglomerate and vivid as possible," Halliburton wrote his father in answer to a letter that he live life in an "even tenor."[23] As always, theirs was a close relationship, but in this they most assuredly did not agree. Indeed, every time his father spoke to him about choosing a steady career and finding a suitable wife, he bristled. At nineteen, Richard was certain he would never settle down and live a conservative life, no matter how many of his friends did exactly that. He had explained this many times to his father.

After his stint on the *Octorara*, the boyishly handsome Halliburton, with his infectious grin, reluctantly returned to Princeton and discovered what little interest he had left for schoolwork extinguished. More often than not he slammed a textbook closed and stared out the window. He preferred socializing in his eating club, the prestigious Cap and Gown, drinking with his buddies and trying his luck in handball tournaments—once he even won the beer-mug trophy. The previous year he'd been elected to the board of the *Daily Princetonian*. The position allowed him a regular outlet to write and sharpen his skills. Eight students had competed for the position, and Halliburton was overjoyed when the board selected him based not only on the quantity but also the quality of his stories.

The demands of the *Daily Princetonian* soon pressed on Halliburton. So consumed was he with his editorial responsibilities that he neglected his studies, barely finding time to squeeze in his Shakespeare, Oriental literature, French, and nineteenth-century poetry. His new job introduced him to the business side of writing, soliciting, and marketing. He excelled at all three. For the *Prince*, he wrote about pushing to increase subscriptions from three hundred to one thousand.[24]

Still, Halliburton grew restless and glum. There were fleeting signs of depression. His bouts of melancholy left him "mentally depressed, restless, and then morbid."[25] He sometimes found himself in tears with frustration. His heart had never been so heavy than when Wesley Jr. died. He just wanted to leave. He craved action and freedom. "Life is not life if it's just routine, it's only existence and marking time till death comes to divorce us from it all," he wrote. While he lived, he wanted to live. He couldn't wait to bust loose from school and let his "restless, discontented spirit run its course." He thought about shoving his desk through the window and becoming a wild man. "I've got in the habit of running instead of walking. Something keeps saying faster, faster—move!"[26]

Halliburton desired an extraordinary life, and travel was his ticket to experience the limitless horizons beyond. In 1920 he, Hockaday, Leh, and Seiberling had visited Montana's Glacier National Park. They hired two Native American guides and spent their days fishing, hiking, and riding horses. He wrote about their trip and *Field & Stream* published the article, "The Happy Hunting Ground," and paid him one hundred dollars.[27] He was hooked. He couldn't stop thinking about seeing his byline and his work in print once again. He planned to turn his future adventures into a book.[28] Later critics would chastise Halliburton for what they perceived as the work of an impulsive, childlike individual, but his early letters showed he pursued his career with intent and purpose.

"And I've a picture of my book—a great melting pot of history, literature, personal autobiography, humor, drawings, paintings, photographs, pathos, romance, adventure, comedy, tragedy, all branching off, but an integral part of the most vivid narrative of real experiences of a very live, open-eyed and sympathetic young man on an unconventional and originally executed circumnavigation of the globe, all bound up in a large and richly covered volume with *Wanderlust* in big gilt letters across the front! There!"[29]

The little town of Princeton bloomed in the soft air of spring. Students studying for final exams sprawled on the quadrangle. Gentle breezes rustled the trees like whispers. Gardeners busied themselves nursing the lawns, plucking weeds, reseeding bare spots, and pruning dead branches. Groundskeepers retouched the peeling paint on eaves and pulled sagging wire fences taut.[30]

Knowing graduation was a mere two months away put Halliburton in a contemplative mood. Rather than reach for his fountain pen, as he normally did, he typed a long letter to his parents. He felt utterly lost now, with little to do aside from prepare for his finals. It was, he remarked, the first time since September he had been able to sit down and write his parents a letter about more than his daily routine.[31] He also directly addressed his father: "I read with interest your paragraph on finding one's self. 'The small voice' you taught me to listen to has worked, I think, and I feel sure, if self confidence and self sufficiency (the two things I've gained in four years) count for anything, I'll find myself out of this trip I'm soon to take. I think about it many times each day. I study the maps and the cities and the places on the maps and am building up a trip in my imagination."[32]

As Halliburton watched the buzz of activity around campus, he wondered whether his four years at Princeton made him a better man, or whether he had squandered his time. While he took biology, geology, math, philosophy, astronomy, architecture, and chemistry, he felt less than proficient in any of them. And aside from French, he knew no foreign language.[33] He felt strongest about his course work in history and European and American modern painting. Decades later, Wesley remembered advising his son about what to do after graduation. "I told him to try out a plan. Quit talking to anyone about it. Then at night, and alone, get on the outside away from the street and people and fill his mind with the subject of what do I *want* to do? I believed the still small voice within each of us would tell him what he *wanted* to do. He did just that and in a couple of months it came to him. The voice spoke to him and it was right."[34]

As school drew to an end, Halliburton thought a lot about his younger brother, dead three years now. On May 31, 1921, Wesley Jr.'s birthday, Halliburton wrote to his mother. "Year by year we drift farther away from the time when he was such a vital part of our family, when

it was impossible to contemplate the four of us being ever any more or
any less, but the succeeding years can never dim the memory of him as
he was at fifteen. He will still be so when we are old. He would have
been nineteen today, almost grown and moulded. We can remember
him always only as a fine-looking curly-haired youth. I always think
about you, Mother, on May thirty-first and I love you more that day.
Well, I do not believe he would have us despond because he is dead,
but he would have us love his memory."[35]

And now there was no more time for second-guessing. In June 1921
Halliburton flung open the windows of the dorm room he shared with
his best friends. A breeze fluttered through the room. He packed away
his black cap and gown. He was as ecstatic to leave 41 Patton Hall as
he had been to arrive.

He and his friends left the quadrangle with its broad-leafed trees
and blossoms. His friends would soon fill "the prosaic mold" into which
they'd been poured.[36] Larry Keyes planned a medical career. John Leh
had studied accounting; he was moving from the dormitory to work in
his father's department store. Chan Sweet became a livestock rancher.
After studying corporate finance, James Penfield Seiberling readied for a
career in selling bonds. All six men would remain in touch throughout
their lives, visiting each other whenever and wherever possible, exchanging letters, phone calls, and photographs. Halliburton visited Akron
on more than one occasion and stayed with the Seiberling family. "It
was a sign of how well these men—thought of each other and how
much they treated each other as brothers that my mother and likely my
uncle . . . referred to them as 'Uncle Larry, Uncle Mike, Uncle Heinie,
Uncle Dick' throughout their own lives," said Cathy Pond, Seiberling's
granddaughter.[37]

Pond recalled how one of her grandfather's many personal letters—dictated, multi-paged, and single-space typed on an IBM Selec-
tric—waited for her in her mailbox when she arrived at college. In it,
Seiberling advised his granddaughter on many things, but above all he
hoped she would find the friendships, and maintain them through the
years, as he had done with his five Princeton roommates.

Apart from his job, Leh was also headed to the altar. In Halliburton's eyes, marriage was akin to slavery. "No fear about my jumping over the broomstick soon," he once wrote home to his father, continuing their perpetual argument about societal expectations.[38] His father countered that a bachelor is nothing more than a selfish egoist. Richard responded that someone is selfish or not by the time he is twenty-one, and marrying would not change him.

And so it was that Halliburton, the student whose fellow classmates voted "most original,"[39] left for New York City. After selling their dorm furniture for cash, he and Hockaday virtually ran from the dorm across campus to the train station. Having made peace with their initial disappointment over their son's intended vocation, Halliburton's mother met the boys in New York City, an ambassador of parental support.[40] Hockaday's parents, knowing he would be home in a few months, had not made the trip to see him off.[41] However, they were most enthusiastic about him going with Halliburton, thinking their son's meticulous nature would prove a necessary counterpoint to Halliburton's "wild imagination and reckless energy."[42]

Halliburton was eager to prove he could make a go of it with little money. After all, the American travel writer Harry Franck had left the University of Michigan in 1900 to vagabond around the world with only $3.18 in his pocket.[43] If Franck could do it, Halliburton thought, so could he. Halliburton and Hockaday headed down to the docks, hoping to find work on a freighter bound for Europe. Any last-minute self-doubts Halliburton harbored about whether he was a better man for school or if it had been a waste of time evaporated in the face of adventure.[44] "Dad, you say that in college I have learned 'to think and analyze and apply thought and analysis to working out my problems.' I hope I have. I get very blue at times because I realize I don't think and analyze, but depend on an impetuous but irrepressibly energetic force to carry me along. I always get there, though upside down sometimes."[45]

Four days after roaming the docks in search of a berth, the young men realized their Princeton diplomas were most certainly not a passepartout for European-bound freight ships. The heat from the concrete seared through the soles of their shoes as ship agent after ship agent turned them down. In their view, the newly minted Ivy League graduates belonged on a ship with shuffleboard decks and striped canvas sun chairs, not shoveling coal into furnaces or swabbing decks.

"In desperation Irvine and I attempted a new method of attack. We gave each other 'soup bowl' hair-cuts, arrayed ourselves in green flannel shirts, and talking as salty as possible descended upon the captain of the *Ipswich*," Halliburton wrote.[46]

After shipping agents rejected the pair more times than they cared to admit, the friends bumped into a family acquaintance of the Hockadays on the sidewalk. In an instant, Sam Pryor changed the young men's luck. As the director of the American Ship and Commerce Corporation, Pryor's father had the right connections. He told the two to present his smartly embossed calling card at the office of W. Averell Harriman, director of the Hamburg American Line.[47] When Halliburton and Hockaday entered the well-appointed office, Harriman reached across his expansive mahogany desk and picked up the phone. By the time he returned the phone to its cradle, Captain R. W. Tucker of the *Ipswich* had agreed to meet with the two young men.[48]

Tucker rolled his eyes when the pair claimed that walking around the Big Apple was the first time they'd stepped on land in twenty-one years, but he signed them on all the same. They would earn fifteen dollars for their work during the crossing, and it wouldn't be light work. They'd have to clean, scrub, paint, and polish.[49] No slacking for the college grads. Eager to work as a deckhand, Halliburton also persuaded Tucker to let the two of them earn extra money serving as lookouts for land. The idea of calling out "Land ho!" tickled Halliburton.

Planning ahead for when they arrived in Europe, Halliburton and Hockaday reached out to Princeton classmate Bernhard Schaefer, who introduced them to his father, J. L. Schaefer, vice president and director of W. R. Grace and Company. Schaefer gave the two a pack of letters introducing them to W. R. Grace offices in more than a dozen foreign ports. "We are attempting to work our way around the world, and you may judge from that what great value your very kind favor is to us."[50]

The letters provided the proper introductions to shipping officials in India, Singapore, and Japan.

On the morning of July 16, Richard stopped to send a Western Union telegram home to his father: "Sailing in an hour. Got your letter just in time. Mother saw me at noon. She is leaving for home Monday night. Will cable from Hamburg. We are all set for anything. Love and goodbye Richard."[51]

Like Keystone Cops, the pair made quite an entrance the morning they boarded. Hockaday had secreted a packet of Mothersill's seasick pills inside his canvas knapsack. While climbing the ladder, he stumbled and dropped his bag, sending the small pills skittering across the deck. Mortified, Hockaday couldn't scoop them up fast enough. Halliburton stifled a chuckle. The crew, which Halliburton later learned included a Yale junior and several high school graduates, watched with amusement as the pair went to their assigned cabin.

Finally the *Ipswich* weighed anchor and left New York. Halliburton already had a deep appreciation for New York City. Later he would write, "If an inhabitant from another world should come to our earth to visit us, which city would most interest and astonish him? . . . I'm sure it would be New York. He would admire the grace and loveliness of Paris. He would respect London's solidarity and grey dignity. He would write home about Constantinople's matchless location, and Rio de Janeiro's gorgeous harbor. . . . And there's the Statue of Liberty, far bigger and more beautiful than its pictures."[52]

The *Ipswich* sailed down the Hudson River and out into the Atlantic. Halliburton bid adieu to the Statue of Liberty as the crenulated skyline slipped away, and the ship set on a northerly course.[53]

In spite of the sun, the brittle cold pricked his fingers as he leaned against the deck's railing. There was no way Halliburton was going to stay topside to write. He clambered down to the cabin he shared with Mike Hockaday. Hockaday had knocked off work early again to lie down. Green with seasickness, he couldn't stop vomiting. Halliburton too felt queasy. Other than oatmeal, he had eaten nothing for the past several meals. Still, he didn't feel ill enough to crawl under the scratchy woolen blanket, and even if he did, he didn't feel he had a moment to spare. *Hurry, hurry* was Halliburton's mantra.

Time pressed upon Halliburton. He aimed to write five hundred thousand words by the end of the trip and intended to sell part of his story to the *Atlantic Monthly*. Aside from working nine-hour days painting rails and scrubbing decks aboard the sixty-five-hundred-ton boat, he wrote at least a thousand words a day in his brown leather-bound copybook. No matter how bone weary scouring and mopping left him at day's end, he wrote.

Since the *Ipswich* rounded the Great Banks off the coast of Newfoundland, the foghorn had blown incessantly. Now the last wisps of fog lifted and the horn stopped. Halliburton appreciated its silence. Life on the cargo boat gave him plenty of time to think about the shape of his itinerary once in Europe.

Halliburton wanted his readers to feel they were along for the ride. He would sail to the Isle of Skyros to visit the grave of the English poet Rupert Brooke, who on his way to serve in the Dardanelles during World War I had died from sepsis aboard a French hospital ship. He yearned to visit Château de Chillon near Montreux, Switzerland, and gaze upon the same gray ramparts that inspired Lord Byron's "Prisoner of Chillon." Like Odysseus in in Homer's *Odyssey*—whom Halliburton preferred to call by his Roman name, Ulysses—Halliburton dreamed of sailing up the Dardanelles to what was then Constantinople and swim against the fierce current of Hellespont in northeastern Turkey. He fantasized about climbing Mount Fuji in the winter—something no American had ever done. And of course it would be a sin to leave North Africa without dipping into the Nile, or part from Asia without gazing upon the Taj Mahal or swimming in one of its mirror-like pools.

Halliburton knew Hockaday considered their trip a long, well-deserved holiday. For the Missourian, it was a last hurrah before settling into a banking career, marrying, and having children. Not so for Halliburton. This trip was the start of his writing career, and he honestly didn't know, or care, when he would go home again. "I do not contemplate with pleasure the difficulties that are sure to come between Mike and me and to end in unavoidable separation. My trip is my occupation in life. I've 'gone to work.' My aim is proficiency in my present task, not to get through on a certain date. It's going to be 'speed up' from Mike and 'slow down and stop' from me. It's unfortunate, but inevitable," he wrote home.[54]

Halliburton recoiled at the thought of spending eight hours a day in an office where secretaries fetched coffee and the only sun he would feel on his face would come through a narrow plate glass window. "I revolt at the idea of being a bank clerk or any other sort of 'beginning at the bottom.' I'm going to be my own boss from the first whatever I do. I can't work for anybody else and not have the reins. I'll never be happy or progressive that way," he'd told his father.[55]

He wanted to earn his own way. Before Richard left, his father had come around to his son's plan and showed C. P. J. Mooney, the editor of the *Memphis Commercial Appeal*, his son's work, including the *Field & Stream* article. Mooney thought the work solid and warmed to the idea of a local son becoming a foreign correspondent of sorts. He agreed to buy Halliburton's articles at thirty-five dollars each. But until he sold his first article, Halliburton would have to rely on an allowance of one hundred dollars a month.

Now, six weeks after leaving New York and close to making landfall, Halliburton felt validated that he and Hockaday had declined their parents' offer of sailing overseas aboard a luxurious liner. He abhorred the idea of checking into a well-appointed hotel and waiting for his soup du jour to cool enough to eat. He loved how he had crammed everything he needed, or thought he needed, into one canvas knapsack. He made sure he had plenty of paper and pens and pencils to document his voyage, and he had packed his camera and several rolls of film.

He was about to start writing "about the world as it is, and as I see it."[56] He hungered for the romance of the sea and foreign ports. He couldn't wait to reach land and find a boat bound for China, Spain, or the South Sea Isles.

Rather than cross the English Channel, the *Ipswich* sailed around Scotland. Never before had Halliburton been so far north, and he thought it exotic to be in a part of the world where the sun set around eleven o'clock at night. The stars barely had time to spangle the sky before the sun rose again.

On the morning of August 1, the *Ipswich* left the rolling North Sea and steamed up the loden-green Elbe River, past the Kiel Canal into Germany. It was a sweltering hot day. The sun glinted off the water. For the last few hours of the trip, Halliburton leaned on the ship's rail, poised in expectation. He saw brightly colored river excursion boats. People on summer holiday jammed the riverside beer gardens. In spite of growing inflation—for the past few days, the wireless broadcast news of the falling German mark—Hamburg bustled.

Although he shared most of his plans with Hockaday, he kept some of his ideas secret, like possibly swimming Hellespont, which connects Europe with Asia. No American had ever swum that stretch of water, where the current is strong and constant, but he knew he could do it. After all, he had long since shed all signs of frailty. Years of swimming, hiking, and handball had transformed Halliburton into a lean and fit youth who stood five foot nine and weighed about 140 pounds. Tough and persistent, personal tragedy had hardened his emotional resolve. He knew firsthand how death could snatch anyone at any time.

That evening, the ship docked in Hamburg. "Safe Happy Hamburg," he wired home.[57] They spent one more seemingly interminable night aboard the ship. Richard Halliburton itched to stretch his legs, heft his knapsack on his shoulder, and stride down the gangway and onto shore. The future beckoned.

2

Romancing the Road

RICHARD HALLIBURTON AND MIKE Hockaday were thirsty. It had been a long six weeks aboard the *Ipswich*. Anxious for a drink, the pair headed straight to a bar. After long days scrubbing and painting, the travelers were in good shape, although neither would ever be described as robust or intimidating. So when they walked into the dimly lit bar, the other men drinking there looked upon the two as easy prey. No sooner had they ordered a drink than a scuffle ensued. As it happened, the crew from the *Ipswich* walked through the doors just as things were getting testy. They saw that their shipmates needed help and swiftly bailed them out. Halliburton and Hockaday's willingness to work hard and without complaint paid off: the lily-white Princeton boys had earned the respect of the crew.[1]

Afterward, Halliburton and Hockaday registered at the front desk of a nearby hotel the crew had recommended to them. Handed keys to their rooms, they quickly went upstairs, threw their bags on the floor, and went to sleep. They left the hotel the next morning with their hobnailed boots tightly laced. The sun shone brightly, the sky glistened. The two waded into the bustle and confusion of post–World War I Europe. The twenty-one-year-old Halliburton was spellbound.

Still clawing its way out from the war, which had ended just four years earlier, Germany made the two men feel uncomfortable. They had trouble reconciling what Halliburton called Germany's brutality and ferocity in the war with the people's "affability, generosity, and kind-heartedness."[2] A current of angst rippled through the city. Yet even if the devastation of World War I and the hollowed-out looks of many young men affected Halliburton, he didn't give voice to those feelings. He only had eyes for new experiences. He had already decided while sailing across the ocean that he and Hockaday would immerse themselves in the city—first on foot and then on bicycles. They spent seven of the fifteen dollars they'd earned as deckhands on twin bicycles. On a whim they nicknamed the bikes "Otto" and "Ophelia."

This was the first time Halliburton had been in Europe since the time he ran away from Princeton on the *Octorara* in 1919. During that trip, he had walked 140 miles from Manchester to London. As far as he was concerned, the only way to get to know a city was by walking along the sidewalks, sitting in parks and cafes, and stopping to talk with its people.

Now, in 1921, American writers were increasingly taking advantage of the possibilities postwar Europe offered, mining the continent for topics to write about, from the destruction to the rebuilding efforts, from the experiences of the soldiers to what life was like on the home front. Halliburton, who was just starting out, had only the one bylined *Field & Stream* article. While he knew he wanted to trade in romance and adventure, not loss and destruction, he also knew he had a lot of catching up to do. He paced himself, setting a goal of writing at least a thousand words each night. Some nights he barely managed five hundred.[3]

Later that year, Ernest Hemingway arrived in France to live and write. While the two shared a continent on more than one occasion and had mutual acquaintances, such as Princeton University alumnus F. Scott Fitzgerald, Halliburton and Hemingway never did meet and took very different approaches to journalism. Hemingway would make a career representing the masculine mystique, pursuing obvious feats of daring and strength such as hunting for big game animals in Africa and deep-sea fishing for marlin and tuna in the Gulf of Mexico. Halliburton would forge his career with an emphasis on escape and optimism, and while he too performed acts of daring and strength, his brand of daring would rub some critics the wrong way; they would look at Halliburton's feats as no more than a schoolboy's high jinks, more manufactured than Hemingway's. Physically, he didn't come close to matching Hemingway, and from a literary standpoint, his prose leaned toward the florid.[4]

On his first trip to France in 1919, Halliburton had seen Paris and visited the trenches of Verdun, where 260,000 men had died. He walked the battlefields of Alsace where Princeton University students had fought and fell. Halliburton never wrote directly about the war. He did, however, write an article about Germany; its sanguinity didn't accurately portray the postwar situation. Halliburton deliberately painted Germany in sunny hues, anticipating that American readers were tired of war and hungry for cheer. He knew he wouldn't be able to sell a story that showed a beaten and economically depressed nation. It would become his hallmark to write around the grimness of life. Halliburton preferred seducing readers with tales of pirates in the South China Sea than alarming them with stories from Bombay's slums.

Unlike those writers who were outraged over the brutal carnage of war and were bleak about the future, Halliburton was not. World War I had not disillusioned him. While in Germany and later in the Netherlands, he absorbed the postwar sights. He listened to people talk about the travails of rebuilding after the devastation. Still he insisted on seeing a world filled with rapidly expanding possibilities. He had every intention of catering to a distinctly American audience, an audience that in the first part of the 1920s took advantage of falling prices and rising corporate profits, and that had more disposable income to buy wristwatches, nylons, movie tickets, and if all went according to Halliburton's plans, his books.[5] Though untested, Halliburton's instincts drove him to separate himself from the Lost Generation writers of the early 1920s. While themes of politics, race, and sexuality dominated the works of Ernest Hemingway, F. Scott Fitzgerald, and William Faulkner, Halliburton refused to follow this trend.[6] And so Halliburton leaped into Europe. He regarded the continent as his personal playground.

After spending several days in Germany, Halliburton was impatient to move on. He tacked a map onto the wall of their hotel room and in an improvised version of Pin the Tail on the Donkey, blindfolded Hockaday. He spun his friend around three times and faced him toward the wall. With arm outstretched, Hockaday planted a finger on the map. Tugging off the blindfold, he shrugged. Not Paris. Rotterdam. The two slung their two-pound knapsacks over their shoulders, hopped on Otto and Ophelia, and started pedaling.

Along the way, the people, children especially, delighted in meeting the Americans. "The moment we landed with our cameras, Irvine and I were singled out as luscious and legitimate prey by a half-dozen well trained and elaborately costumed little girls. Our cameras rivaled the Pied Piper's music in collecting children."[7]

Halfway to Amsterdam, they paused in the hamlet of Nenndorf and then continued on toward Hanover, "a most meticulously cultivated piece of land" to Halliburton's eye.[8] They continued through to The Hague. By the time they reached Amsterdam, where the houses were set as close to each other as kernels of corn, Halliburton had written more than twenty-five thousand words about Germany and Holland.[9]

Each afternoon or evening, Halliburton devoted at least two to three hours writing long letters home on hotel stationery, asking after his parents and Ammudder. In his curving script, he outlined and shaped his book ideas. Even before he had sailed away, he had a clear idea of what he wanted to write. He was also quite sure he would finish what he started. "There can *be no failure!* There'll be a book. No, I don't want a Baedeker, nor a Harry Franck, nor a Mark Twain, nor a Frederick O'Brien, but something of each, plus chiefly of me."[10] Early on in the trip, he not only started to think like a writer but also called himself a writer when asked.[11]

Harry Franck, who started writing his travel books at the turn of the century, had long been a source of inspiration for Halliburton. Franck's first book, *A Vagabond Journey Around the World*, was published in 1910. While still a student at Princeton, Halliburton heard Franck was scheduled to give a lecture near Lawrenceville. Halliburton charmed himself into an invitation. He wanted to learn how Franck, nineteen years his senior, had launched a career in adventure writing.

That evening Halliburton sauntered over to Franck's table. Afterward Halliburton wrote about the encounter in a short piece called "Dinner with Harry."[12]

Later on in his postcollegiate adventure, Halliburton would arrive in India and visit the Taj Mahal, and ask his guide to take his photograph in front of the alabaster mausoleum. It's nearly an exact duplicate of a portrait of Harry Franck standing before the Taj Mahal. Later, the picture of Halliburton would strike a chord with readers, one of whom summed it up like this: "I like the photo of you standing before the Taj Mahal. There seemed to be something so dramatic and symbolic about it, —a touch of gay, careless boyishness, —youthful confidence facing the future with a smile, and an ancient tomb, emblem of immortal love."[13]

For now, however, Halliburton and Hockaday took several day trips in Amsterdam. In Haarlem, Halliburton couldn't resist buying a pair of wooden clogs for his father. Eventually they sold their bikes and sneaked onto a train bound for Zermatt, Switzerland. They rode through the Valais, a fertile plain nestled between the Alps that yields the bright apricots that become jams and jellies, schnapps, and tarts. Looking through the windows, the travelers spied ancient forts and stone farmhouses with steeply pitched roofs.

The travelers arrived in Zermatt. Fewer than six thousand people lived in the village at the base of the Matterhorn, one of Switzerland's highest peaks. From the railway station, they rode the yellow post bus to the mountain village. Halliburton decided there might be more enchanting spots in Switzerland than Zermatt, but "for inspiring missed grandeur, it is unparalleled this wide world round." He penned his musings in a softcover journal, squirreling them away to harvest later when he sat down to write his first book.[14]

To save money, Halliburton and Hockaday rented rooms in a rundown little hotel. Ever the aesthetic, Halliburton found the porcelain washbowl in his room decorated with hand-painted cow lilies charming in an Old World sort of way.[15]

The Matterhorn straddles the border of Italy and Switzerland, rising 14,692 feet high. The Italians call it Monte Cervino; the French call it Mont Cervin. On the Swiss side, the mountain rises like a solitary triangle, an "imperious sweep into the blue heavens."[16] There are no easy ascents and the weather is fickle—sudden snowstorms and violent winds make climbing it a dangerous undertaking. To maximize safety, alpinists try to stick to the climbing season, which runs from mid-July to mid-August. It was now September. In the village, frost already tinged the early morning autumn air.

Halliburton and Hockaday asked around until they found a pair of mountain guides, Adolph Schaller and Roman Perone. They introduced themselves to the guides, both of whom had grown up on the mountain, and asked them to take them to the summit.

"Of course you have climbed other mountains?" Schaller asked.[17]

"Oh, many," the two said. The young men dared not reveal that climbing cathedral stairs and steep countryside paths in Germany was just about their only training. They also walked the six miles to the summit of Gornergrat, a rocky ridge overlooking the Gorner glacier, to build their stamina and muscle strength.

The guides snorted in disbelief when they learned Halliburton and Hockaday's equipment consisted of a toothbrush and a safety razor each. "You are not climbing Mt. Olives, you know. It will be cold," Schaller said, referring to the olive grove–covered mountain that lies just east of Jerusalem's Old City.

Halliburton looked at their equipment list. They needed cleated mountain shoes, socks, leggings, mittens, and an ice ax. "We begged, borrowed, and stole equipment and rented three-ton cleated Alpine shoes from our guides," Halliburton wrote.[18]

The day before the climb, Schaller and Perone invited the two men for a walk through Zermatt's churchyard. They wanted to give them a chance to reconsider their plans. After all, scaling the Matterhorn was not a simple Alpine stroll. Scores of alpinists had died or were severely injured attempting to summit its chiseled face.

Halliburton and Hockaday walked through the little cemetery, a sort of Alpine club for the dead. There was a stone to honor W. K. W., who fell to his death from the Matterhorn in 1870. There was one for

Edward Whymper of Great Britain. He hoped to be the first to summit the mountain. Instead he plunged to his death alongside four members of his team. Another stone was inscribed, "B. R. B. with two guides on June 10, 1891, slipped from the shoulder of the Matterhorn and fell 3,000 feet."[19]

From the cemetery, the four stepped into the village's alpine club museum, and Halliburton and Hockaday considered its collection of climbing equipment, including ice axes, cleats, and helmets. If the guides hoped to dissuade the two college graduates, they had failed. Walking among the weathered stones and through the museum, the invincibility of youth won. They tramped back to the inn to get some sleep before the big day.

They awoke in darkness. They pulled on woolen pants over thick long underwear. They rolled on wool socks and laced their boots. They shoved their arms through jackets and made sure their caps covered their ears. They carried their borrowed gear. Their quiet matched the predawn hush. The first bits of silver light were just peeking through when they joined their guides.

They started out, heading toward the Hörnli Ridge. While tough, this part of the climb was not technical. They passed the ridge and tackled the steep and rocky way that led around and above the moraine, the Furggengletscher. They could see the ice-covered Breithorn, which stands at the end of the Matter Valley, 13,661 feet high. Halliburton's legs quivered and burned. Hockaday's back screamed from the weight of his pack. Still the two climbed. They followed a zigzag path to reach a promontory, trying to reach a warm refuge. The air now hovered near zero degrees Fahrenheit. The wind howled and snowflakes stung their frozen faces.

Gingerly, they put one foot in front of the other. At times there was only a twelve-inch-wide, snow-covered edge to walk on. Handholds were hard to find. They swallowed their nerves and pushed forward. Schaller and Perone "soon saw we were not the chamois goats we had pretended to be in Zermatt."[20] At 10,700 feet they reached the Hörnli

Hut, built by the Swiss Alpine Club in 1880. It had taken them more than half a day.

They ducked inside the rustic cabin, where they found thick woolen blankets and bunks. Even with their heavy clothes and a fire, it took several bowls of piping hot soup to warm them in the night. Schaller and Perone woke the pair at 3:30 AM. They breakfasted and a half hour later Halliburton and Hockaday were roped, each man to one guide. They stepped back into the freezing air. "Feeling very much like pet poodles being led by a chain, I barked in response to Adolph's call, and Irvine in response to Roman's."[21]

Inch by inch they moved forward, at times pressed against the cliffs, which were slick with ice and formed a sheer wall rising several feet on either side. The walls seemed to grow higher and "come oftener as we labored upward and we had to use elbows and knees and teeth and toes as well as hands and feet to gain every yard." Schaller swung his ice pick, stabbing handholds into the ice. Just six hundred feet from the summit, Halliburton grabbed onto a stone and lost his footing. In an instant, the rope around his waist tightened and stopped him with a jerk.

It was painstaking. With each step Schaller and Perone made sure Halliburton and Hockaday were safely ensconced in some crevice, whereupon their guides would scale the rock wall to a point twenty to thirty feet past with the agility of a mountain goat. Upon their signal, Halliburton and Hockaday resumed their climb.

Now just a hundred feet from their goal, the four men were ankle deep in snow. One last step and Halliburton stood on the summit beneath a cloudless sky. Mont Blanc rose in the west and the Jungfrau to the north. Two young, inexperienced climbers, unskilled in every way, had accomplished what only a few men had done before. They spent all of ten minutes on the narrow summit, looking around and briefly basking in their achievement. Then came the truly hard part—the descent.

The young men had been so busy climbing, concentrating on looking up and reaching the top, they never thought about how steep the descent would be. But once they stood on the summit and looked down they got nervous; it was going to be the most challenging part of the adventure. "It was the quality of the Swiss guides that got them through—the guides could carry them down if need be. The fixed ropes they'd passed on the way up didn't seem too sturdy," recounted Hockaday's son, Irvine Hockaday Jr.[22]

On the way down, Halliburton and Hockaday slipped several times on the icy shoulder, despite the crampons affixed to their boots. Only the quick reaction of one of their guides saved them from careening off the icy face. Their arms ached deeply. The fierce wind stung their faces. Halliburton would later write, "I shall refrain from giving all the details of our descent. The complete disappearance of the seats of our corduroy pants tells eloquently enough how we really came home to Zermatt."[23]

Back in the village at the inn, they very nearly had to chip off their ice-crusted clothes. Halliburton drew a hot bath, pulled off his wet socks, and sank into the water. Later, after hot drinks and hot food, they fell into their beds. "It took derricks to get our painful limbs out of bed, and we groaned to think of the aftermath of the Matterhorn."[24] Hockaday reveled in his accomplishment. For Halliburton, the work was just starting. He needed to write about it—the smell of the cold, the feel of the granite beneath his fingertips, the tug of the lifesaving rope. He penned an entry in his journal, and then he shared a more fully developed story in a letter to his parents. The climb would come as news to them. "I didn't mention it before because I knew you would worry yourself sick but, now it's all over, congratulate me on the feat."[25] It was a signature Halliburton move. He always waited until after the fact to tell his parents about a dangerous escapade. After Wesley Jr. had died, it had become an unspoken agreement that Halliburton not unnecessarily cause alarm.

In the morning Hockaday and Halliburton packed their knapsacks and took the post bus to the train station. They bought third-class tickets and boarded the train. Just before it reached Lausanne, Switzerland, they decided to part ways for a bit. Hockaday looked forward to spending some time in Paris, but Halliburton still wanted to visit Château de Chillon, the medieval castle at the foot of the Alps that inspired Lord Byron's poem "The Prisoner of Chillon." The two friends agreed to meet in the City of Light in a few days.

Halliburton hopped off the train near Montreux, a hillside town in Suisse Romande situated on the banks of Lake Geneva. Halliburton strolled to the château. Over the bridge, he entered the keep. Once upon a time, archers stood in the galleries and balconies running above, poised to defend the castle. He trotted down the worn stone steps to the dungeon where Byron had once etched his name on a stone pillar. Halliburton spent hours in the dungeon with the vaulted ceiling, gazing at the lake through the bars on the narrow windows. Across the lake lay Evian, France, and the Alps. After a spell, Halliburton walked to the lake's shore, climbed over some boulders, stripped off his dusty clothes, and dove into the chilly water. He climbed back out and, while drying off in the cool air, read Byron's poem. The Alps on the other side were now silhouettes against the crimson sky. He cried, feeling the full weight of what he had accomplished thus far. He wrote about this with ease, unembarrassed to show emotion when it came to describing his reaction to his surroundings. But rarely would he show emotion like this about his personal life, particularly about his brother's death. Those feelings resided too deep.

Halliburton held a particular fondness for Paris. He rejoined Hockaday, and the few days there gave him a chance to dine and catch up with friends. Halliburton and Hockaday spent an enchanted evening dining with the lady-in-waiting for Empress Eugénie. They also spent time with a former cabaret dancer with the Folies Bergère.[26] Halliburton also mailed home an article about the Matterhorn climb so his father could hand deliver it to Mooney at the *Memphis Commercial Appeal.*

Hockaday's grand adventure ended on October 9. He could no longer ignore his mother's calls for him to return to Kansas City, Missouri, and start work. "He came home like a good son. He had a Midwesterner's sense of duty," said Irvine Hockaday Jr. decades later.[27]

Thus the Princeton friends bade each other adieu. Hockaday went home via Marseilles, and on October 29 Halliburton finally—after postponing his departure so he could work on additional articles about his

Matterhorn climb—went south to the walled city of Carcassone, follow-ing in the footsteps of the Knights Templar, one of the most wealthy and powerful of the Western Christian Military Orders that dated back to the First Crusade. He enjoyed a brief stop in Carcassone and then crossed the Pyrenees in winter. "I decided to make the venture—it was too delightfully insane to miss," he wrote.[28]

Meanwhile, back home in the United States, Babe Ruth broke Roger Connor's mark for 138 home runs in a career. Red Grange dominated the football field, and also won the Illinois state title in long jump. Helen Wills took the California Women's tennis championship, and President Warren G. Harding would soon complete his first year in office.[29] Across the country, in all facets of life, people chased and reached new heights, be it in sports, politics, or entertainment. Each record ignited a sense of optimism, a feeling that the nation was stepping forward and leaving the gloom of World War I behind. Halliburton had yet to set records, but he too would spark the spirit of the general public.

Next stop: Barcelona. The noise, energy, and art pulsed through Catalonia's capital. Halliburton had taken a room in a small inn after being turned down by one hotel after another on account of his dishev-eled and dirty appearance.[30] He had neither changed clothes for several days nor had time to shave. Notes from a fast-paced song came in through the open window. Down below in the Plaza de la Paz, circles of dancing men whooped and cheered. Halliburton took the stairs two at a time and joined the merriment.

After the crowd dispersed, he noticed a man flipping through the red-jacketed *Baedeker's Spain and Portugal.* Halliburton introduced him-self and struck up a conversation. The tourist introduced himself as Paul McGrath, a twenty-seven-year-old architect from Chicago. "We were both a little embarrassed, but agreed not to tell. . . . He . . . is the best company since Mike left, as solitary as I, so we have been inseparable except while I'm writing."[31]

What exactly they were embarrassed about Halliburton never said. It could be that each thought he was alone in dancing with locals. It could be each was unsure of the other's sexual orientation. Nevertheless, a careful read of Halliburton's time here suggests the two likely became lovers.[32] Together the two traveled through Spain, parting once in late December when Halliburton took a train to Granada. "I shall be here till after Xmas, for Paul is going to stay a month and I would not care to miss his company on Xmas Day just to save two or three days," he wrote home.[33] He wrote about how he and McGrath wandered into the gypsy quarters, where the fountains splashed and the blue sky reflected off the marble-edged pools and how "never have I been so happy in a quiet, restful way."[34]

Of course, Halliburton couldn't publicize their relationship, in either his books or his letters home. Thus the raconteur reduced McGrath to an amiable acquaintance.[35] To further conceal his sexual identity, Halliburton started weaving fantastical romantic liaisons with women into his stories. He wrote about a young woman he named Mademoiselle Piety for her modesty but also of how he discovered that she was actually the "queen" of the Folies Bergère dancing girls harem. He wrote about winning a radiant young woman's heart when he clasped a circle of cherry-red glass beads around her pale neck.[36]

In future interviews Halliburton would describe his perfect woman. He spoke about how he had little time for romance when attending Princeton but had since had the chance to experience many foreign women. French women were the "most fascinating" and Spanish women possessed an "ardent temperament." In the end he concluded America produced "the ideal girl." But, he confided—in a stage whisper of sorts— that he would never marry any of them, for he still had too much distance to cover.[37]

A month after whirling around Barcelona, Madrid, and Granada, and celebrating the New Year in Cádiz peeling and eating mounds of oranges with McGrath, Halliburton took a ferry across the Bay of Algeciras to British-controlled Gibraltar. His well-worn knapsack was slung over his shoulder and his Kodak camera hung from his neck. McGrath would follow in a day or so.

Today about thirty thousand people live on the two-and-a-half-square-mile peninsula. At the time of his visit, tourists, mostly European, came to enjoy the La Alameda Gardens and the Moorish Castle. They were, however, most certainly not free to roam the military installations that stood tall above the narrow straits where the Mediterranean Sea joins the Atlantic Ocean. That restriction tantalized Halliburton, who had a somewhat prickly relationship with the law. "I began to wonder," he wrote, "if here, in such moonlight, on one of the world's most dramatic stages, some delightfully indiscreet adventure was not awaiting me. Prophetic instinct whispered that there was."[38]

After dinner and time spent writing in his red leather-bound copybook, Halliburton slipped out of his hotel, camera in hand. He made his way toward the fenced-in perimeter that wrapped around the fort. The tap of his footfalls echoed through the winding streets. He snuck through the gate. Inside he snapped forbidden photos of weapons emplacements. If climbing the Matterhorn showed grit, his exploration of Gibraltar, ever the symbol of universal indomitability, showed his rebellious side.

The next morning, thunderous pounding on the door jolted Halliburton awake. A British military police officer barged into the room and arrested Halliburton, whose hair was still tousled from sleep, and hauled him to headquarters. Suspicious that the American only had a knapsack rather than a steamer trunk plastered in stickers like most tourists, the prosecuting officer accused Halliburton of spying for Germany and demanded he surrender his film. Having hidden a second roll of film on the window ledge outside his hotel room, Halliburton relinquished only one roll to the authorities. Sensing the authorities were not amused, the traveler asked that the trial be postponed so he could better prepare his case. He hoped McGrath would arrive in time and help get him out of jail. The judge agreed to a delay, and ordered Halliburton locked in a cell inside the city prison. His twenty-second birthday came and went.

A day later, McGrath arrived from Cádiz and heard from the innkeeper that his friend was sitting in jail. He met with Halliburton, who told him about the hidden film. McGrath assured the writer he would search the ledge and gutter outside the hotel room for the other roll. In the interim, the police developed eighteen photographs from the first roll. They interrogated Halliburton again. They checked with the American consul, who vouched for the validity of his passport. Four days later, sorely needing a shave, Halliburton again appeared before the judge. The judge let him off with a fine of ten pounds or thirty days in jail and a stern reprimand. Fine paid, warning heeded, the irrepressible peripatetic and his companion Paul McGrath left the rock before sunup, now abloom in hyacinth.

After Halliburton left Gibraltar and said goodbye to McGrath, who returned to Chicago, he sent the photographs from the second roll to the British authorities. The military headquarters of Gibraltar later informed Halliburton that "there will be no objection to the publication of those numbered 3, 4 and 5. The remainder must not be published."[39] Later he included some of the photographs from the hidden roll in his book *The Royal Road to Romance*.

In a *Time* magazine story about the incident, Halliburton played the story for all it was worth. He didn't embellish—there was no need—but he knew how to weave just the right amount of tension and humor into his final manuscript. He presented himself as someone ready to push the envelope and do what was necessary to find a story for his book. He was self-deprecating to a fault. To his parents, and later to his readers, Halliburton downplayed the gravity of the situation, writing sardonically how he "was held there until the military court found that the 'dangerous American spy' was only a young American student out to see the world, a student who took poor snapshots of all the interesting sights he encountered—cannon and castle included—to send back to his family in Memphis, Tennessee."[40] In *The Royal Road*, he chose his words more judiciously, striking a balance between rebellion and respect.

Halliburton arrived in India at night after several weeks traipsing through Egypt, where he slept atop a pyramid and swam in the Nile. It had been a circuitous journey. After his Egyptian interlude had ended, Halliburton went to Port Said in northern Egypt and signed on as a seaman aboard the American oil tanker *Gold Shell*. He sailed across the Indian Ocean and around the toe of India until the tanker made port in Calcutta. While in the teeming city he bought two tailor-made white cotton suits, though he had little use for them as "I *live* in my boy-scout short pants and shirt so that the heat concerns me not a whit. With my helmet I prowl about at midday all over town and am honestly not the least uncomfortable."[41]

He awaited the arrival of a new traveling companion, David Russell, three years his junior. Halliburton had met Russell back in Delhi and found him to be a "made-to-order" companion,[42] as he too was working his way through Southeast Asia and was more than used to harsh conditions. The two were eager to trek through the Ganges Valley, Kabul, Kashmir, and Katmandu. Anticipating the heat, Halliburton left his pack at the YMCA in Calcutta. He had a tailor sew large pockets inside his khaki shorts to carry his passport and wallet so they wouldn't fall out.[43]

But before tackling the pass they stopped in Agra, a city of more than one million people in Uttar Pradesh. Home to the Taj Mahal, the city was a festival of color. Women garbed in saffron-yellow and hibiscus-pink saris pushed through the markets. Great jugs filled with oil, sacks of grain, and jars of spices crowded the markets. The greasy odors of cook shops pervaded the streets. Fruit and vegetables tempted taste buds. Changing out of his shorts, Halliburton dressed in linen pants and a loose-fitting shirt, donned a hat to block his fair skin from the sun and his trusty hobnailed shoes, and met his guide, Ahmed. Together they walked toward the Taj Mahal.[44]

Halliburton stood before the bejeweled mausoleum, Shah Jahan's tribute to his immortal beloved. Though later disgraced for squandering his kingdom's wealth, the shah's monument has stood the test of time. For Halliburton, it was as if the illustration inside his ink-stained, frayed-edged schoolbook had leaped off the page and materialized before his eyes. "The Taj Mahal had been deified in my mind ever since that childhood day when I had first looked upon an oil painting of the fairy tomb and read the immortal story of its creation," he later wrote.[45]

Enchanted, Halliburton lingered, well after the last tourists and pilgrims had made their way to dinner and bed. The sky was a confection of color as the sun set. The scent of clematis and honeysuckle hung heavy in the air. Halliburton slipped into the shadows and waited in a willow grove. Night fell. The last sentry left his post after locking the gates to the mausoleum. When the grounds seemed clear, Halliburton slipped off his shoes and socks and walked barefoot over to the deepest lily pool. He sat for a long moment on a marble bench beside the pool, mesmerized by the fluffy white lotus blooms floating on the water. He paced back and forth, casting a long shadow on the ground. He stripped off his clothes and jumped into the languid water. The moon shimmered.

"This was a page from the Arabian Nights, a reversion to the fabled luxury of ancient emperors—this, at last, was romance," he wrote of the swim.[46] The plush prose would find an audience. But it would also receive sharp criticism. Halliburton naively left out details such as the fact that the pool was five feet deep, more than deep enough to allow a grown man to swim. Had he included these salient points he might have prevented several book reviewers from accusing him of inventing the whole experience, insisting the pools were too shallow. One of his most spiritual experiences would later become one of his most critically challenged.

Nevertheless, Halliburton cherished his time in India. He adored the children and talking with people on the street. His later film, *India Speaks*, and its accompanying publicity suggest a casual racism and acceptance of stereotypes. To be sure, bigotry sometimes punctuated Halliburton's letters home. Back when he was in France with Hockaday, he wrote about spending time in Coblenz to "investigate the French occupation and the tales of horror spouted against the Negro troops by the whining Germans . . . We visited the black barracks. The blacks are impudent and undesirable but are perfectly behaved and cause less actual trouble than the white soldiers."[47]

Halliburton put more footsteps on the map as he and Russell headed toward the Khyber Pass. On July 21, 1922, local officials granted Halliburton and Russell permission to visit the Khyber Pass, a historic mountain pass "filled with the ghosts of armies so thoroughly soaked with romance and battle and blood."[48]

Along the way the two men met British soldiers. Halliburton told them how "we were adventuring about the world on the money we made as we went along and that we had not the means to burden ourselves with superfluous luggage. 'You know!' the son of Britain replied, 'only an American would do that.'"[49]

After the romanticism of the Taj Mahal, Halliburton hankered to visit Leh in Tibet. Home to the Ladakh people, it is one of the highest inhabited cities in the world. He planned on a ten-day hike through twisty canyons. Ever the master of traveling light, his pack weighed less than six pounds when he left.[50] Had he remembered to discard his old shoes, it might have weighed about half as much. Anyway, Russell had lugged a bag filled with a flashlight, a tripod, bedroom slippers, pillow, a nightgown and other superfluous items, "all of which however (with the exception of the nightgown) I used frequently, ridiculing him all the while for carrying them around.)"[51] Halliburton also had a cook, two packhorses, and a guide to accompany them on the nearly three-hundred-mile trek.

Poplars and honeysuckle populated the sparse country. Snow-frosted mountains rose in the distance. Once in Leh he spent time with the Ladakh, who agreeably posed for several photographs with the young American.

Halliburton breathed in deep the scent of spring as they tramped across the Kashmir highway. "On every hillside branches of white pea and pale pink almond blossoms dipped into stretches of yellow mustard. Green wheat and freshly plowed fields mottled every landscape," he wrote. The landscape changed when they reached the Zoji La pass, for at 11,575 feet it was the "land of eternal snow."[52] He found hiking in the Himalayas taxing: "not mere Sierra Nevadas these, not more Mont Blanc and Matterhorn, but Himalayas 16,000, 18,000, 26,000 feet."[53] From the top, the mountains appeared to spread hundreds of miles in all four directions. In his letters to his "Dear Memsab and Sab," as he teasingly called his parents in some letters home from India, he described a remote quarter of the earth carpeted in white, yellow, and pink wild roses, and beds of purple iris.[54]

Toward the end of their stay in the Kashmir Valley, Halliburton and Russell spent days on a fully furnished houseboat with four servants, for $1.15 a day. The two parted ways in Calcutta, Halliburton wanting to venture further into Southeast Asia.

Halliburton left for Burma and sneaked aboard a Singapore-bound ship with thirteen dollars in his pocket, but he proved an unsuccessful stowaway. The ship's captain caught him soon after they got underway. The captain lowered a skiff into the water, dropped a rope ladder, and ordered the brazen writer off the ship. Back in port, Halliburton talked his way onto another boat.

The trip was now starting to wear on him. It was September 1922, more than a year since he and Hockaday had sailed out of New York Harbor on the *Ipswich*.

He didn't wallow in his melancholy for long. The Malay Peninsula and its ever-present steamy rain waited. He was determined to tramp across. The Andaman Sea lay on one side, the Strait of Malacca on the other. In between lay two hundred miles of thick forests, home to boa constrictors, scorpions, and leeches. Once again, Halliburton lacked the proper gear. When the mud pulled at his shoes, he bound them to his feet with rattan creepers. Men steered dugout canoes in the false twilight. At one point, Halliburton climbed into a dugout and spent a day or so in Taplee, a village deep in the jungle.

A few weeks later, he reached the other side covered in fiery bug bites and scratches. He wrote home, realizing he was "doomed to seek, seek, all my life, never content with what I have, despising it after I have it, seeing a higher place and greater fame every step upward."[55] As his friend Mike Hockaday told his own son, "He was always looking for the next vista."[56]

All bets were off when Halliburton arrived in Hong Kong. At the American Express office, he picked up an envelope containing $500 from the sale of newspaper and magazine articles, including the one he sold to the *Commercial Appeal* about his Matterhorn trip, complete with pictures. He also had $100 from Ammudder, Mary Hutchison.[57] He promptly spent $400 on gambling and jade in Canton on the appropri-

ately named Jade Street. He bargained for the stones, which he mailed
home, and in telling his parents how he drove a hard bargain he again
showed his prejudice, this time against Jews: "Of course, you can jew
'em down, but even at that jade is no pastime for a vagabond . . . I
never enjoyed 'shopping' so much."[58]

Then he took the *Sui An* from Hong Kong to Macao, where he
planned on spending the afternoon at a casino. When he was down to
his last dollars, he boarded the boat with more than three hundred other
people. Ten miles out of Macao, a band of Chinese pirates seized the
vessel. Some boarded the *Sui An*; others had hidden themselves among
the passengers dressed as tourists. In the chaos, passengers flattened
themselves on the decks and hid in cabins. Under the command of Lai
Choi San, the "Dragon Lady," the pirates went from cabin to cabin,
stealing watches, wallets, hats, and shoes. Halliburton lost his money,
hat, coat, vest, and belt to the bandits. He even lost his Camel cigarettes.

Halliburton filed a story about it to the *Commercial Appeal*. It marked
one of the first times the author was the subject of a news story rather
than solely the author. Halliburton, it turned out, made good copy.[59]

In Cambodia he visited Angkor Wat, and his descriptions were
ethereal and slightly reverent. "I saw a curious gray cloud with blos-
soming towers . . . no by heaven it was not a cloud. It was stone—it
was what I had come to see, the wonder of wonders, the most colossal
and perfect monument ever build, the prodigious temple of Angkor."[60]

As soon as Halliburton saw the graceful sweep of Japan's Mount Fuji
rising above Yokohama, he declared the summit would be his. Others
he met dismissed his idea as folly. "In Yokohama, the headquarters for
a climbing expedition, the 'can't-be-done' sentiment continued to be
expressed," Halliburton wrote.[61] The Tennessean took this as a challenge.
As in Zermatt, Halliburton found himself once again borrowing gear,
but he was less shy this time. Halliburton borrowed woolen leggings,
crampons, cleated shoes, and a helmet. Of course, he also needed a
guide. The latter proved slightly more difficult to find, since he spoke

no Japanese. Eventually, Halliburton found someone to take him up the 12,388-foot summit.

Though more than two thousand feet lower than the Matterhorn, Fuji, a dormant volcano, had its peculiar challenges. Savage blizzards often swept the face of the dormant volcano, driving climbers off the side to their deaths. Halliburton and his guide trekked through ever deepening snow until they reached the five-thousand-foot shelter as dark fell. With gloved hands the two men cleared the heavy snowdrifts from the door and once inside lit a fire.

After a fitful few hours of sleep, Halliburton took a swig of brandy, lashed spikes onto his snowshoes, and attached an ice ax to his wrist with a six-foot rope.[62] It was four in the morning. The team took several hours to reach the snowcapped and windless summit. "In the dim light the ghostly peak before me, barren of all vegetation, glimmered like a colossal cone of white sugar," Halliburton wrote. A field of stars dotted the sky like sequins on velvet.[63]

Neither a hot bath nor twelve hours of sleep in a warm bed after the climb saved his toenails or the skin of his nose. In all, Halliburton considered them very minor battle scars for the experience and ensuing story. The Japanese mountaineering society verified his climb, and he sold the story to newspapers across the United States, including the *Kansas City Star* and the *Oregon Journal*.

And then his trip came to a close. All told, his six hundred days overseas were an amuse-bouche of a lifetime of adventure to come. For more than a year he had pursued whatever caprice struck his fancy. He indulged in the freedom to search in the farthermost corners of the earth for the beautiful, the joyous, and the romantic.

But now Halliburton was happy to sign on as a seaman on the *President Madison* and sail for home. It was time to make good on his promise to finish a book.

3

Feats and Marvels

A FTER MORE THAN A year abroad, Richard Halliburton returned to America. He had literally come full circle, having sailed from New York aboard the *Ipswich* and arriving on the West Coast aboard the *President Madison*. He first stopped in Seattle, Washington. There he stayed with the son of a Lawrenceville man he had met aboard the ocean liner. He spent time with Lucy Belle McPherson, the widow of Lawrenceville's late headmaster, Simon John McPherson. He and the widow reminisced about their Lawrenceville years and Halliburton's younger brother Wesley. "It was a reunion of memories," he said.[1]

With the money he earned selling a couple of stories to the *Oregon Journal*, Halliburton bought a ticket for Denver, Colorado. From there he stayed with Mike Hockaday in Kansas City. He had last seen his friend on a quay in Marseilles, France. Halliburton updated his friend on the adventures he'd had after they parted ways. While the young men joked around at the kitchen table, Hockaday's mother patched and darned Halliburton's threadbare socks.

His earnings from the *Kansas City Star* article covered his train fare home. Finally, he crossed into Tennessee and opened the door of his parents' Memphis home.

He spent days in his old bedroom at his boyhood desk, writing friends and publishers. He spent nights catching up with his parents and Ammudder. Richard took long walks with his father and had long

When Richard Halliburton visited his parents in Memphis, he stayed with them in this house. Sometimes he would work on a manuscript in his old bedroom. *Author's collection*

talks with his mother. He swam endless laps at the YMCA to keep fit. Yet, accustomed as he was to living out of a knapsack and not knowing what the next day would bring, the slower pace of life in Tennessee shortly chafed him. So after weeks of pointedly not talking about what he planned next, Richard called a family council.

Staying in Memphis would not advance his career.[2] And he did consider it a career: after reviewing his expenditures, Halliburton calculated he had earned $300 more than he spent during his travels. In his mind that made the trip both financially and professionally successful. Still, he imagined editors bidding on his manuscript. Instead, multiple rejections stuffed his parents' mailbox outside the white clapboard house on Cortland Street. Impatient, he decided to go to New York City and personally knock on publishers' doors. At the family meeting, Richard told his parents that while he treasured being home, he was starting to feel a tiny bit restless. With his parent's blessing, he packed his typewriter, manuscript, and photographs and took the next train to Flint,

Michigan, to pick up his new $900 1923 Buick roadster, a gift from his father. He headed east.

Halliburton was happy to be back in New York City. He parked his mud-spattered car in a garage for three dollars a night, the cheapest he could find, and walked to the YMCA on Fifty-Seventh Street near Central Park.[3] Halliburton took a garret room on a high floor. Staring out the window, he thought how "nowhere in the wilds of Asia was I more homesick than I am tonight. No one with whom to discuss what seem momentous problems—only a little garret room with 7,000,000 people I do not know and don't want to."[4] Soon he would share a room, and split the rent, with Cecil Crouse, a good friend and classmate from Princeton who happened to be a rather talented amateur pianist.

At the start of his career, before having the means to stay in swankier hotels like the Roosevelt and the Duane, Halliburton frequently lodged at the YMCA when visiting New York City. The YMCA organized reading groups in its libraries and had swimming pools and gymnasiums its residents could use; it was ideal for single, young professional men between the ages of twenty and thirty. By the 1920s, the seven YMCA residential hotels in New York housed more than a thousand young men.[5] That single young men stayed at the Y appealed to Halliburton, who was just starting to explore his sexuality. Nevertheless the aspiring author kept his homosexuality hidden, navigating the thin line between his private self and public self.[6] He knew if his secret got out, he would be personally and professionally ruined.

Of course he had little time to socialize, focused as he was on selling his books. His doodle of a running man on one of his letters home said it best: he was "simply spinning!"[7] For weeks Halliburton doggedly pursued one publishing lead after another. He met with editors at Charles Scribner's Sons and the Bell Syndicate. He gathered his Gibraltar photos in a neat stack and took them straight to the Hearst Syndicate. There he received a "cordial reception but negative answer."[8] Halliburton opened up to his parents in a long letter. He was unhappy. Indeed he felt more homesick in this city of chrome, steel, and concrete than he had trekking through the tangled vines and steamy air of the Malay Peninsula. Nonetheless, Halliburton wouldn't think of surrendering his dream of becoming a published author.

Pursuing his goal was costly. The twenty-three-year-old depended on the allowance he received from his father and though grateful for the help, it embarrassed him. Wanting to support himself, Halliburton thought if he sold some articles to magazines he could supplement his income until he sold his book idea. That too proved futile. The Hearst Syndicate unambiguously rejected Halliburton's proposal to write a series based on his European and Asian expedition. However, the editors did suggest he try the *American Magazine*, a human-interest periodical founded in 1906 by muckraking journalists Ray Stannard Baker, Lincoln Steffens, and Ida M. Tarbell.

Halliburton met with a junior editor there, and at last, had a success. The editor agreed to pay him ten dollars for his story on the Chinese bandits. He wanted a three-part series, but his offer was contingent on Halliburton delivering the first of three installments within two hours of their meeting.[9]

Next Halliburton approached the McClure Syndicate. Not interested, they said. He pressed on, and took a taxi over to the National Geographic Society, where he met with the magazine's illustrations editor, Franklin L. Fisher. Halliburton pitched every story in his quiver, giving special weight to the ones about Bali, Fuji, and Asia. Fisher considered running Halliburton's piece about summiting Mount Fuji in winter, side-by-side with another writer's story about climbing the storied peak in summer. Fisher ruminated. Halliburton sat. The moments ticked. Fisher deliberated some more. Ultimately he turned down the younger man's proposal.

Each rejection twisted Halliburton's guts. Deflated, he couldn't fathom why no one seemed interested in his story. No one in Halliburton's circle of friends or extended family had worked as a writer or reporter, so not only was there no hope of networking there, there was no one to advise him on the best track forward. He was exasperated. "I abominate this life but it's necessary, perhaps for two weeks more," he wrote home. "Things have gone so much more slowly than I hoped for. I get terribly impatient at the way my book is progressing."[10]

Aside from fending off feelings of melancholy triggered by the endless rejection parade, he was also busy brushing off repeated inquiries from his father about girlfriends. His father wrote faithfully every Sunday, each letter a combination of news, advice, and questions about how his son planned to get on with his personal life.[11] Ever elusive when it came to discussing his romantic life, Halliburton repeatedly gave his parents vague assurances that he would someday marry and give them grandchildren.

With virtually no income coming in, the balance in Richard Halliburton's bank account dwindled fast. In what would later prove to be a stroke of marketing genius, Halliburton reckoned he could earn a fair living wage lecturing. He decided to call upon the Feakins Agency. He knew the premier lecture bureau had hundreds of speakers on its roster and so he asked William B. Feakins, the founder and head of the prestigious agency, to hear his proposal.

Over lunch, Halliburton shared his photos with Feakins; by dessert he agreed Halliburton must try out. Feakins wanted to see an audition in real time. The Fifty-Seventh Street YMCA offered Halliburton the use of its huge lobby as a venue. Shortly before the event, Halliburton learned Feakins had been called away on other business and would miss the lecture. Williams's son Albert, who was also a partner in the agency, would attend in his father's stead. He looked forward to the event, anticipating that Halliburton and his stories could be highly marketable.

The evening arrived. Halliburton dressed in a freshly pressed suit and shoes shined to a pitch-perfect gloss. His wavy hair was brushed back, his face freshly shaven. At 7:30 PM he strode to the podium, set in the back of the spacious hall. He felt confident. After all, he had taken an advanced public speaking course during his undergraduate years at Princeton University. He thought capturing the attention of a New York crowd would be easy. He was wrong.

"It was the worst ordeal I ever endured," Halliburton wrote about lecturing in the YMCA's lobby. "People were passing and talking and sitting and departing, a piano banged in the reading room, and a bag-piper advertising something or other stopped outside to compete with me. It was almost impossible to hold contact and, in consequence, it was not an impressive talk."[12] Feakins's son let him down gently. Regrettably, he couldn't offer him a spot based on the evening's performance.

Another setback, another rejection; Halliburton needed a contract and a steady income. It wasn't that his parents were pressuring him to get a job, but he felt pressure nonetheless. Each of his peers were settled into jobs and earning money. He loathed the rut of a nine-to-five job, but he wanted financial independence and he wanted to say he was a professional author. He tried to tamp down his despair and frustration. The last thing he wanted was to crawl home to Memphis and work for his father selling real estate.

Halliburton went back to Feakins's offices shortly after the YMCA fiasco. Albert Feakins thought the earnest young man had potential; he just didn't think he was quite ready for the lecture circuit. So he told him about an opportunity at a publication Halliburton later remembered as *Boy Scout Magazine*—it may have been *Boys' Life*. Its editor was looking for new writers, so Halliburton met with several of the publication's executives for drinks inside the richly paneled Algonquin Hotel on Manhattan's west side. Perhaps a little of Dorothy Parker and her roundtable might rub off on Halliburton. Although the editor expressed great interest in Halliburton, the plan never materialized. In part, Halliburton hesitated to commit to such a large-scale project; the position involved lecturing, traveling, and some motion-picture work.

Several weeks after the botched audition, Halliburton decided to give it another go. He persuaded the lecture agency to give him another chance; fortunately both William and Albert Feakins conceded the lobby of the YMCA was far from the ideal place for a lecture.[13] Acting upon William's suggestion, Halliburton contacted Charles Powlison, who was general secretary of the National Child Welfare Association. Powlison invited Halliburton to speak at the Sheltering Arms Orphan Asylum, an all-boys orphanage in New York City. Halliburton called Feakins back, thanked him for the introduction, and invited him to attend.

After returning from a trip to Hoosick Falls, about two hundred miles from New York City, Halliburton arrived at the orphanage in time for dinner. Then, at 7:30 PM, the children sat, bellies full, and waited for the program to start. With no lecture notes in hand, Halliburton walked to his place behind the wooden podium. Feakins and Powlison sat in the back row, looking like a pair of judges. He knew he had to deliver an engaging talk or else wait at least another year before Feakins might possibly reconsider him for his roster of speakers.[14]

Halliburton thought about what parts of his adventure he should highlight. He would tell them the wildest stories in his repertoire. He would definitely tell them how he and Hockaday slid and skidded their way down the Matterhorn. The children would likely get a kick about how he had hidden from the guides at the Taj Mahal so that he could take a moonlight swim. Halliburton considered his audience. Three hundred boys aged five through fifteen sat on the floor, some with legs tucked under them, others with legs stretched out, all with heads tipped up and eyes locked on him. Subtly he cleared his throat and began speaking—trying to modulate his voice and keep it steady.

The children sat wide-eyed, no one made a peep—until the end. Raucous applause filled the room. He had done it. He had connected with the kids. "I knew I had them, for not a person moved. Their eyes were big as saucers, and I saw that Feakins saw *that*," Halliburton said.[15] Powlison sprang from his seat and rushed the podium. He told Halliburton it was hands down the best talk anyone had ever delivered to the children.

Feakins hired him for one engagement at twenty-five dollars, to take place in the autumn of 1923. It was a start, Halliburton told himself. In short order, Halliburton became one of the most compelling and captivating speakers in the Feakins stable.

With this accomplishment in his pocket, Halliburton took his manuscript out for another look. He had written an introduction, but the rest now seemed to be pages of disorganized notes. He started on it again, taking it one chapter at a time. Meanwhile he sold a few articles to *Travel Magazine* about his trek across the Malay Peninsula. He sold photos to the *Tribune* for forty dollars and a cartoon for fifty. Every cent he earned proved he could become a professional writer. After having woken up one morning in June with nary a nickel to his name, he didn't take these sales for granted.

In mid-July he met his parents in Princeton. During the past year Richard often spent weekends in the college town with his pals John Leh and Edward "Larry" Keyes. The friends "danced till six and I was surprised how much I enjoyed it. The new dances are really lots of fun."[16] Now the three Halliburtons rented a house for the remainder of the summer and took many short day trips. At summer's end his parents drove his new Buick back to Memphis, the car a luxury he could ill afford in New York City.[17] Once back in the city he didn't miss the car, but he did miss his parents. "You know exactly what I've been doing since you left—the same as before, only lonesomely [*sic*]. We had such a good time, the *best* we ever had, together. I used to lie awake nights on my trip and long to be situated just as we've been here in Princeton."[18]

Throughout the fall of 1923 Halliburton lectured in Philadelphia, St. Louis, and Buffalo. In December he spoke at Lawrenceville Academy and received one hundred dollars, bringing his monthly earnings to $1,160. He loved every minute of it, but the strain of the schedule started to show. His eyes looked tired and his frame thinner.

Halliburton spent a delightful Christmas at home in Memphis, but it was clear to his parents that their son was worn down. Wesley also worried the demanding lecture schedule coupled with a full social life distracted Richard from doing the work the book required. Richard had to admit his father was right. New York was proving to be a difficult environment in which to work. There had been far too many diversions the past year—from seeing Anna Pavlova dance with the Imperial Russian Ballet to dining out with his roommate Cecil Crouse at the Princeton Club (where he became a member) and from attending the Vassar prom with his old friend Martha Love to passing a day with twenty nuns in a Jersey City convent: "The girls were from six to eighteen—a rather hard variety. Everyone had a *grand* time, including me. The abbess was as human and gracious as anyone I ever saw. We were friends immediately."[19]

Halliburton realized he needed to cloister himself if he was seriously going to write his book. So in August 1924 he packed his notebooks, typewriter, and some clothes. He slid behind the wheel of his Buick and drove to Hyannis, Massachusetts. The ferry glided over Nantucket Sound and docked at Straight Wharf. Halliburton rented a small place in Siasconset, a village on the eastern end of the island.

Piles of notes lay scattered on the floor near his writing table inside his cottage. Notes and sketches filled his softbound copybooks. Blue and black ink crossed out paragraphs and scratched out words. Halliburton wrote upside down on some pages and up the margins on others.[20] These longhand manuscripts show a writer's mind at work; he crafted as he wrote, deliberating over phrases and verbs. True, his prose tended toward the florid, particularly at this nascent stage in his career, but his revisions showed that he was already beginning to exercise editorial judgment.[21]

Halliburton knew the first lines of his book were essential. If the readers didn't like what they read, if they had to think too much, or if they were confused, they would abandon the book. For the better part of nine weeks Halliburton sat before his desk for up to nine hours a day.

In August, as the summer sun warmed the waters off the island, Halliburton felt the familiar health problems of his adolescence creep into his body. The rapid heartbeat and fatigue had returned. Halliburton made an appointment with a local doctor on the island who diagnosed him with goiter, a thyroid disorder. That didn't sound right to Halliburton; the symptoms felt too similar to his youthful ailments. He took the ferry back across the sound to Hyannis and drove to New York City. Ammudder, who had spent a few weeks with him on Siasconset, traveled with her dear Richard. The New York physician diagnosed him with hyperthyroidism and recommended Halliburton return to the Battle Creek Sanatorium for treatment.

Ammudder went with him into the heartland. Disobeying his doctor's orders and ignoring Ammudder's admonishments to put his notebooks and typewriter aside, Halliburton viewed his month-long stay as a sort of writer's retreat. He labored on his manuscript, and by the end of September had produced nearly 145,000 words. And he had his health back: "Don't get discouraged even *yet*, Dad, about your inability to raise boys. *This* one is going to be a prizewinner, despite everything. All this present mess is one more lesson I hadn't learned and needed to."[22]

In October, Halliburton met his father in New York City. Together the two "tore the old manuscript to pieces."[23] They whittled away several thousand words. Wesley hired a professional typist to transcribe Halliburton's longhand. Once that was finished, they had the work bound and boxed. On November 10, they mailed it to the first publishing house on their list: Boni & Liveright. Established in 1917, the New York City–based firm would publish Ernest Hemingway, e. e. cummings, and William Faulkner. They would not, however, publish Richard Halliburton. The editors rejected his manuscript outright.

And so Richard and his father went down the list, one house after another. They tried Century Company to no avail. One rejection after another reached the would-be writer. Halliburton sighed with frustration and started preparing for the next lecture season. Wesley returned to Memphis with "a nice lot of rummage," pictures, manuscripts, circulars, and clothes his son had carted around since freshman year at Princeton.[24]

In June 1925 Halliburton dove into a punishing schedule, crisscrossing the country on trains and in cars. For his entire career Halliburton submitted to a grueling lecture schedule, giving far more of himself than any other author of his time. Certainly how much he believed he owed his readers his time. "Halliburton was hugely regarded and in demand. He was, according to my father, a riveting speaker. He attracted a lot of crowds and his appeal was widespread," Irvine Hockaday Jr. said.[25]

In Lafayette, Indiana, Halliburton checked into the Fowler Hotel, which advertised itself as a modern establishment with 217 rooms, each with a toilet and bath.[26] After the engagement, Halliburton stopped off at the Indianapolis headquarters of the Bobbs-Merrill Company, a publishing house established in 1838. He had sent them his manuscript ahead of time. After a brief meeting with David Laurance Chambers, an editor at the publishing house, Halliburton headed back to New York City, stopping in Memphis on the way. While he was there a telegram arrived from Thomas R. Coward, an editor in Bobbs-Merrill's New York office. Coward liked the manuscript and hoped to meet with him upon his return to New York. Halliburton rang and scheduled a meeting.

Halliburton had come to Coward's attention through Chambers. A member of the Princeton University Class of 1898, Chambers was flipping through the alumni magazine when he noticed Halliburton was scheduled to speak at the Princeton Club in New York City. Chambers decided to hear the young man speak. He phoned the New York office of Bobbs-Merrill, housed at 185 Madison Avenue, several blocks from Macy's Herald Square, and invited Coward to come along.

The young man's storytelling ability captivated Chambers and Coward. They found his enthusiasm contagious. His gift of connecting with the room convinced Chambers and Coward to invite Halliburton to further discuss the book idea. Halliburton felt nervous, excited, and he admitted to himself, just the tiniest bit hopeful. But he didn't want to get too hopeful. There had already been too many rejections to count.

Pleasantries aside, Coward got straight to the point. He and Chambers loved Halliburton's lecture at Princeton and they and the publishing house saw great promise in his manuscript. Coward, a Yale graduate, told Halliburton how much he loved the manuscript's originality and capricious spirit.

As Coward had noted in their preliminary communications, "We are all enthusiastic about your manuscript and want to publish it. However, the entire Editorial Force and the outside readers are unanimous in thinking that it should be cut about 80,000 words."[27] Additionally, they wanted Halliburton to change the title. They felt *The Royal Road to Romance* too cumbersome and flowery for a book authored by a young man.

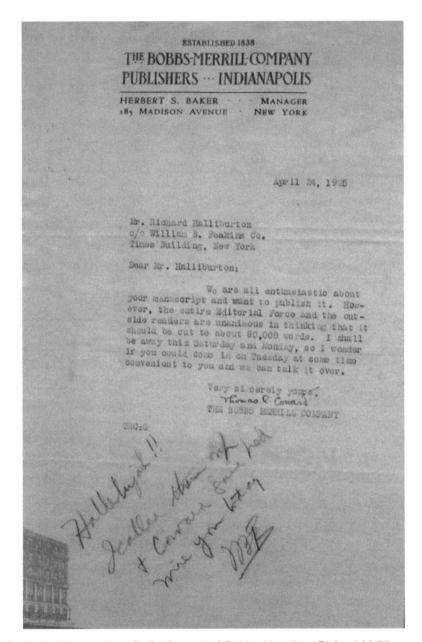

Book deal! Letter from T. R. Coward of Bobbs-Merrill to Richard Halliburton announces the publishing house would very much like to work with the aspiring writer. The letter is now at Rhodes College, Memphis. *Courtesy of the Halliburton Archives, Barrett Library, Rhodes College, Memphis, TN*

On this point Halliburton was unrelenting. He insisted the title captured his soul and the book's essence. That stubbornness taught his publishers a lot about Halliburton. Yes, he was young, and yes, he was inexperienced, but he had vision. The editorial staff offered Halliburton a contract. Halliburton had walked into that office an aspiring writer. When he walked out, he could say he was an author.

Following through on Coward and Chambers's advice, Halliburton contacted Hewitt H. Howland, the Indiana-based editor. Halliburton returned to Lafayette and received "a royal welcome."[28] He thought Howland affable and easy to work with. The two delved into the work and spent ten days rewriting and reshaping the manuscript.

Getting the contract with Bobbs-Merrill was a coup indeed. Halliburton entered into a book trade just on the cusp of prospering. Since the end of World War I, publishers were competing for new authors. Some, such as Knopf, Viking, and Random House, started the relatively new practice of paying advances. For the first time, authors could live on the income provided by a publisher's advance.[29] Over at Scribner, Maxwell Perkins, the chief editor, brought in F. Scott Fitzgerald, Ernest Hemingway, and Thomas Wolfe. In a few years *Ladies' Home Journal* would count Halliburton as one of its most regular contributors.[30] Hemingway and others in his cadre of writers, including F. Scott Fitzgerald, might ridicule Halliburton for contributing to *Ladies' Home Journal*, but with sales topping more than $2 million, it was fast becoming one of the largest circulating magazines. A byline in the magazine went a long way toward raising a writer's profile.

Book editors competed to win over American youths, a demographic fast asserting itself as a new consumer market. Editors at Bobbs-Merrill, including Chambers and Coward, sensed something fresh in Halliburton. Their instincts told them the Princeton graduate had the requisite daring to interest young readers. They knew he had the looks to attract female readers and enough of the maverick in him to interest male readers. Bobbs-Merrill correctly predicted that adventure stories, and ones with a touch of rebelliousness in them, authored by someone of Halliburton's generation, would reel in hundreds of thousands of readers.[31]

Early that summer, nearly three years to the day since he had flung open the dormitory windows of 41 Patton Hall, the dust cover of *The Royal Road to Romance* was ready for Halliburton's approval.

"I gave it reluctantly. The jacket is gorgeous in color and artistry— the picture of the Jap coolie and horse crossing a bridge in silhouette with Fuji in the distance—but it suggests so strongly a travel book on Japan which I hated—but the salesmen convened while I was there were so enthusiastic about the sales possibility of the cover I withdrew my objections. After all let's have anything on the jacket that will sell the book."[32]

The note is striking for several reasons. First, it shows Halliburton's trust in the Bobbs-Merrill sales force. Second, he shows his own keen marketing sense, which he had begun honing back in Princeton during his tenure as editor of the *Pic*. Third, the note shows the nonchalance with which Halliburton used racial slurs. This may not have been unusual in the time period in which Halliburton lived, but it nevertheless begs consideration. For as many miles as Halliburton would eventually accrue in his trips around the world, he would never lose his deep sense of white Anglo-Saxon man's superiority.

Later in the year, while Halliburton was already out of the country on his second grand adventure gathering material for another book and another lecture season, Bobbs-Merrill would release *The Royal Road to Romance*. Halliburton dedicated his first book to his four Princeton roommates: Irvine Oty Hockaday, John Henry Leh, Edward Lawrence Keyes, and James Penfield Seiberling, "whose sanity, consistency, and respectability as Princeton roommates drove me to this book." Halliburton later told a fan that choosing to dedicate his first book to his friends was easy, as he "loved all four of them to death. They were the only one-and-inseparable-now-and-forever type friends I'd ever had or hope to have the rest of my life, but the stamp of correct, standardized propriety which they followed and which I abominated prevent me ever winning their complete approval as a roommate."[33]

The reviews started coming in and the lines of demarcation were clear: the public loved him, the literary critics abhorred him.[34] *Time* attacked his language, complaining about Halliburton's flowery prose. The *New York Times* declared the book "juvenile" and picked at his exaggerations. They felt the first-time author wasn't a reliable narrator. The *Saturday Review of Literature* called it superficial. However, the *New York World* described it "full of life and positively delightful." E. B. White wrote a piece about Halliburton for the *New Yorker's* Talk of the Town. The debut book captivated the *Columbia College Spectator*, which called it the "next best thing for those who couldn't travel."

The book commanded attention; one could not read it and remain neutral. The widespread press helped sales; *Royal Road* sold one hundred thousand copies in its first year and shot to the bestseller list, where it remained for years. The publisher's sales force was agog over the book.[35] Halliburton's work soon announced itself overseas. The book was published in Czechoslovakia, Denmark, France, Germany, Holland, Italy, Norway, and Sweden. Halliburton eventually earned $70,000 in royalties from *The Royal Road to Romance*.

His work enchanted women who were expected to be satisfied housewives, and thrilled adolescents seeking independence. As Corey Ford, writing under the pseudonym John Riddell, said in *Vanity Fair*, middle-aged suburban housewives, impressionable girls, graduates, Thursday afternoon bridge clubs, and sex-starved librarians flocked to Halliburton. He was "a figure to legions of worshipful adolescents, a dauntless hero whom women of various eligible ages longed to marry."[36]

The famous noticed *The Royal Road to Romance*. Carrie Jacobs-Bond, the popular American singer and songwriter, sent Halliburton a fawning letter. The sixty-three-year-old woman especially loved the chapter about his Matterhorn ascent. She was not shy in declaring her adoration of the young writer: "There are so many things I want to say to you and I should like to write them, but my trembling hands forbid, so I will have to ask my secretary to tell you that I have chosen you, providing your mother is willing, to be my boy too and there is just one other boy besides my son, that I should like to think I am his second mother, and that is dear Lindy [Charles Lindbergh]. Your book just came and I have only read to page 98, but in the wee small hours this morning, I was lying awake . . . and I went with you up into the clouds and froze and shivered with you on that peak and wondered if the cheese was as bad as you said it was."[37]

Likewise, Halliburton offered a taste of adventure for men who wanted to climb mountains but only climbed managerial ranks. His writing fascinated a younger generation that relished adventure. These younger readers likely took no notice of his inattention to detail. Indeed he took poetic license to enhance his narrative, admitting in letters to his parents that he would embellish his prose and sometimes insert fabricated stories, particularly about romantic encounters with young women. Some reviewers overlooked this quirk and considered his style delightful. Most readers closed Halliburton's books quite confident he had done the things he said he did. That he dressed up his adventures simply added to the excitement. "He was simply a college boy on the loose, a little bit crazy with romantic enthusiasm," concluded *Time*.[38]

Halliburton was not a foreign correspondent per se; he didn't cover war and economic crises. Instead, he positioned himself as a travel reporter who followed his guts and relied on his wits from story to story. He left politics and religion to others. None of his letters reveal his personal views about politics, domestic or international. When the 1925 Scopes Trial took place, he refrained from entering the debate about teaching evolution in schools. When the Spanish Civil War broke out, he said not a word. If people wanted to read about war and its impact, they could open the *New York Times* or the *International Herald Tribune*. If people wanted to read about the growing Dust Bowl, an environmental disaster attacking the nation's heartland, they could read all about it in the *Los Angeles Times*.

But if people wanted a moment of respite, or if they wanted to immerse themselves in another region, or go where others dared not, they could read *The Royal Road to Romance*. His writing was decidedly, and deliberately, apolitical and inoffensive.[39] People gravitated to the new book's sense of high adventure, danger, and wonder. He won over a generation of readers young and old.

"I have just begun your *Royal Road to Romance* and am sharing your experiences with equal enjoyment, though you are leading me to lands where I have never been. I am a fireside traveler now and I thank heaven for just such books as yours," wrote Nicholas E. Crosby. High praise indeed from a reader who just happened to hold a PhD from Princeton.[40]

And so Halliburton would achieve star status with this first book. The public mobbed bookstores and lecture halls. Without checking with his boss, a secretary working for the *Red Star Line* invited Halliburton to lecture passengers on a trans-Atlantic trip. The military attaché at the American embassy in Paris sent him a long letter just to say he loved the author's "fluency and 'tourneau [*sic*] de phrase.'"[41] He spoke at the National Geographic Society to four thousand people in Washington, DC. Halliburton's world was fast becoming one of the rich and famous. Dr. and Mrs. Charles Mayo hosted him in Rochester, Minnesota. He met Herbert Hoover in the Oval Office and met Huey "King Fish" Long, former Louisiana governor.

Like a wandering minstrel, Halliburton traveled from town to town, city to city, regaling audiences with tales of escapades and near-death experiences and a touch of the illicit—sneaking onto trains. When he spoke, he took people away from the mundanity of the real world.

"Richard Halliburton that dashing, modern Don Quixote, whose gay vagabondage to the far corners of the earth in search of romance and adventure has put his books into the bestseller class. . . . Whenever and wherever he lectures, countless husbands eat a late cold supper," wrote Dorothy Dayton in an article for the *Illustrated Love Magazine*.[42]

Despite the tendency for his voice to climb a few notes when he spoke, even becoming a tad reedy, the trim young Princetonian was developing into a most effective and magnetic speaker. The "human dynamo," as one audience member remarked, had learned to control his arms and hands while he spoke; he rammed them into his pockets to keep them from windmilling.[43] He also made each member of the audience feel as if he or she were the only person in the room.[44] He seduced his audience. As Dayton put it, "He isn't 30 yet, and he isn't married. He is tall, well-built, good looking, with a charming manner and a smile that still retains a boyish enthusiasm and eagerness."[45]

The way Halliburton beguiled his audience comes as no surprise to Harriet D. Chapman, recounting her mother's memories of Halliburton. Chapman's grandfather, J. Penfield Seiberling, was one of Halliburton's Lawrenceville and Princeton roommates. "My mother remembered her 'Uncle Dick' fondly, influenced both by her memories of meeting him in childhood but also secondhand, through the comments my grandfather made about him over the years. He was definitely charismatic," Chapman said.[46]

After nearly two years stateside, the thought of shaking another hand, smiling before another women's club luncheon, or dodging one more question about girlfriends from reporters made him skittish. He needed to escape. He decided to follow one of the oldest and most fascinating literary paths in history, that of Homer's Ulysses. Halliburton came up with the idea when reading Homer that "there I resolved that some time I should do it, that no office desk could bar me from it." He read the *Odyssey* and immersed himself in stories of Greek gods and mere mortals.[47] He talked over his idea with Chambers at Bobbs-Merrill. Chambers approved wholeheartedly of the idea.

As the 1920s settled in to the mid-decade, intolerance and social conservatism increased.[48] So although his lecture tours afforded Halliburton many chances for fleeting trysts here and the occasional dalliance there, he was forever discreet. No one ever saw a female lover on his arm or seated across from him at dinner. Yet, he continued to insert the idea of numerous liaisons into his serialized magazine pieces, books, and lectures. When he sat down for a lengthy interview with Dorothy Dayton in the *Illustrated Love Magazine*, he spoke all about his ideal girl. His double life pained him, but there was no one with whom he could talk. It drove a wedge between him and his parents. During his visit to

Memphis, Wesley and Nelle sensed something unsettled their son. He seemed emotionally vacant at times. But of course they wouldn't know what tormented him until several years later.

"My trip home was so beautiful in most ways and so unsatisfactory in a few—unsatisfactory because the emotional cage I've been in seemed to tighten about me," Halliburton wrote home. "I was hungry for your affection—I needed it so badly and wanted to express my profound love for you and yet some inhibition built a wall all around me and then allowed me to ache because I was unapproachable. I don't know what's the matter with me. I know I love you both with all my heart and soul—and sometimes a hunger for you and a remorse that I was so disagreeable and distant in Memphis sweeps over me and adds to the turmoil my mind is in. This dreadful state is surely only a stage, a period, through which I hope I emerge sometime with a freer and happier spirit. Don't be hurt, please, at my apparent disregard for you. I'm frozen inside against every thing and everybody—but there must be a way out and surely I'll find it."[49]

Once back in Manhattan after spending time with his parents in Memphis, Halliburton checked into the Shelton Hotel. He yearned for a change in his mood: "If this Odyssey of mine doesn't lift me out of the slough I've been in for a year, then nothing can and I shall be in despair indeed."[50]

Halliburton hoped the intense activity of the past weeks would have cured any mental depression. It did not. Instead he prepared for this new adventure without the slightest bit of enthusiasm, forcing himself into making the necessary arrangements. The twenty-five-year-old hoped if he went through the motions, true happiness would follow.[51]

4

Following Ulysses

"DEAR LONESOME DAD, IN about 10 hours more we're off and when this ship sails the Bay I'll be thinking about you—and loving you Dad—and hoping you're comfortable and busy and so happy as possible with Mother."[1]

On July 4, 1925, Richard Halliburton sailed from New York aboard the *Mauretania*, the 790-foot-long sister ship to the *Lusitania*. Roderic Crane, a Lawrenceville classmate, joined him on the first leg of the trip. The Omaha, Nebraska, native had taken a leave of absence from his job as a school administrator, thinking he'd spend between one and two months with Halliburton. Of course, that hinged on how well they got along. Halliburton told his father that "Rod's going to get on my nerves if I let him—which I won't . . . with a sort of lack of finish and a religious complex . . . but he's cheerful and good natured and pliable to my direction which overcomes a multitude of religiosity."[2] Halliburton's mother, Nelle, was also aboard the ship acting as chaperone for a group of seven Memphis college women on a month-long tour of Europe.

The small party shared many a repast together as they crossed the Atlantic Ocean.[3] In the Verandah Café the author and his friend relaxed in white wicker chairs enjoying the way the skylight diffused the morning sun. One afternoon, seated on deck chairs, wearing heavy coats, Halliburton, Crane, his mother, and her young charges posed for the camera, the sun illuminating their faces.

Heavy twill pants, work shirts, a hat, pens, pencils, notebooks, and his trusty Kodak camera filled Halliburton's canvas pack. On board, he favored his black suit, black shoes, and black socks. His dress, reminiscent of an undertaker, reflected his mood. Although he projected good cheer in photos taken during the voyage and found much to laugh at when spending time with Crane, his mother, and her students, he was often beset by gloominess that, while he couldn't pinpoint the cause, built up while he was in the States. "I pray the next six months will cure my mental diseases, and when I've flown my cage. It sweeps over me . . . at times I become murderous and suicidal and have to fight desperately to keep the matter to myself."[4]

Indeed, in the weeks before his trip, Halliburton felt overwhelmed with a pressing need to abandon what had become a too familiar life of lectures and teas, luncheons and book signings. The newly minted writer feared he would sink into the trough of banality if he weren't careful. He hoped the intense work that lay ahead coupled with a change of scenery would lift his spirits.[5]

This time Halliburton looked to Homer's *Odyssey* to provide the map for his journey. After Troy fell, it took Ulysses ten years to return to Ithaca and his bride Penelope. Halliburton had a mere five months to see what Ulysses saw, including Troy, Athens, and Ithaca. He had promised William Feakins at the Feakins Agency he would return to the lecture circuit by year's end.

After a "smooth as silk" crossing, the ship docked in London.[6] Halliburton said good-bye to his mother and her students. He and Crane crossed the English Channel and spent but a moment in Paris before boarding a train to Zürich. At the Zürich Hauptbahnhof, the city's main train station, situated in the heart of Switzerland's financial capital, they caught another train to Innsbruck, Austria. The train sliced through a torrential downpour as it pulled into the station. Halliburton and Crane reached for their luggage, stepped off the car, and made their way to a taxi. The driver deposited them in front of the Hotel Tyrol.[7] Hours spent sitting on the train left their legs begging for exercise, so despite the pouring rain, they climbed a nearby hill. They returned to the hotel, their clothes drenched and their shoes squishing with each step. Then it was on for a brief stay in Vienna.

Halliburton and his companion checked out of the Grand Hotel in Vienna and boarded still another train. Leaning against the headrest, Crane wrote to Halliburton's mother, Nelle. Although his friend's animated personality had yet to fully return, Crane noticed a change in his demeanor. The angst and restlessness seemed to be lifting. Crane wrote that Richard, or Dick as he called him, read a lot on the train, gazed out the windows, and had become "quite his old handsome self—the result of several nights of good sleep, so sleep is our slogan from now on."[8]

The train chugged east, carrying the two to "the full, dirty capital of Serbia," as Halliburton described Belgrade.[9] And then it was forty-eight horrible hours on the Orient Express; conductors asked for tickets every fifteen minutes. The food and drink were tolerable at best and the cars jammed with people. The two young men arrived in Constantinople awash in fatigue.

Halliburton rose at dawn. He liked getting an early start so he could walk through a city or village just before the first rays of sunlight touched the buildings. He climbed the Blue Mosque's great minaret as the sun burst forth from the Bosporus Strait. As the muezzin called the Muslim faithful prayer, Halliburton thought to himself that he was a long way from Memphis. Then one Turkish bath in Turkey later, Halliburton's quest to follow Homer officially began.[10]

Halliburton considered the sapphire waters of the Hellespont. They might be the Dardanelles to the rest of the world, but he preferred calling them by their name of antiquity. Of the many rivers he'd so far seen—the Ohio, the Rhine, the Nile, the Volga, the Thames, and the Jordan—Halliburton awarded "first place to Hellespont."[11] Here nature was at her most capricious, sending the Black Sea rushing past Constantinople through the narrow channel of the Bosporus.

According to Greek mythology, Leander swam these waters every night to visit his beloved Hero, a high priestess imprisoned in a tower in Abydos. With a lamp held aloft, she lit Leander's way from Sestos. One night, a sudden gust of wind snuffed out the lamp and Leander lost his way, perishing beneath the black waves. Distraught, Hero leaped from the tower. This kind of dramatic love story enticed Halliburton. That and knowing his literary hero Lord Byron had swum the strait at the age of twenty-two made the idea of swimming across irresistible.

Unfortunately for Halliburton, the swim almost didn't happen. Once again Halliburton's tendency to antagonize authority reared itself. On August 9, the day before the swim, Halliburton and Crane lugged the movie camera up Xerxes Hill. They wanted to film the area Halliburton planned to swim. Halliburton had just started turning the handle of his camera when fifteen soldiers sprinted from a guardhouse at the foot of the hills. They seized his $400 camera, arrested him "à la Gibraltar as spies," Halliburton said. "It took a lot of explanation before I could regain my freedom."[12]

For thousands of years, the straits had served as a military strategic waterway and it was now heavily patrolled on the Asiatic side. The Turkish authorities didn't care if Halliburton and Crane saw how the hill overlooked two ancient forts. But they did mind that from the hill the two men could see where the Turkish military had excavated a pit, reinforced it with concrete, and stored modern artillery. This was a flagrant violation of the treaty governing the Dardanelles. Turkey lost the Dardanelles after World War I. However, the 1923 Conference of Lausanne returned it to Turkey so long as it didn't fortify the area. Hence the Turkish troops eyed Halliburton with suspicion. It was highly plausible they considered him, with his fair hair and skin, a British spy.

After a lot of pleading, and even more explaining, Halliburton sorted the problem.

On the morning of August 10, Halliburton stood on the banks of the Hellespont; the churning water looked ready to boil. A phalanx of reporters and photographers stood by—they'd gotten wind of the American's plan and knew it would make good copy for readers in the

States. Knowing he would spend hours in the water, Halliburton ate a light breakfast: he peeled open a tin of sardines and swallowed the contents. Wiping his face with the back of his hand, he looked up as Crane stepped into the fishing boat that would carry him alongside Halliburton during the swim.

Halliburton took a deep breath. He knew he possessed the mental stamina to meet the challenge. However, he wasn't certain he was fit enough to succeed. Swimming the Hellespont means battling against a strong, constant current that flows from the Marmara Sea to the Aegean. At one point the stretch of water narrows to just under a mile wide; there the force of the current is merciless. He silently reassured himself; the boat would be there should he exhaust himself.[13]

After a round of publicity pictures, both motion and still, Halliburton squared his shoulders and dove into the water. The icy cold shocked him. The galloping waves broke over his head; the wind bore down; Halliburton would need to fight for every stroke of the four-mile swim. The placid waters of the Taj Mahal pool were a distant memory.

"I didn't know whether I had got more than two hundred feet when I was the most surprised fish in the Hellespont to look around after a solid hour of swimming and find I was about a mile from shore—as well as being 1½ miles from my starting point," Halliburton wrote home.[14]

Severe cramps nearly paralyzed his legs. Each time he took a breath he swallowed salt water, leaving him thoroughly nauseated. Up came the sardines. From the support boat, Crane fed Halliburton brandy-soaked lumps of sugar, hoping they would give him warmth and energy. Now and again Halliburton took a swig from the flask. Still "the intense cold of the water to a great extent neutralized its effect." When his blood started circulating again, he let go of the boat. Halliburton took a stroke through the water. Then another and another. He felt reinvigorated, "amazed at the ease with which I swam. I doubled, trebled my speed as we approached the last third of the distance." At long last, his foot struck the sandy bottom. Crane dragged his exhausted friend into the boat, gave him more brandy, and buried him under blankets. Halliburton's knees shook. His hands trembled so violently he couldn't hold a glass of water or light a cigarette.[15]

Later that evening Halliburton relayed the story to his father, omitting nothing. Just as when he and Mike Hockaday climbed the Matterhorn, Richard hadn't prepared his father for this feat. "Very dear Dad: You have the honor to be the father of the *first* and *only* American in *history* to swim the Hellespont. Leander was the first Greek—Lord Byron the first Englishman, and Richard Halliburton the first American. Of course I was headed straight for Hellespont the moment our ship sailed from New York. As with the Matterhorn, I said nothing about it in advance for obvious reason, but now that this is 3 days past and except for a terrible sunburn—I'm just as before, I can confess the truth."[16]

At least Halliburton's truth. The young author, who was now an object of media fascination, had tried to fake his death. He thought orchestrating such a publicity stunt would promote his debut book. It started when Halliburton convinced Dwight Moore, an American friend living in Athens, to write to the *New York Times* to say he feared Halliburton had drowned mid-swim.[17] At the same time, Halliburton had mailed letters to his father and David Laurance Chambers at Bobbs-Merrill with instructions on how to react when reporters started calling. Those letters never arrived in time.

As promised, Moore wrote to the *New York Times*. The reporter ran with the story, not bothering to verify Moore's account at the source. "It was on the reverse swim that it is feared Mr. Halliburton met his death," reported the *New York Times*. A sudden squall sprang up and, the article continued, Halliburton's friends feared the strong current had swept him out to the open waters of the Aegean Sea.[18]

Moore's version then took a fantastic turn. He told the *Times* reporter that while Halliburton struggled with the waves and the rain, he spied a Greek fishing boat. Halliburton reportedly screamed for help and the fishermen heard his cries over the noise of the storm. Working together, the fishermen dragged the exhausted swimmer aboard. Once they saw Halliburton was safe, they continued on their course to Troy. Stuck in Troy, Halliburton had no way to reach his friends, Moore said.[19]

Just as Halliburton predicted, the reporters came calling, and when they did, his deception was unmasked. First they called on Wesley Halliburton Sr. and then they called on David Laurance Chambers at Bobbs-Merrill. They also called on William B. Feakins, Halliburton's manager at the lecture bureau. Feakins told journalists the last he had heard from Halliburton was an August 4 letter announcing his plan to attempt the swim. Without going into details, Feakins said communication in that part of the world was so poor it was entirely possible Halliburton had left on a trip through Macedonia or Thrace without notifying his friends.

The story of the drowning didn't hit the newsstands until early September; about three weeks after Halliburton had successfully swum the strait and had left Turkey. In fact, by the time the news broke in the United States, he was ensconced in a small, unremarkable hotel in Athens, Greece, working on his book. The story of his death persisted for several days. As such, he had no inkling of the initial media firestorm.

When he did finally face the press, Halliburton bluffed his way out of the conundrum. The twenty-five-year-old told newspaper and magazine editors that a violent tempest struck about a half mile into the swim. He spoke of waves that galloped like horses and sea swells that rose too high for him to swim through. He stuck to his story that a one-masted Turkish fishing boat, bound for the island of Imbros, rescued him eight miles from his starting point. He maintained the boat's captain lent him a keffiyeh, a red fez, and sandals. And he repeated the line about living with Turkish peasants for three days before finding a boat to Constantinople. That's when he was out of touch and word was sent that he was drowned.

Halliburton miscalculated the reach of his celebrity, the interest at home, and the displeasure he caused his editors.[20] The young author needed to make amends. To start, he wrote qualified letters of apology to the *Memphis Commercial Appeal*, which had gone to great lengths to support his budding career.

He also wrote his editors at Bobbs-Merrill, both apologizing and justifying his actions. "Feakins, my mother and father, are apparently all three nervous wrecks, and have succeeded in making me feel that I'm the most disreputable blackguard unhung. [Halliburton is using an old term to describe a servant in a royal household.] In fact, I'm considering a visit to Rome for to see the Pope in the hope he'll absolve me from my sins. But I still claim despite all the broken heads and endangered reputations it was a good and timely piece of publicity," he wrote.[21] Halliburton noted the *Memphis Commercial Appeal* ran the story across the front page; an editorial about his swim accompanied the article. The Associated Press broadcast both the story and the denial and the *New York Times* published a lengthy article in the magazine section.

Halliburton spun the story so it seemed he had no choice but to resort to this stunt. He told Chambers he had hatched the plot because he was genuinely concerned *The Royal Road to Romance*, which had been released shortly after he arrived in Europe, receive its fair share of publicity. "Not being able to afford a press agent, I have to put, sometimes all sense of modesty behind me and in cold blood court the front page. There's a risk of such behavior cheapening me—and therefore I beg of you that in regard to publicity of this and future books you carefully weigh all my advertising suggestions with your more experienced and discriminating eye in order that we may help our books on a plane of high dignity."[22]

He stubbornly refused to fully apologize. Rather he said he regretted that the stunt hadn't worked the way he'd planned. He blamed the press for trying to verify the story and the slow mail for not getting his letter to his family on time. "I'm broken-hearted over it, for that report properly broadcasted would have had tremendous value for us at this time. I wrote my family and Mr. Feakins a week in advance of the report to tutor them in the simple role they were to play—and there for some mad reason the report got there first—the Times pounced avidly upon them for verification to the complete root of all my evil plans. Serves me right, I suppose—but I only wanted to be dead for a week or ten days."[23]

Many of Halliburton's critics never forgave him for the publicity stunt, considering it proof of Halliburton's artifice. Meanwhile, though relieved Halliburton was alive, his fans never understood why he did it. Roderic Crane told his friend that high jinks like this were a waste of his time, intelligence, and talent. Moreover, he told Halliburton that pretending to be lost and found was to engage in too much "romantic nonsense." Halliburton rebuked his friend, telling him the world needed romantic nonsense; people needed to dare and to push their limits. As if proving his point, eager copycats dove into the Hellespont. Three college women, Lucy Hancock of Vassar and Eleanor Stutley and Eugenie Paterson of Smith College, were among those who ventured to repeat the challenge.

Those who knew Halliburton knew he didn't believe he was an amazing diver or swimmer any more than Ernest Hemingway considered himself a great bullfighter. He swam the Hellespont purely to feel what Leander felt, because it would make a good anecdote, and because it was there. Had he stuck to that simple narrative, he would have had a fine story without press backlash. That he felt he had to exaggerate shows his naïveté at this early stage in his career.[24]

And so Halliburton retreated to his garret in Athens, drumming his fingers on his desk. He rented the shabby quarters to save money. He needed money for food and enough money to see the expedition through, an expedition that, aside from the Hellespont hiccup, had so far exceeded his wildest hopes.[25] The author-adventurer spent a lot of time thinking of better ways to publicize *The Royal Road to Romance*. Halliburton envisioned an advertisement that included a picture of him standing atop a Grecian pedestal and, in typically plump prose, telling readers "here is a gay and spirited Odyssey of genuine adventure written by an impish young satyr who sings and fights and laughs his vagabond way from one delightfully mad experience to another."[26]

But advertising would have to wait. With his notes piled high, he doubted whether he could string together letters and words into coherent sentences. Crane harbored no such doubts. So impressed was Crane with his friend's talent that he spoke of it in a letter to Nelle Halliburton. "Dick's Odyssey already exists intact in his own subconscious creative mind and this trip is gradually bringing these ideas to light. So as we go along he just develops the film of his thought and, looking ahead, I can see it's to be grand success."[27]

It was time to continue on his journey. Halliburton prepared for a highly anticipated pilgrimage to Rupert Brooke's grave on the Island of Skyros. Ever since he was a student at Lawrenceville Academy, Halliburton wanted to pay his respects to the English poet-soldier whom he considered a kindred spirit. Brooke died in 1915 aboard a hospital ship anchored off the Dardanelles. He was twenty-seven. To Halliburton, Brooke represented the brevity of youth and, like his brother Wesley Jr., the brevity of life. As Winston Churchill said, Brooke's life "closed at the moment when it seemed to have reached its springtime."[28]

Halliburton and Crane spent eighteen hours sailing across the Aegean Sea to the island, a blistering, sleepless, and vermin-ridden ride.[29] The friends passed the hours talking with an American Greek expatriate. Once they arrived on Skyros, he invited them to his house, and offered to take them to the gravesite in the morning. The trio rode mules for two hours until they reached his house. The grave lay ten miles from the village, so the next day they rode five hours more to the marble tomb. As they rode, buzzards flew above the scrubby and rocky landscape, and wild goats grazed alongside the road.[30] By the time they arrived at the grave, night had fallen, and the full moon poured white light upon the ghostly marble. Halliburton was transported. For the writer, even meeting someone who knew Brooke was awe inducing: "like meeting one of the apostles." Although the Englishman had authored only a few short poems, Halliburton considered him one of the most gifted men of the twentieth century, his works "immortal to any one who values emotional expression in poetry rather than intellectual."[31] He longed to write an authorized biography of Brooke.

He wrote to Rupert Brooke's mother, Mary Ruth, and told her he would be honored to call on her at her home in Rugby, England. She sent a vaguely worded response, neither inviting him, nor rejecting him. Halliburton interpreted her ambiguity as a yes and decided to pass through Rugby at the end of his personal odyssey.

After seeing the grave, Halliburton and Crane moved on to the village of Thessaloniki, near the Macedonian border. Halliburton was fixed on scaling Mount Olympus, which at nearly ten thousand feet was the second-highest mountain in the Balkans. Climbing the mountain of the gods would be one more way to revive Homer and his hero Ulysses. Today, scores of people crawl and scramble over boulders to reach the summit. However, in 1925 few ascended the barren peak.

Halliburton hired a guide for him and Crane. He knew the climb wasn't as difficult as the Matterhorn or Fuji, but as he was unfamiliar with the terrain, he decided to err on the side of caution. On the way up, they passed a three-foot-high cairn, which the Swiss mountain climber and photographer Fred Boissonnas had left behind in 1913 on his way to become the first European climber to reach Greece's highest peak. In a nod to Lord Byron, Halliburton and Crane carved their names onto one of the bottom rocks. The men pushed their way through cold and fog. At the top, feeling tired and pleased, Halliburton and Crane joked about making an offering to Zeus. "I should have liked to sacrifice Roderic's mustache, but it was undetachable."[32] The two spent the night tucked into sleeping rolls, shrouded in mist. In the middle of the night they awoke to the crack of thunder and snap of lighting. It was, Halliburton thought, the perfect melody.

Halliburton's cheeky letter home about the excursion stressed his safety. He told his parents that no fewer than eight soldiers and six shepherds escorted them all the way to the summit.

After his thunderous night atop Mount Olympus, Halliburton loitered a week in the Vale of Tempe. He climbed Mount Parnassus for inspiration. There is a photo of Halliburton at the Parthenon taken that September. With a broad grin, hands in pockets, he stands proudly atop a crumbling column, and three complete columns stand sentinel in the background. Thousands of tourists have walked up and down the marble steps, but no one is allowed to sleep on the grounds. That didn't hinder Halliburton from spending a "Taj Mahalish night alone in the Parthenon. Never was anything so divine, so clear, so alone—human, so chastely perfect as these haggard ruins. I'd been up to the Acropolis 10 times, but in the moonlight everything was changed."[33]

Richard Halliburton poses atop a column at the Parthenon during the trip that became *The Glorious Adventure*. *Author's collection*

However, as far as the book editor at *Time* was concerned, everything had already changed. To the magazine, this trip was "a professional set piece: a stunt following-out of the wanderings of Ulysses," while in the trip that resulted in *Royal Road*, Halliburton had "neither put on a show or concocted copy."[34]

Nonetheless, soon after that night, Crane sailed home on the *Majestic*, unable to postpone his departure date. He needed to return to Omaha and to his job as a school administrator. Halliburton helped his friend pack and saw him off on the first boat to Naples. "Rod's gone. I miss him but am too busy to have time to miss him much. We got along with absolute harmony—it would have been impossible for two people to travel more agreeably together, and with less friction. He was made to order for this particular . . . trip."[35]

At this point, Halliburton had mended his clothes so many times there were few original threads left, and dirt had turned his gray suit black. Newly arrived in Italy, he asked a local Sicilian launderer to dry-clean his suit, but the owner told him it would take at least ten days for the job. That was too long for Halliburton, who would likely be gone from Sicily in a few days. Ever resourceful, Halliburton set a ceramic bowl of hot water, a bar of soap, and a brush on his room's table. He attacked his suit, scrubbing his coat and trousers as he would a kitchen table. They "looked like the devil" after air-drying overnight, but he figured a few passes of a hot iron would reshape the garments.[36]

During Halliburton's brief stop in Sicily, he endeavored to swim the three miles across the Strait of Messina, between a rocky shoal and a whirlpool that were considered the inspiration for the mythical Scylla and Charybdis. According to legend, Scylla and Charybdis were two deep-sea monsters. In the *Odyssey*, Ulysses had to choose which hazard to confront when sailing the straits. To pass Scylla, a rocky shoal depicted as a many-headed monster, would mean losing a few sailors. To pass Charybdis, a whirlpool, would mean losing the whole ship. Ulysses chose to sail past Scylla.

Halliburton knew the tale and still ventured forth. To his knowledge, no one had ever successfully swum through the roiling waters.
Any time Halliburton could claim to be the first at something was a
good day; however, aside from the dangerous whirlpools, terrific currents, and frigid water, there was the heavy shark rope the fisherman in
the accompanying boat insisted he tie under his arms. He yielded after
going a third of the distance.

If he couldn't test himself in the water, he would settle on another
climb. Mount Etna, Europe's most active volcano, sits on Sicily's east
coast. It has been the source of myth and legend for centuries. According to Greek myth, Hephaestus and the Cyclops forged Zeus's thun-
derbolts deep inside the mountain. Virgil describes it in book III of
the *Aeneid*.

Halliburton hired a motorcar to drive him to a village situated ten
miles up the lower slopes. There he slept. He rose before dawn, ate
a hearty breakfast, and at 6:00 AM, he, a guide, a mule boy, and two
mules started their ascent. Chestnut groves, golden in the early morning
light, yielded to great wastes of black lava on both sides. Halliburton
plodded through knee-high snow for the last two thousand feet of the
ten-thousand-foot climb. Lavender and rose light splashed the volcano
in the gloaming.[37]

"The guide and I climbed this last distance but the wind was so
strong and so cold and I was so ill prepared for it, we just had a look
over the crater rim and hurried back."[38] He spent the night in a mountain refuge under a mound of blankets—cold, damp, and unimpressed.
Lazily, he watched the sun rise in the morning and "slid home again
down the lava ashes."[39] The climb most definitely did not compare with
his Matterhorn and Mount Fuji climbs, but he knew it would make a
good story nonetheless.

Taking a ferry across Homer's wine-dark sea, Halliburton arrived
in Malta. There he faced one of the most terrifying experiences of his
journey. He, the American Consul, and a Miss Adams lunched in a
four-hundred-year-old palace, after which they drove all over the island
sightseeing. On their way back to the consulate, a twelve-year-old boy

darted in front of the speeding car. "We struck him with a sickening thud. I've never experienced a more dreadful moment," Halliburton wrote home. Sprinting from the car, Halliburton picked up the limp boy, who bled from a dozen places, his clothes shredded. They sped to the hospital. On the way, the boy regained consciousness and "to our relief could move all his limbs. . . . We went to see him Sunday night and found him quite all right. But it was all very heartbreaking. Why he wasn't killed I simply do not know."[40]

In Tunis, Tunisia, for Thanksgiving Day 1925, Halliburton wrote to his parents that he dreamed of having a new dinner coat made, though he had no dinner to attend, a sure sign he was losing interest in the trip.[41] His adventure was almost over; soon he would start for home. He took a combination of boats and trains to the French coast and by the time he crossed the English Channel, his mood was sour. Again, the ease with which he used derogatory phrases showed itself: "Morning—what a ghastly night! It being only one night I took second-class on this ship. My cabin, shared with two wops, was just below the after decks on which 20 cows were being transported."[42] The rocking of the ship threw the cows back and forth, their hooves ricocheting on the steel plates above his head.

In England, he looked forward to calling on Rupert Brooke's mother. Arriving in London on December 6, Halliburton hopped on the last train to Rugby. The small town sat near the River Avon in Warwickshire. He checked into an inn, donned his gray suit, and at 8:00 PM knocked on the door of Mary Ruth Cotterill Brooke.

Stoic and mannerly, she held her distance. She was alone now, her husband long dead, and all three of her sons also dead—the war claimed two, illness the other. Halliburton kept his visit brief. He talked with Brooke about his wish to write the story of her son's life. She listened politely and seemed interested in Halliburton. Although he left feeling he'd learned nothing about Brooke that would serve a biography, he felt the visit was worth it because meeting his mother was "next best to meeting him."[43] He returned to London and sailed for New York aboard the *Republic*.

A cheery Memphis welcomed back their native son, and Halliburton settled in for the holiday season, pleased to see his stocking hung from the Christmas tree, just as he had asked. He relished the time with his parents and a hug from Ammudder. The four sat around the table, trading stories and gossip.

He had clinched his celebrity journalist status. Reporters mobbed him while he visited his parents.[44] In February, during signings and parties in Chicago, he stopped off at Brentano's bookstore for an event. In the shop window, a large poster emblazoned with the words OUTSTANDING TRAVEL BOOK OF THE YEAR leaned behind a stack of Halliburton's first book, *The Royal Road to Romance*. By February, the black clothbound book ranked number two on Chicago's bestseller list.[45]

Speaking at the Nineteenth Century Club (where his mother was president) Halliburton encouraged a predominantly female audience to "find a spirit of wanderlust in herself. . . . Don't be Penelopes, pray God, may you never be steady women!"[46] In Pittsburgh, more than six hundred people came to hear him speak in a lecture hall that had capacity for five hundred. A gardenia adorned his lapel and he wore a blazing turquoise ring for the "blue ribbon occasion."[47]

Indeed, Halliburton made every effort to treat each speaking engagement as a "blue ribbon occasion." His suits were freshly pressed, his shirts starched, and his face closely shaved. He often carried his polished walking stick and buffed his shoes to a high gloss. Sometimes Halliburton added spats to the ensemble. It's what the public expected to see. They never saw the actual adventurer—the one with a full and dirty beard, the one whose hair was a tangle atop his head. The one who wore several days of sweat and dirt like a second layer of clothing.

As he sped from one lecture to the next, he considered his parents at home, wanting them to feel his success. Sometimes he'd slip a check into an envelope for his mother and father, urging them to "buy a new hat or gasoline."[48]

Winter made way for spring. Halliburton relished his busy schedule. It kept him from completely sinking into depression's dark embrace. He felt himself teetering on the edge of becoming a national figure. This excited him because he felt the only cure for whatever he suffered from was his rise to stardom. "I have to keep climbing furiously to keep my mental balance."[49]

Nonetheless, a month later, the slump he had been fighting had succeeded in pulling him down. For a man so often surrounded by hundreds if not thousands of people, he felt alone. "But I confess to my mudder and Dad and Ammudder, I'm lonely. My affections are absolutely dead—I've no time to care about people—wish I could fall in love. It would add some sweetness and sparkle to all this brass materialism. I lead an absolutely loveless life, friends and acquaintances too many, but all of them could disappear and I wouldn't know it."[50]

He dwelled in melancholia through the summer. Once autumn arrived and he began lecturing, his gloom sloughed off.

"The lecturing since seeing you has been a series of semi-riots," Halliburton told Chambers.[51] The biggest crowd in the history of the Milwaukee City Club turned out to hear him. In Memphis, five hundred people stood to hear the author, while two thousand more were turned away; the Goodwyn Institute never knew such a mob. He addressed an audience of twenty-five hundred teachers Friday night, and he expected at least the same number for his talk at the New War Memorial Hall in Nashville.

Halliburton also reconnected with some of his Princeton friends. Just after New Year's Day 1927, he saw Mike Hockaday in Kansas City. Halliburton was shocked to learn Hockaday's father had committed suicide after "a terrible physical, financial and physiological sickness had produced a chronic melancholia which affected his mind."[52] Heartbroken, the newly married Hockaday looked "so old and worn."[53] A call from Chambers wrenched Halliburton from his friend's side. The editor asked him to go to Indianapolis to work on more publicity for the *Royal Road to Romance* sales campaign.

In April Halliburton's attention turned home. The Great Mississippi Flood, the result of excessive summer rains, drowned as much as twenty-seven thousand square miles of land, submerging some places under thirty feet of water. In Memphis, sandbags along the river could not keep the waters from flooding downtown. "My dear flood sufferers," Halliburton wrote home, enclosing a check for thirty dollars from a Mrs. Charles Bond of Boston for the flood fund. "People up here seem really impressed and flood funds are being collected everywhere."[54] By May the river below Memphis would be sixty miles wide.

Between speaking engagements and concern for his fellow Memphians, Halliburton worked furiously to turn the notes from his latest journey into his second book, *The Glorious Adventure*, to be published in 1927. After the Hellespont debacle, Chambers kept a tight leash on Halliburton as far as content and accuracy were concerned. He nurtured Halliburton's literary voice, which tended to gush. While Halliburton's tone drew in readers, Chambers advised the young author to keep the material simple and not get lost on too many tangential stories. He wanted more Homer and less Halliburton.

For example, in the proposed last chapter, Halliburton tried to draw a parallel between Ulysses and Penelope and himself and a young woman named "Fifi." Chambers viewed the parallel "so incongruous as to be ridiculous. Alas, it isn't even funny! It's the failure to establish that kind of parallel that makes one doubt the wisdom of putting Fifi in, at all. Not that you have fallen down in the way you've handled it. But it just can't be done. The material itself is lacking. As long as Fifi was just used for light comedy as in Chapters 19 and 20, I thought we might get by, but from the beginning of 21 where you have an irate husband writing Fifi, and Fifi cabling him for money for you, the fun isn't there. At least your literal-minded readers would never see it as you do. They'd call it bad taste."[55]

However, Fifi was the least of Halliburton's editorial problems. According to Chambers, the biggest snag was that aside from the Homeric story—the Hellespont swim, the climbs up Mount Olympus and Mount Vesuvius—the material seemed thin. Chambers was concerned that Halliburton padded his other stories with imaginary incidents. "Indeed they are so patently manufactured that they may cast doubt on the things you really did; doubt that you swam the Hellespont or climbed Mount Olympus. And that would be calamity," Chambers said.[56]

Halliburton worked over the book with Hewitt Howland, the same editor who helped on *The Royal Road to Romance*. Like that first book, *The Glorious Adventure* shot to the bestseller list. The reviews came quickly: from the *Catholic Vigil, Springfield Republican*, and *Saturday Review of Literature* to *Time*, the *Saturday Evening Post*, and the *New York Herald-Tribune*.

Wesley Halliburton Sr. employed a service to gather media clippings, and Richard also sent home reviews. The notices arrived faster than Wesley could cut and paste them into his leather-bound scrapbook. His son took a peculiar delight in his negative reviews. "That is one explanation of my comparative success I suppose that success and flattery honestly bores me—but opposition and ridicule interests and rouses me profoundly. In fact I find myself just a little disappointed if there's no disapproval in reviews."[57] His detractors egged him on.

Halliburton, who once met F. Scott Fitzgerald and his wife Zelda at a dinner party, decided to send his fellow Princeton alum an inscribed copy of the new book. Fitzgerald poked fun at the gesture, suggesting Halliburton staged every escapade right here in the United States. "I hope this will reach you before you disappear into Brooklyn to imagine and write another travel book—because don't think I really believe you've been in all these places and done all these things like you say. . . . Your friend, Scott Fitz."[58] Fitzgerald went on to say that he thought the book was better planned and written than *Royal Road*.

Fitzgerald considered Halliburton a poseur and mocked his exploits. True, the novelist's friend Ernest Hemingway had manufactured adventure to some degree—driving an ambulance during the Spanish Civil War, climbing Mount Kilimanjaro, deep-sea fishing off the coast of Florida's Key West. Yet, neither Fitzgerald nor anyone else doubted his exploits. In part this was because physically the two men could not be more different. Halliburton possessed what some critics called a slight and unsubstantial physique compared with Hemingway's sturdier and more muscular frame. It was also in part because Halliburton announced his plans, and appeared to seek publicity in a way Hemingway did not.

Writing for *Esquire* in 1940, George Weller summed it up this way: Hemingway was trying to sell "absinthe and cognac" while Halliburton was trying to get them to "take nectar, liberally watered."[59] The literati set, particularly those writers for the *New Yorker* and *Vanity Fair*, took aim at Halliburton. They viewed him as an attention getter, not much different from the likes of Gertrude Ederle, who at nineteen became the first woman to swim across the English Channel, and Joan Lowell, an actress who in 1929 published *Cradle of the Deep*, a memoir that turned out to be entirely fabricated. Comparing him to women was a deliberate shot at Halliburton's masculinity.

In some respects this criticism represented a larger, growing concern about the feminization of American men. In the mid-to-late 1920s Hollywood celebrated men who were rugged but also androgynous. In response, an increasing number of men turned to "strenuous recreation, spectator sports, adventure novels and a growing cult of the wilderness" to prove their manhood. Popular culture continued to idolize prizefighters, cowboys, soldiers, and sailors, heralding them paragons of virility.[60]

Halliburton smashed that mold. Reticent he was not; he wrote with emotion and adornment. He wrote with enthusiasm because he wanted his audience to feel what he felt. As the English writer Beverley Nichols put it, "If you were to ask an Englishman why he swam the Hellespont, he would probably reply 'to reach the other side.' If you were to ask him why he ran to Athens, he would doubtless say 'because there was no bus.' . . . He'd never say it was because he just 'felt' the need or call upon 'mysticism of the East.' Yet Richard Halliburton really felt these things, and it was fortunate for him that he did so, because he was able to transfer his orthodox emotions to 120,000 American readers through the medium of his pen, and to some 500,000 American lecture-goers through his voice."[61]

Halliburton's escapades offered an escape from a weakening economy. Fan mail crammed his parents' mailbox and was sent to him in batches every four days or so. Some admirers begged the writer to take them along on his next adventure, some pitched story ideas for Halliburton, and besotted teenage girls proposed marriage. Some wrote inviting him to join in adventures of their own devising. Still others, men included, made unabashedly romantic overtures toward the author.

In March 1927, Jack Gibson of Ohio, Illinois, invited the author to meet him. It's impossible to know whether Gibson knew Halliburton was homosexual, but clearly he harbored feelings for this man he had never met. Since Gibson first read about Halliburton in *American Magazine* he could not stop thinking about him. "I believe in destiny, and I truly believe that you and I are to meet, and for the good of both of us," Gibson wrote. "My guarantee is just myself. I stick by a fellow, even to the giving of my life, and I expect the same from the other fellow. Dick do you believe in caring for a fellow that you have never seen? I have only your picture but you seem now as a pal to me. I am hoping you will be. You see my former Pal I lost during the War. We went together for eight years, and I thought I would never hook up with another fellow again. You are the first one I have asked of such a request." Gibson enclosed a photo of himself in military dress, the only one small enough to slip into the envelope.[62]

Whether Halliburton replied is unknown. He likely kept the letter from his parents and friends. As always, Halliburton jealously guarded his private life.

When Thanksgiving came, Halliburton sent Chambers a teasing note, trying to make him feel guilty for his favorite author who spent the holiday alone, "off in the wilds of New Jersey," where he "dined all alone on ham and eggs at a Greek quick lunch counter" before returning to his desk to rewrite *The Glorious Adventure*.[63]

By 1928 Halliburton was delivering as many as fifty talks a month. In February, he spoke before eight different audiences in five days. He was so busy he barely had time to write. "Mother dear & Dad, You would be probably badly worried about me—and this long letterlessness if you hadn't learned from long experience that I'm always quite alright and only furiously busy."[64] With the exception of the actor Will Rogers, Halliburton drew the biggest crowds of anyone, or so he boasted.[65] Nevertheless, the Tennessean considered it a miserable audience unless all the standing room was taken. He still remembered an event a year before where he had two hundred books on hand to sell but only sold twenty-five.[66] Overall, he thought lecturing "all great fun and tremendously thrilling—and I was happy to find I could be aroused by a howling audience," he wrote.[67]

Seven years after he graduated Princeton University, Halliburton was a fixture of the *New York Times* society pages. He dined with movie stars like Rudolph Valentino and sipped cocktails with Mary Pickford. He went to the same parties as Raymond Hitchcock, a silent film actor who starred in John Ford's 1927 film *Upstream*. He "teaed [*sic*] with every famous movie actor there is. A few of them are nice enough," he wrote home.[68]

Occasionally while on the road, Halliburton phoned home, delighted by the clarity of the connection: "Mother & Dad Was happy to have talked to you last night from Fort Smith. Wasn't it fun? You seemed only a block away."[69]

As the year unfolded, Halliburton's old, and for now unfounded, fear returned: he worried his popularity was waning. Fretful the public might be "fed up with Dick Halliburton's juvenile antics," Halliburton thought about a time when he could write a book (the Rupert Brooke biography) where his name only appeared on the spine.[70]

Halliburton felt the all too familiar push-pull of travel. "I find myself moving slowly but surely toward a yearning for escape and friends and calm," he wrote his parents. "I'm at the ragged edge of literary oblivion unless I do the right thing. I have full faith that when the time comes I'll do it."[71]

This time, Halliburton didn't want to relive anybody's life—alive or dead, real or imagined. This time he wanted to go "semi-vagabond," starting in Paris, crossing the Alps, visiting the Holy Land, and then voyaging on to South America. "The idea struck me with a finality that I suppose will prove irresistible. I'm going to buy an Atlas tomorrow and route myself."[72]

5

Glorious Panama

I N SPITE OF HIS enormous success, Halliburton couldn't slow down. He decided there could be no better cure for his anxiety than to follow the trail of Spanish conquistador Hernán Cortés through Mexico.

It hadn't been his first choice for his next book. For the better part of a year, he'd considered writing about Richard III and the Crusades. However, his editor David Laurance Chambers was lukewarm to the idea, thinking it lacked the wide appeal essential in keeping his fans happy and attracting new readership. He wanted the publishing house's prize author to stick to what was so far a winning formula: take a familiar figure—or two—from history or literature and follow their path.[1] "We've never had an author who gave us such wonderful cooperation, to whose interests we could feel more personal devotion, to whom we have felt more closely bound. You have made a royal road into our hearts, my dear fellow, and all our contact with you has been a glorious adventure. More power to you, to both the books, to all of us!"[2]

Halliburton's books had power indeed. The first two sat on the bestseller lists alongside George Bernard Shaw's *The Intelligent Woman's Guide to Socialism and Capitalism* and Thornton Wilder's *The Bridge of San Luis Rey*. This next adventure, which he now broadened to include Vasco Núñez Balboa's hunt for the Pacific Ocean and an excursion to Machu Picchu, would also gather Mayans, Aztecs, and Incas into one hardbound book. He and Chambers were confident it too would rise to become a bestseller. Additionally, the writer just signed a contract with Loring Schuler of *Ladies' Home Journal* to do a series of articles.

This time the twenty-eight-year-old asked his fifty-seven-year-old father to join him on his voyage to the Southern Hemisphere. Surprise gave way to nostalgia for the past; Wesley Halliburton Sr. remembered the yearly getaways they'd taken together each Easter when his son was young. They'd visited Civil War battlefields, walked the woods of Chattanooga, and played golf at the Grove Park Inn in North Carolina.

Richard was thrilled that his father—or Père, as he sometimes affectionately called him—said yes. He hoped to bridge some of the space that had crept between them of late. Some of that distance had arisen because Richard sensed that his father—more than his mother—fretted whether he would ever marry, have children, and settle down. His son's personal life remained a mystery.

It was late May when father and son said good-bye to Memphis and hugged and kissed Nelle farewell; she was preparing to accompany another group of young women abroad. The two Halliburton men sailed from New Orleans across the Gulf of Mexico to Vera Cruz, a port city on the eastern coast of Mexico. During the crossing, they read, walked on the deck under periwinkle skies, and ironed out the itinerary. Richard thumbed through William H. Prescott's *Conquest of Mexico*. An American science historian, Prescott focused on Mexico's political and military affairs. Richard's basic knowledge of Cortés and his conquest needed a refresher if he were to write an authoritative but entertaining book.

Richard and his father carried little extra in the way of personal baggage, although Richard naturally lugged his typewriter along; not wanting to waste space he sometimes stuffed it with extra socks.[3] Richard also carried letters of introduction from the US State Department requesting he receive "such courtesies and assistance as you may be able to render, consistently with your official duties."[4]

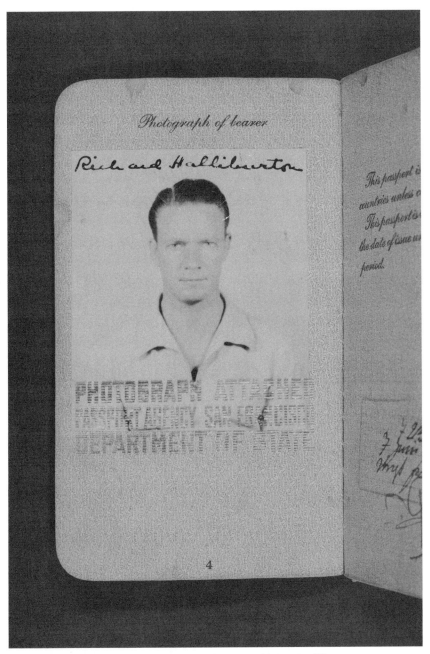

Passport photo of Richard Halliburton. *Princeton University Library*

Father and son stayed in Vera Cruz just long enough to hire an interpreter who was willing to go with them the more than 250 miles to Mexico City. Richard was antsy to begin following the very same route Cortés and six hundred soldiers followed in August 1519. And like Cortés, they'd walk. They wound their way through Xalapa, Tlaxcala, and Cholula. Hot, dry air sucked the moisture from their skin. Richard's light brown hair turned flaxen under the sun. On their last day, the small group covered nearly thirty miles, passing the twelve-thousand-foot saddle between Popocatépetl and Iztaccihuatl to Mexico City.

Upon reaching their destination they checked into the Hotel Regis, a three-hundred-room hotel with 280 baths and, according to the hotel stationery, every other modern convenience.[5] Immediately after registering, Richard wired his mother in Memphis to tell her they had arrived. A longer letter to "My Sweet Mudder" followed, describing their pilgrimage from Vera Cruz to Mexico City. "You got our wire yesterday and know that we're safe,—so far, so good, and *what* a time we've had! It's really been one of the most original adventures I've ever had."[6]

Richard felt rejuvenated. He had been positively drained before, having overextended himself lecturing, and if he were honest with himself, walking hundreds of miles under the scorching Mexican sun was taxing. But there was something about being immersed in a project, surrounded by magnificent scenery, that fired his strength. And although Wesley seemed to weather the long march all right, he felt more sapped than he let on. His bushy eyebrows drooped with fatigue. The two retired early and after a restful slumber, the elder Halliburton rallied. After breakfast father and son climbed Mexico City's Metropolitan Cathedral's bell tower, which sits atop the site of the ancient Aztec Templo Mayor. During his Mexican conquest, Cortés and his Spanish missionaries razed the Aztec temple and used the stones to erect the new cathedral.

The second item on Richard's checklist was more daunting. He meant to climb the 17,802-foot high Mount Popocatépetl, North America's second-highest volcano and one of Mexico's most active; its Aztec name means "smoking mountain." (Popocatépetl erupted in 1994 after fifty years of dormancy; it has since been closed to climbers.)

The temperature rose sharply shortly after starting out, and soon it was very hot indeed. Wesley's legs started aching and his breathing grew labored. He doubted he had the fortitude to reach the top. Not wanting to burden his son, he turned around and headed back to the hotel. And then there were two. Richard and his interpreter continued on.

Once atop the steep-walled crater, Halliburton reached for his own camera and started snapping away. He needed photos for the articles he was under contract to write for newspapers and magazines, including *Ladies' Home Journal*. The shutter jammed. Head hanging in frustration, the writer hiked down Popocatépetl and met his father back at the Regis. He took out his stress on his typewriter, jabbing at the keys until a skeleton of a story formed. A few days later, Wesley left for home, carrying a first draft of his son's Cortés story. He would mail it to Chambers once he got back to Memphis. "I felt like a poor lone widow woman after Dad's train pulled out—and it got worse all day. But I stuck to my desk and have drowned my loneliness in work," he wrote his mother, adding that he "was disappointed to death Dad wasn't able to bring you this bronze bull we found."[7]

Meanwhile Halliburton prepared to climb the peak a second time. Taking no chances, he took along a professional photographer who had also climbed the volcano twice before. Halliburton wanted a panorama picture of the summit, with him as the centerpiece. He wanted the sunlight to hit him just right, and so at 12:30 AM Halliburton left the warmth of the Hotel Regis together with his interpreter, guide, and the mules. They ascended in darkness, aiming to reach the summit at daybreak. The wind whistled through the cold night. At 3:00 AM, a summer blizzard surprised the little knot of climbers. They couldn't see more than ten feet ahead. Taking baby steps and feeling their way, they made it to the top. The trio shivered in the glacial dark for more than an hour until the first shards of light poked through the sullen gray sky. After the photographer took several shots of Halliburton, the group turned around and went down, slowly and deliberately, taking care to avoid loose stones and shifting earth.[8]

Back in his hotel room, Halliburton changed clothes, flexed his writing muscles, and started reworking the draft of his Cortés story so he could use it for the book. He had become quite familiar with the repetitious nature of writing—the writing and the rewriting. He had already filed a story about climbing Popocatépetl with his father for the *Memphis Commercial Appeal.* The story tickled Chambers so much he wrote Wesley, "It's a peach! I see that if Dick decides to stop adventuring and mountain climbing we'll have to persuade you to pinch-hit for him. I suspect he'd find you a dangerous rival, too, for this is certainly a bully story."[9]

While Halliburton missed his father, he wouldn't be in want of company for long. He planned to meet Fred Healy, a friend of his from New York who worked for G. P. Putnam's Sons, in Progreso, on the Yucatán Peninsula. After squaring his bill with the hotel clerk he returned to Vera Cruz. Now that he was done playing Spanish conquistador, he could travel by car rather than on foot or horse and make the trip in a day. He spent three miserable days—by his description—moored in Vera Cruz "for a terrible Mexican boat and ride on it 48 hours across the Gulf. There were cows aboard and Mexicans. But I worked hard at my Cortez [*sic*] and tried not to notice the smells," he said, shameless about using pejorative language.[10]

In Progreso, Halliburton met up with Healy and the two rode on to Mérida, the capital of the Yucatán. There he met the "Ruling American," who was most enchanted to meet the famous writer and get his copies of *The Royal Road to Romance* and *The Glorious Adventure* signed. After a lovely tête-à-tête, Halliburton went back to his hotel, closed the door to his room, and worked on a second draft of his Cortés story.

Meanwhile Fred Healy recovered from his inoculation against typhoid fever and Halliburton collected necessary letters from governors, military commanders, and other officials to ensure their safe passage through the Yucatán Peninsula to Chichén Itzá.[11]

The car bounced along the dirt road on the way to the great Maya ruins of Chichén Itzá. At its apex, the ancient Mayan civilization extended from Guatemala through the Yucatán Peninsula and controlled a vast network of trade cities extending as far south as Panama and as far north as Central Mexico. The Mayan civilization flourished in the north until the sixteenth century AD, when Cortés and the conquistadors arrived wearing shiny armor and carrying razor-sharp swords and disease. Halliburton's articles and forthcoming book *New Worlds to Conquer* would gloss over the atrocities the Spanish conquistadors inflicted on the region. Instead his work would focus solely on the colors, smells, and sounds and, naturally, his formidable stunts.

Along the way Halliburton saw cactus-like vegetation growing with stiff and sharp-pointed leaves. He saw rows of sisal and yellow masses of fibers drying in courtyards. Finally he arrived at the ruins sweaty and dusty. While the still unwell Healy stayed behind in Mérida, the celebrity journalist spent the next three days exploring the ruins. The sight of Chichén Itzá overwhelmed the young man from Memphis. His blue eyes took in the Temple of Warriors and the 225-foot-wide and 545-foot-long ball court where players tried to hit a nearly nine-pound rubber ball through a scoring hoop hewn from stone. The court had no ceiling and its acoustics were phenomenal. Whispers at one end could be heard at the other end. Halliburton walked past statues of a Chacmool—a reclining god on whose belly priests occasionally presented bloody sacrifices to summon rain—until he stood before the Temple of Kukulkan.

The ancient edifice rose from the heart of the site. Built for astronomical purposes, the pyramid marked the vernal and autumnal equinoxes. There are 91 steps on each side of the pyramid, and the top platform is the final step. Thus the total number of steps equals 365, or one for each day of the year. Halliburton climbed to the top. Heavy clouds hung in the sky like drawing-room drapes. From the top of his 75-foot-high aerie, the writer spied the *sacbe*, an 886-foot-long and 100-foot-wide raised road, otherwise known as the white road.[12] It lured the writer; he knew that just beyond lay the Cenote Sagrado or Sacred Cenote.

The Mayans believed cenotes were mouths leading to the realm of Chaac, the god of life-giving rain. There are thousands of cenotes across the Yucatán; underground rivers carved them out of the limestone. Not all were used for human sacrifice; some were used for collecting drinking and bathing water.

Darkness shrouded Chichén Itzá. Halliburton balanced on the balls of his feet, just on the edge of the Sacred Cenote. "The water's surface far below stirred the spirits of the Rain God's brides and his phantom worshippers."[13] He felt an irresistible urge to leap into the water-filled cavity. He drew the damp air deep into his lungs. He sprang. Aiming his body like an arrow, he dove seventy feet into the sacrificial pool. Surfacing, Halliburton stared up at the pool's sheer sides and wondered if he was about to become another human sacrifice. Today divers use rope ladders to scale the cenote's vertical walls. No such assistance awaited Halliburton; he had to free climb. Sheer will propelled him upward, ten feet, thirty feet, sixty feet. Finally, he was up and over the top, his feet planted firmly on the ground. Water dripped from his body, creating runnels in the cream-colored sand.

It was Halliburton's misfortune no one bore witness to his nighttime jump. Without photographic proof, his critics would certainly cast doubt on his account. Ever the master of public relations, Halliburton repeated the perilous jump two days later. "The realization of the dramatic possibilities for a story made me go back and do it again. I must have evidence for the doubting reviewers," he wrote his parents.[14] And so he dove again. This time he brought along two photographers, one of whom had a movie camera, and two reporters. He paid the photographer $150, but always calculating, he figured he would earn $2,500 from the story—*Ladies' Home Journal* would salivate over it.

"The second plunge in no way harmed me, except my hand striking the water strained a muscle across my chest," he wrote, adding that, like the first time, the shock of hitting the water caused a terrific headache. Later he joked he repeated the jump solely to retrieve his moccasins.[15] Though either dive could have injured or killed Halliburton, he paid little mind to that fact. In fact, he seemed ever insouciant toward his own death.

The leap was merely a prelude to his biggest claim to fame.

Halliburton returned to Mérida and showed the film from his dive to an excited audience. Healy was still ailing from his inoculation, but not so much that he couldn't continue. The two set off on "an unspeakably filthy" sixty-ton sailboat, which took nearly three days to inch along the coast from Mérida to Cozumel.[16] With the sun beating down on his head, Halliburton handed Healy his nail scissors and asked him to crop his hair close to the scalp. Looking in a mirror Halliburton decided he resembled a newly released convict from Sing Sing.[17]

In Cozumel the two enjoyed a few days swimming and sunbathing on a beach fringed with palm trees. Relaxed and refreshed, the two boarded another sailboat. They weren't the only passengers; they had a hundred giant turtles for company. The two sat and slept sandwiched between the four-hundred-pound creatures all the way to Belize, where they caught a fruit steamer to Guatemala. From there they took the USS *Cleveland*, a naval battleship, to Panama, the Western Hemisphere's youngest republic.

At 480 miles long and between 32 miles and 118 miles wide, Panama is slightly smaller than Ireland. Inside the small country, the points of the compass seem twisted, the sun appears to rise in the west and set in the east.[18] Aboard the *Cleveland*, Halliburton mused aloud about swimming the canal. Well-meaning passengers tried to talk him out of so bold a plan with a litany of warnings. It was too long, too cold, and the currents were too strong. And, by the way, there might be sharks. The possibility of coming up against a shark was enough to convince Halliburton he absolutely had to do it.

In Panama City, Halliburton and Healy registered at the posh Hotel Tivoli. The crisp white building contrasted nicely against the emerald green of the surrounding foliage. Upstairs, Halliburton stepped onto the tiny balcony off their room and gazed upon a sea of rooftops, the closely set tiles resembling scales on a fish. He enjoyed an uninterrupted view of the ocean. It had been three weeks since Healy had clipped his locks; his hair was now spiky as a cactus.

On his first morning in Panama, Halliburton strolled along the canal, the humid air caressing his skin. Pelicans glided overhead and as the morning mist burned off, the distant trees appeared as a solid green wall. Halliburton considered the murky water. It took laborers forty years to hack through the thick jungle lowland. Cholera, dysentery, smallpox, and yellow fever claimed the lives of tens of thousands of people during the canal's construction.[19] In 1928 most people wouldn't venture to the Panama Canal as tourists, but as one of the seven wonders of the modern world, it held tremendous appeal for Halliburton. He knew there was only one way most of his readers could experience its magnitude: he would swim its length from the Atlantic to the Pacific, locks included. Halliburton would not be the first person to swim the canal; that honor belonged to zone employee Wendell Greene, who in 1916 swam the canal in thirty hours. However, Halliburton would be the first person to pass through the three sets of locks, rather than get out and walk around them as Greene had done. Such a tour de force would earn him a place in recorded history.

Shortly after his arrival, Halliburton called on Brigadier General M. L. Walker, the governor of the canal, at his residence. Stepping inside the mansion's cool interior, Halliburton told Walker of his plan. An enormous fan of the adventure writer, Walker agreed, although not without issuing a set of caveats. First he strongly suggested Halliburton be vaccinated against typhoid before taking the plunge. Because alligators swam in the waters, Walker authorized a launch to accompany Halliburton from Colon to Balboa and pass through the locks toll free. "A photographer, rifleman, newspaper reporter, and one companion are permitted to accompany the launch on this expedition. It is understood that any expenses in connection with this expedition will be borne by yourself and that the Panama Canal will not be held responsible for any damage sustained by you," Walker stipulated in writing.[20]

Halliburton accepted the terms.[21]

On the afternoon of the swim, Halliburton stood in front of the Foreigner's Club at Limon Bay. More than five hundred people gathered to cheer the American as canal officials measured and weighed him, just like they did for any ship passing through the canal. The "SS

Halliburton" paid thirty-six cents in tonnage. It remains the lowest toll paid in the canal's history.[22]

A herd of reporters positioned themselves at the canal's edge, angling for a photo or pithy remark from the adventurer. The press now covered Halliburton with a zeal usually directed at film stars and politicians, to the point that Halliburton now sported several nicknames: Daring Dick, Romantic Richard, and Handsome Halliburton. Every exploit garnered a headline, from his Hellespont swim to his Well of Death dive. The papers reported nearly every appearance, be it his attendance at the Catholic Actors Guild in the Hotel Astor or a lecture at Princeton University. "Newspapers printed thousands of columns of his exploits and plans for exploits. About nearly all of them there was an element of bravery and an element of bravura," according to *Time*.[23] Although he didn't always feel the press gave him a fair shake, Halliburton indulged the crowd and made several impromptu remarks. He told everyone he planned to swim the canal in stages. He reminded the reporters and columnists, as well as the crowd of locals, that he knew he wasn't the first to swim the canal. However, Halliburton emphasized he would be the first person to pass through the locks, which would prove to be a punishing ordeal since the strength of the currents would make it seem like Halliburton was swimming in place.[24]

And with that short announcement, the twenty-eight-year-old reached for a tub of lanolin and greased his body against the cold. At 2:40 PM Halliburton dove into the water. Army sergeant Thomas Wright, a marksman in Company E, 14th Infantry, rowed ahead, his eyes scanning the water for barracuda and alligators. Wright enjoyed his stint as bodyguard, later writing to Halliburton about how fun it was and how he was "plum scared" when they saw a shark in the harbor.[25]

Four hours later, or two and a half miles from the Gatun locks, Halliburton emerged from the canal, his muscles rubbery from the exertion. He had swum just over three miles, covering only a half mile in the last hour. At 5:30 PM a freshly bathed Halliburton sipped hot coffee from a mug. Reporters, notebooks in hand, peppered him with questions. He confessed the swim was not as easy as he thought it would be, but that didn't surprise him. After all, he'd not trained for this swim, nor had he swum anything of consequence in the past two years.[26]

On the second day Halliburton mentally steeled himself to pass through his first set of locks and begin the long swim through Gatun Lake.[27] He knew alligators lurked in the bottomless black of the artificial lake. Engineers created the lake after closing the Gatun Dam, which once spanned the Chagres River. The subsequent overflow submerged 165 miles of lowland. Here and there dead *cedro* trees pierced the water's surface. What appeared to be islands in the lake were formerly summits of high hills.[28] Vines and creepers trailed near the water's edge. And just beyond a riot of scarlet hibiscus, purple orchids, and fuchsia passionflowers was the wild unknown.

At 7:45 AM, after a light breakfast, Halliburton jumped back into the canal at the entrance of the Gatun locks. The powerful current made him feel as if he were swimming through molasses. After much struggle, Halliburton reached the lock. The ponderous steel gates, each weighing fifteen hundred tons, slowly opened. Thirty billion cubic feet of water rushed in and raised Halliburton eighty-five feet from sea level to the level of Gatun Lake.[29] The force of the water nearly drowned Halliburton. When the current subsided, Halliburton entered the thousand-foot lock chamber.

It had taken four years to construct the locks that raised and lowered Halliburton like a bathtub toy. If posed upright, each lock would fall just 250 feet shorter than the present-day Empire State Building.[30] Operators control the flight of locks from the second floor of the control house. They stand before a long, flat, waist-high counter, upon which the locks are represented in miniature. Everything the actual locks do the miniature do—from the rise and fall of the fender chains to the opening and closing of the gates.[31]

Halliburton struggled as he approached the lake; he felt a raging fever coming on. Crowds on the sides laughed at his style—part sidestroke, part paddle. In the distance, passengers on cruise ships waved as they passed the young man. He ignored all of them and concentrated on the work ahead. Halliburton swam three and a half miles through

Gatun Lake. The blistering sun painted his neck, ears, shoulders, and back crimson. He took to wearing a brimmed sailor's cap to ward off the fierce rays.

At 6:30 PM, finished swimming for the day, Halliburton spoke with reporters, as was becoming the daily ritual. Among the journalists present was Fred C. Cole of the *New Yorker*. His article about the swim skewered Halliburton and misled readers. "So thoroughly had he impressed me with his quiet strength that I fully expected to see him plunge into Limon Bay (Atlantic side), take a few bold strokes of what is called the Australian Crawl, and emerge smiling and triumphant, from the peaceful blue of Panama Bay (Pacific side). Did this happen? No, brother; it did not happen," Cole wrote.[32]

Cole withheld the salient fact that Halliburton had always been forthright about his intention to swim the canal in stages. Instead, Cole misled readers into thinking the Tennessean was simply weak.

"The shock came when Richard had negotiated three and one-quarter miles. At this point he clambered into his boat, put out an anchored marker, and set sail for the shore, quite done in. 'But, Mr. Halliburton,' I cried, 'I understood you to say that you were going to swim through the Canal, not *at* it.' 'Tomorrow,' he assured me, 'is another day. I shall take to the water where I left off today.' With that enlightening statement he was whisked away in a high-powered Chevrolet to his suite in the Washington Hotel. You see, it was teatime. Ladies' Clubs were waiting. The courageous Mr. Halliburton would abandon most any project, I am convinced, ere he would keep a delegation of matrons waiting in idle suspense."[33] One last dig closed the article: Cole wrote that one could easily navigate the entire Pacific Ocean in the same piecemeal manner Halliburton was swimming the Canal.

Throughout the swim, sharpshooter Wright balanced inside the escort boat scouting the water for alligators. On the seventh day, while Halliburton swam through the Gaillard Cut, an alligator surfaced a mere twenty-five feet away from the writer. Wright pulled Halliburton into the launch in one fell swoop. In the next instant Wright sighted on the alligator and fired. The reptile bellowed and sank. Wright nodded an all clear and Halliburton slid back into the uncomfortably cold water.

Alligator dispatched, Halliburton had but a moment of calm before a tropical deluge hit. Halliburton couldn't see more than ten feet ahead and got separated from the launch. He heard the propellers of a number of ships passing in the channel, but he couldn't see them for the rain and fog. Aware the blades could shred him to bits at any moment, he took it one stroke at a time.

Alligators and rain notwithstanding, Halliburton completed the six-mile swim through the Gaillard Cut in six hours. It was his best time yet. The hardest part of Halliburton's swim was now past. The tranquil waters of Miraflores Lake, situated between the Pacific locks, waited.

Halliburton had so far completed thirty-one miles of the nearly fifty-mile swim. In one day he had swum five and a half miles from the naval radio station at Darien to Gamboa. Rising six hundred feet high into the sky, the station's towers could communicate with stations from San Francisco to Arlington, Virginia, and from Valdivia, Chile, to Buenos Aires.[34] It is from these towers that news of Halliburton also reached the States.

Nine days and fifty hours in the water later, a sunburned and hurting Halliburton finished his swim. "Swam Canal Nine Days Easily Pleasantly Hotel Tivoli Panama City Wire Mother," announced the cable he sent to his father.[35]

Halliburton became the first swimmer in history to swim the length of the Panama Canal, locks included, and wrote about the experience in a much longer letter home. "The past 3 weeks have been a bit overwhelming. My cable explained my long silence—my canal swim. It's over. I'm not harmed one speck. The sunburn and sore limbs are departed. I'm just where I was before beginning . . . it was the supreme adventure of my life and not likely to be duplicated by anyone," Halliburton wrote his parents. "I'd had no swimming since the Hellespont and was amazed how well I stood up to the ordeal. . . . Over 1,000 people watched the unique experience and I'm the only person in the canal's history ever to be so sent through."[36]

Today tourists can visit the Panama Interoceanic Canal Museum, which documents Panama's history. A photo of Halliburton hangs beside a plaque describing him as an adventurer who swam the canal in the 1920s. His record stands.

Fred Cole was not the only writer to mock Halliburton for swimming the canal in stages. The tone of their articles suggested this was akin to taking a dip in the local swimming hole. They didn't report on how uncomfortable and sick Halliburton was the entire time. They never mentioned the blisters, fever, and dehydration.[37] John Nicholls Booth, a fan, met Halliburton in 1933. In 1939, sometime after Halliburton's death, he visited the Panama Canal. Well aware of the mixed tone of the press coverage, Booth was curious to hear directly from Panamanians on how they viewed the famous author's swim. "They were all derisive at first, but then when they [the support on the boat] brought him in absolutely a wreck after the first day, it was clear that the swim was no picnic," Booth said. "The critics I read were really far off base."[38]

Booth once asked Halliburton why he never told audiences about the grueling side of his adventures. Why, Booth wondered, did he omit it from his books and skip over it during lectures. Halliburton quickly answered. "'I try to present to my audience like a bouquet of roses, like roses with the thorns cut off,'" Booth remembered the author telling him. "'They don't want to hear about the dark side of what I do. They don't want to hear about skin falling off, not sleeping properly.'"

Halliburton believed his audience didn't want to hear about the blazing sun or how he had to swim through the sewage discharge of the ocean liners. Halliburton knew he was a competent swimmer but not a superstar. It wasn't all romance for him, but he made it sound that way.[39] His audience wanted glamour and gloss, and he obliged.

In the meantime, Halliburton's wallet was once again empty. His three *Ladies' Home Journal* stories about Cortés needed a rewrite, and he wouldn't be paid until he submitted the revisions. Chambers and Loring Schuler, his editor at *Ladies' Home Journal*, sent him several letters urging him to finish the job. He had to borrow $200 from a local bank to cover his Panama hotel bill. Considering his famous name collateral enough, the bank approved the loan. Bobbs-Merrill covered the bank loan and advanced him another $2,000. Though Halliburton spent money as quickly as he earned it, he often found it easier to blame income taxes for his poor financial health. "What's the use of making so much money if the government grabs it all away?" he once complained to Chambers.[40]

With borrowed money in hand, Halliburton headed south to San Miguel, where he planned to rejoin Healy. It was time to reimagine the Spanish explorer Vasco Núñez Balboa's expedition.

Halliburton was determined to find the precise spot where in 1513 Balboa "claimed the Pacific and all lands and waters it touched for his queen."[41] In San Miguel, Halliburton paddled forty miles in a dugout canoe up the murky and mysterious Tuira River to the base of Mount Pirri. Halliburton climbed the peak, now wilder and more desolate than it was in Balboa's day. He camped halfway up the mountain. In the morning he woke to find a baby ocelot had crawled into his bed. He tucked the spotted wildcat in his rucksack and carried it with him to the top of the mountain.[42]

Throughout his career some critics charged Halliburton played loose with the facts. The Balboa story was a case in point. Halliburton "disagrees with local historians that Mount Pirri is the place, asserting that after climbing six thousand feet on this peak he could not see the Pacific, which is fifty miles away." He found another peak "which he contends he found only one hill from which the Pacific could be seen."[43]

And that was that. The debate over from where exactly Balboa spied the ocean and claimed it and all its shores for Spain proved tedious to Halliburton; in a huff he and the ocelot boarded the Panama City–bound seaplane sent courtesy of the US Navy. Later, Halliburton presented the ocelot to the Bronx Zoo, and he visited it whenever he was in New York City.

Halliburton cruised to Peru aboard the *Santa Maria* to discover Machu Picchu for himself. Fred Healy came along, but bowed out of climbing Machu Picchu. He was still too weak from his recent bout with malaria. All of Peru seemed to admire Halliburton. The local papers loved Halliburton. Even the dictator Augusto Leguía was a fan. He invited Halliburton to the Lima presidential palace and over drinks he asked Halliburton to retell the story of his Panama Canal swim.

Halliburton agreeably posed for pictures, granted some more interviews, and mailed copies of the Peruvian newspaper articles to Chambers, who loved the stamps and the "picture of yourself surrounded with dignitaries at whose top-hats I've gazed with admiration and awe. I don't quite make out what's happened to your hair unless that's the latest Peruvian style of cut and the beard seems so far to be a moustache—otherwise it's fine!"[44]

Halliburton led Chambers to believe everything was fine. However, he ended up staying in Lima for three weeks . . . although not for pleasure. Rather "one blasted thing after another has held me here. I had to go to the hospital for a week for another damned hemorrhoid operation—had been getting worse for months—and decided I'd best get it over with where there *was* a hospital."[45] Halliburton's father later deleted Halliburton's explanation for his extended stay.

After he recovered, Halliburton boarded a freight train and spent three days in a boxcar as it wound its way to Cuzco, once the center of the Inca Empire. He spent an afternoon exploring the burnt umber city before hiking over an eleven-thousand-foot ridge. On the other side of the ridge, he trekked sixty more miles down the Urubamba River canyon. He then ascended a twenty-five-hundred-foot cliff; before him lay the Incan wonder of Machu Picchu.[46] The white granite stones weathered to a honey color. The entire range of the Andes disappeared into the horizon. As Halliburton admired the view, "black clouds raced over the tops of the distant amphitheater—the thunder bellowed among the imprisoning walls—several rainbows flung themselves across the canyon—the late sun piercing the clouds for a moment struck the granite city—and the river half mile below on 3 sides roared and rumbled down the hill."[47]

Halliburton had now gathered enough stories for his third book. It was time to go home. He hoped to reach Memphis by Christmas.

En route he and Healy stopped in Buenos Aires for a bit of rest and relaxation. But true to Halliburton's nature he couldn't stop moving or finding things to write about. He worked on articles for *Ladies' Home Journal* and the *Memphis Commercial Appeal*. Taking a respite from his writing, Halliburton plunked down his last few dollars on a trained monkey and a broken hurdy-gurdy. He christened the monkey Niño and gleefully performed in city parks and on city streets. Once again, such whimsy earned Halliburton a night in jail since he lacked a street performer's license. He thought it was a small price to pay, since he gained a story and enough money from his musical performances for a boat ticket.

He and Healy sailed to Rio de Janeiro, where they enjoyed three days in Copacabana, getting drunk on sunshine. As for Niño, the little monkey didn't fare so well. It died en route. The story touched the heart of one Al E. Ruger, all the way in Menominee, Michigan. "I have just finished reading your monkey business story, and must say that it had a very peculiar effect on me. I am 76 years of age but I simply could not help shedding tears over the doings of little Niño," Ruger wrote. "He seemed to be human in his love and trust in you, and then his death came, and his fragile little hands crossed over his eyes. We are an old couple living in this place to which we moved a few years ago from Texas, and by the way we feel almost acquainted with you."[48]

Halliburton showed American readers like Al Ruger the world, and in turn showed the world how embracing Americans could be. Although Halliburton abstained from the political and religious in his books, he was an unofficial ambassador for American interests. Without sermonizing, he encouraged people to open themselves to the world, either through their own travel or reading about his. He never preached, he never told readers where to eat or where to stay or which route was the prettiest—there was Baedeker's for that. Rather he recorded how people dressed, the smells, the colors, and the feeling of where he was. All of this allowed people a glimpse into the lives of others in distant lands. By the time *New Worlds to Conquer* landed on bookshelves, President Franklin D. Roosevelt's Good Neighbor Policy, a US government initiative for better relations with Latin America, was well underway.[49] In his way, Halliburton contributed to the expansion of an American empire around the world.

Writing home from the *Pan American*, a steamship liner, he expressed his incredulity that after thirteen full days of tropical seas where he and Fred sunbathed and swam, he was going to soon be snowbound.[50]

Halliburton never made it home in time for Christmas; indeed, he wouldn't reunite with his parents and Ammudder until February, when he was in Springfield, Missouri, for a speaking engagement. Instead he arrived in New York City on January 15, and the Feakins Bureau insisted he hit the lecture circuit straight away. He rang in the New Year with a $900-a-week guarantee from the Feakins lecture bureau. His first two books continued to sell well. He needed to finish his *Ladies' Home Journal* obligation. He wrote about his three-week stint on Devil's Island in French Guiana, where he convinced the warden to let him live undercover as a convict and "in the faces and the hearts of those outcast thieves and murderers I found a living, aching picture of much that is wrong with the world."[51] He collected hundreds of letters from these men and briefly considered turning them into a book.

When he arrived in New York City, he had also been pleased to find a $2,000 bonus from *Ladies' Home Journal*, a show of appreciation for the way his stories had boosted their circulation. After that he took a room in Atlantic City to write. *The Royal Road to Romance* was written in elevators and Pullman cars, at two o'clock in the morning and sequestered in Nantucket. So too was *The Glorious Adventure*. *New Worlds to Conquer* would get the same frenzied treatment.

6

Hollywood Lights

IN A JANUARY 1929 article, *Ladies' Home Journal* declared: "Everybody Ought to be Rich."[1] Ten months later, on October 28, 1929, the stock market crashed, and in just one day the market lost $14 billion.[2] Richard Halliburton personally lost 80 percent of his stock portfolio, which had been valued at $100,000. Likewise, father Wesley's real estate business suffered. Halliburton felt more obliged than ever to financially support his parents. So as he had done for the past several years, he often ensured they received a portion of his royalties so they could buy a new car, new clothes, or pay off part of their mortgage. Sometimes he sent money so they could treat themselves to small luxuries: "Mother Dear, this AM I sent you a note with a $200 check. Now you must buy a pretty hat for yourself."[3]

The year was off to a frenetic pace, Halliburton's calendar a kaleidoscope of engagements and writing. One of his more memorable events took place at the University of Notre Dame, where he hypnotized two thousand young men, aged seventeen to twenty-two, with his tale of swimming the Panama Canal and his thoughts on the poet Rupert Brooke. "We had a regular riot. I don't think I ever had a more intent audience," he wrote home.[4] In Chicago he spoke before the Curtis Publishing Company of advertising men and sub-managers, and then in February he met his mother, father, and Ammudder in Springfield,

Missouri. A reunion with his Princeton friends Chan Sweet and Mike Hockaday followed. And so turned the weeks and months.

Then, on November 27, 1929, just one month after Black Friday, Bobbs-Merrill published Halliburton's third book, *New Worlds to Conquer*. Like its forerunners it received mixed reviews. The *New York Times* chided Halliburton for refusing to don the mantle of adulthood. "Let us, therefore, dub him Peter Pan Halliburton and laugh at his pranks, even while secretly holding that there is becoming a surfeit of them. Who knows? Perhaps this Peter will some time grow up, and then, as so often the elders do, we shall wish we had the child back."[5]

Unsurprisingly, Halliburton's reading public, which now numbered in the hundreds of thousands, ignored such book reviews. Even so, the book's sales never matched the levels of *The Royal Road to Romance* and *The Glorious Adventure*. Early reports from Bobbs-Merrill pinned sales figures at just around thirty thousand, compared with one hundred thousand for *The Royal Road*'s debut.

"The difficulty is this general nationwide depression in business. Bookstores are experiencing the worst slump in twenty years and not daring to buy five-dollar books by anybody," Halliburton wrote home.[6] At least he had had the presence of mind to ink a contract in September with Garden City Publishing Company to publish low-priced mass market editions of his books.

However, Halliburton believed there was more at play here than the rapidly souring economy. He believed negative articles about him, like the one Fred Cole wrote for the *New Yorker* about his Panama swim or the one Corey Ford wrote for *Vanity Fair* under the pen name John Riddell, called "The Adventure Racket," contributed to his diminished sales.[7] In his piece, Ford pretended he was Halliburton calling on readers: "Hearken middle-aged suburban housewives, impressionable girl-graduates, Thursday afternoon bridge clubs, sex-starved librarians and the rest of my fluttering, feminine, middle-Western audience. Look, I'm calling you."

This caricature of Richard Halliburton suggests that the author was simply a fixture on the ladies' club circuit. *Courtesy of the Library of Congress*

Inwardly, this kind of coverage stung Halliburton. Outwardly he turned the other cheek, but as these last few reviews seemed to come with more frequency, he vented his frustration in a letter to Chambers. "I'm sure we've not lost a sale that was due us. We've got to face the fact that besides [the] Depression I've suffered from no end of personal hostility—the Corey Fords . . . but it's inevitable and part of the game."[8]

Even with the disappointing sales, Halliburton knew the numbers could have been worse. Chambers had considered releasing *New Worlds to Conquer* in the spring of 1930. At that point a scarce few would have shelled out money for the book no matter how magnificently Bobbs-Merrill advertised it. The publisher had pulled out all the stops to promote the book. Weeks before publication, Bobbs-Merrill took out a full-page advertisement in newspapers across the nation, including the *New York Times* book section.[9] Halliburton's editor also planned a launch party in New York City. His mother, Nelle, joined her son for the celebration and then accompanied him to other book parties in Chicago, Indianapolis, and Cincinnati.

Of course the stagnating economy also affected his other sources of income. Where Halliburton once commanded $300 an engagement he now earned between $150 and $200. Halliburton was powerless to change this, but in any event, the lectures allowed him a way to personally promote the book. In the first few months of the year he stopped in South Beach, Florida; Chicago, Illinois; South Bend, Indiana; and Philadelphia, Pennsylvania.

In March, Halliburton went to Ohio, and as he often did, he stayed with his old Princeton friend J. Penfield Seiberling in Akron. They visited Stan Hywet Hall, the country estate of Penfield's grandparents. Built between 1912 and 1913 the Tudor revival had the distinction of being one of the largest homes in the United States. Halliburton enjoyed playing croquet and horseback riding on the elegant grounds. Before he left he took a moment to sign the guest book: "Sun and wind and beat of sea, Great lands stretching endlessly, Where be bonds to bind the free? All the world was made for me! That's the way I always feel when I come back home to the Seiberlings, and especially on the sunny Sunday March 10, Dick Halliburton."[10]

And then he was off: another city, another book talk awaited.

With the azaleas in bloom, Halliburton enjoyed a springtime visit to Memphis. While there he visited his friend Mary Goodwin Winslow in nearby Raleigh. Her mother, Anne Goodwin Winslow, was at the time a fairly well-known author of poems, essays, short stories, and books including *The Dwelling Place*. That afternoon she and her children, Mary and Randolph, entertained a small group of friends with a life-mask party at their family home, Goodwinslow. Halliburton was one of the guests at the caramel-colored stucco house. When his turn came, he stretched out on the dining room table, his head resting comfortably on a pillow. The others carefully placed strips of linen soaked in plaster of paris on his face, which had been slathered with petroleum jelly. Slowly they lifted off the mask, which wore an ever so slight grin. Halliburton had to leave before his mask was completely dry. According to Goodwin family lore, nobody remembered to give him the mask the next time he came through Memphis. Hence the mask, with its jade-green velvet turban, remained in the family's possession for decades.[11]

Winslow's granddaughter, Margaret DeVault, who now lives in Mississippi, knew about the mask her entire life. "When I was about 11, at Miss Hutchison's School, one of my teachers read Richard's description of his swim in the sacred well at Chichén Itzá, and I was fascinated. In the 8th grade, our teacher read aloud from *The Flying Carpet* and I was hooked," DeVault said. "I finally made the connection that the Richard who wrote those things was the same Richard whose plaster face reposed in the corner cupboard in the parlor."[12]

Decades later, long after Halliburton died and DeVault married, her mother, Anne, gave her the piece of art. No one else in DeVault's family appreciated the lifelike mask, and after Halliburton died, his grieving parents did not want to see it. In time, both mother and

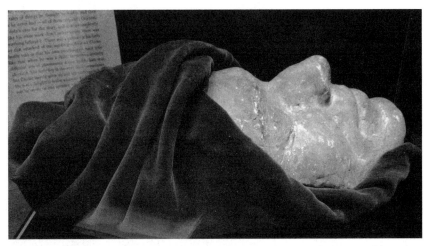

Richard Halliburton's life mask is now on display at Rhodes College in Memphis, Tennessee. *Courtesy of the Halliburton Archives, Barrett Library, Rhodes College, Memphis, TN*

daughter decided the mask belonged at Rhodes College in Memphis, which already housed a significant collection of Halliburton's papers and personal effects.

The worsening economy sent Halliburton in a new direction—literally—to seek and find adventure. He had some money in his pocket left over from a print advertisement he had done for Lucky Strike cigarettes nearly a year before. It was not uncommon for film stars and society beauties to be a shill for products, but it was a bit different for a writer, especially one who didn't smoke. "There's real health in Lucky Strike . . . for years this has been no secret to the men who keep fit and trim," read the ad.[13]

In January 1930 Halliburton ducked down to Bermuda for some sun and procrastination. Writing to his "Mamma, Papa, and Ammudder" he let them "know I'm hale and hearty, despite my advancing years. I've only six more days to stay here, and I'm sick about it. It's perfectly grand. Don't remember when I've been so enraptured with a place—sun—sun all the time. I've been so busy absorbing sun I've not done half the writing I'd like to have—but the sun was more important. I'm typing my first story and have half written the second."[14]

After a fortnight of swimming and sunbathing, Halliburton could no longer postpone work. He headed to Los Angeles, where the fifty-foot-high sans serif letters spelling HOLLYWOODLAND rose from Mount Lee. Halliburton drove toward the sign, which was meant as a real estate advertisement but to him seemed like the *X* that marks the spot on a pirate's treasure map.

By the early 1930s, Hollywood studios were turning out more than eight hundred feature films a year, or 80 percent of the world's total. Halliburton banked on selling *The Royal Road to Romance* to a movie studio. Having been in the business of selling escape, adventure, and romance for nearly a decade, it was inevitable Halliburton went there to peddle the brand that was his name.

Audiences were especially fond of adventure films, from Frank Capra's *Flight* to Allan Dwan's *The Iron Mask*. Halliburton did his research and knew that as far as directors and producers were concerned, the ideal Hollywood adventure hero was handsome, polished, athletic, shrewd, witty, strong, and charismatic.[15] To his readers Halliburton was exactly that; he figured these traits would easily translate onto the screen. Indeed, by every rule in the book, Halliburton should have landed a contract in Hollywood. But it didn't work out that way. Call it a conflict of personalities between the celebrity journalist and various studio heads, call it artistic differences, whatever the explanation, Halliburton ultimately came up short in his quest to see his name roll with the credits.

In the early years of the Depression, the conventional wisdom held that the film business was "Depression-proof," since for less than a quarter people could enjoy a few hours of relief from the decade's mounting miseries. The thinking was wrong. By 1932 Hollywood studios were handing out pink slips, cutting salaries, closing theaters, and nipping production costs.[16] RKO and Paramount were just two of many studios that fell into receivership. Hollywood, like the rest of the nation, was hurting.

Nevertheless, it was with high hopes that Halliburton checked into Hollywood's Roosevelt Hotel on Easter Sunday 1930. After a restful night's sleep, he shaved and combed his thick hair into place. Under clear skies he drove to the Fox Films studio to meet with president William Fox and the studio's executive producer Malcolm Stuart Boylan. Halliburton aimed to sell the rights to *Royal Road* for $50,000—he figured his name was worth at least that much.[17] Fox, on the other hand, wanted him to script an original screenplay for half that amount.

It was a rather testy meeting, but Halliburton kept his annoyance in check. Although he was known to be quite amiable, not everyone fell under the Halliburton spell. Boylan became more irritated with Halliburton as the meeting went on. The executive producer and the author had actually met in 1927 and never quite clicked. Halliburton thought Boylan an "odd sort (ugly, heavy) . . . but very bright and good company."[18] However, Boylan found Halliburton to be a bit of a playboy—a bafflingly astute playboy, but a playboy all the same.[19] Boylan was skeptical Halliburton could deliver.

Frustrated, Halliburton took a meeting with executives at Universal Studios. He met with Cecil B. DeMille, whose reputation for flamboyance and a tyrannical approach to movie making preceded him. Unfazed, Halliburton sat down with the consummate showman. After the meeting, he entertained and rejected an offer from DeMille: Halliburton wanted $50,000 and a starring role in any movie that would come from *Royal Road*. DeMille offered less than half of that and no role.

Halliburton diligently chased one lead after another. Over time, his disillusionment and disgust with the film industry intensified, which brought out a nasty streak. In a letter to his parents, laced with anti-Semitic comments, Halliburton complained about Hollywood: "Last Wednesday I wobbled out to Universal City—a big movie outfit and met one of the big Jews who runs the joint. He seemed aware that *Royal Road* was a book and said he thought something should be done about it—so I'm busy writing out (dictating to a secretary) the movie story from *Royal Road* to show them what can be done—that a talkie *can* be made from the book."[20]

He dreamed of seeing his work on the silver screen, but deep down he deemed Hollywood a shallow town out of touch with reality. The money thrown around at meetings simultaneously amazed and appalled him. "People of the commonest, stupidest type get $5000, $7000, $10,000 a week. Any actor or director or writer receiving less than $1000 feels ready to join a revolution. At the same time people are absolutely starving by the thousands. There's the worst depression in history here. I'm dodging hungry and desperate friends half my time."[21]

The economy was in rough shape; people were losing land. There were 134,000 foreclosures in 1929 and about 1.5 million unemployed, and that number would triple by 1930 to 4.5 million. The auto industry was operating at one-fifth of its capacity and agriculture was hit hard, too. Nonetheless, neither Halliburton nor his friends, nor anyone in his social circle, experienced anything that could be described as desperate straits. In fact, Halliburton spent quite a bit of his time dressing for elegant dinners and trading gossip at sophisticated teas. He twirled across the dance floor with President Woodrow Wilson's daughter Eleanor Wilson McAdoo. "She took me to the theater and *dancing*, imagine! She's enormously charming and intelligent and I'll see her again," he wrote home. As it happened her husband, California senator William Gibbs McAdoo, was ill and Halliburton didn't chance to meet him.[22] One evening he attended a lavish party hosted by one of his fans, the American songwriter Carrie Jacobs-Bond, who wrote the song "A Perfect Day." Among the guests were the novelists Charles Norris and his wife Kathleen Norris. A great admirer, Kathleen invited Halliburton to dine with her at the beautifully appointed Fairmont Hotel. At another event he met Wei San Fang, a Chinese actor who happened to graduate from the University of Tennessee. The two enjoyed comparing notes about the state.

Occasionally, in between meetings with various studio executives, Halliburton motored up the coast to Pasadena to stay at his millionaire cousin Erle Halliburton's ranch. Once he was invited to spend time at the Bohemian Grove, an all-male club north of San Francisco that dates back to 1872. He spent the entire stay among writers, authors, and business leaders clad in nothing more than scarlet silk pajamas embroidered in emerald dragons.

Halliburton eventually scored a film deal in 1932. Producer Walter Futter signed the author to star in his photoplay *India Speaks*. Born in Omaha, Nebraska, Futter produced and directed about fifty films before he died in New York in 1958. Futter filmed most of the movie in Yosemite National Park in under a week.[23] Rose Schulze costarred alongside the adventurer. She played the part of an Indian maiden in need of rescue; Halliburton played himself. Futter, who had also made the 1930 photoplay *Africa Speaks* starring Paul Hoefler and journalist Lowell Thomas, told Halliburton more acting would be required of him than to be himself.[24] Of all the films in his repertoire, *India Speaks* was an unqualified box office flop. Even the hardback book of black-and-white movie stills, published by the New York–based Grosset & Dunlap as a promotional for the movie, fell flat.

The film would open at the Roxy Theater in New York City in May 1933. The film left movie critics flabbergasted. The *New York Times* critic described it as "a curious concoction of fact and fiction which now on exhibition . . . although there is no denying the interest of the authentic scenes of 'the land of drama and romance' it is somewhat disconcerting to be called upon to believe what the screen voice is saying at one moment and then appreciate that in the next breath one is listening to a fanciful escapade. It is a mixture which does not 'jell.'"[25]

Not only did it bomb, but no remaining copies of the film exist, except for a garden scene in which Halliburton can be seen walking hand and hand with his costar in the "jungle." She wears diaphanous robes and a sheer veil, strands of beads draped about her neck. He wears pleated white linen trousers, a tennis sweater, and white shoes.[26]

During Halliburton's Hollywood interlude, his father became wistful. Once again he asked his sole surviving son when he might marry and father children who would carry on the Halliburton name. As usual, Richard brushed off such questions. "Don't be so downcast about your lack of grandchildren Dad. There's lots of time as I grow more tired of this headlong life. I'll grow more hungry for domesticity—the current gets stronger that way every year. What I want now is financial security—so I can do what I want, and not what I must."[27]

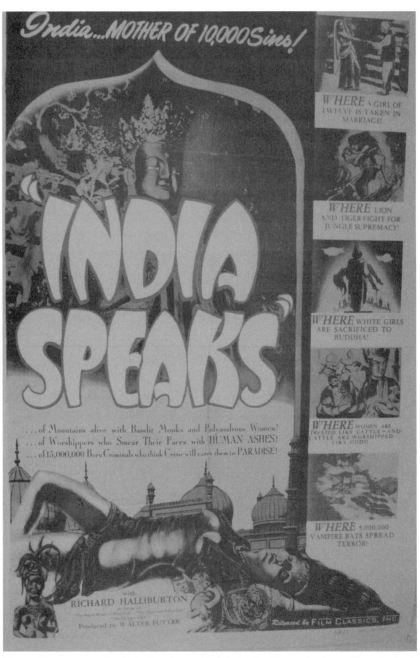

This publicity poster for *India Speaks* couldn't help the film in the box office. *Author's collection*

Although Halliburton deemed Hollywood tedious from a business perspective, he continued to find amusement in the people he met and the company he kept. Florence "Pancho" Barnes, a barnstorming, airfield-hopping, adventure-prone woman, took an immediate liking to Halliburton. Her husband, Reverend Calvin Rankin Barnes, was a respected executive head of the Episcopal Church in Pasadena. She earned the sobriquet Pancho after she worked on a commercial fishing ship posing as a man. Working as a technical director on Howard Hughes's *Hell's Angels*, she captured authentic audio of airplanes by flying past tethered balloons with sound equipment attached to her own plane. She also consulted for George Hill's *The Flying Fleet*, which starred Ramon Novarro, Ralph Graves, and Anita Page, and also advised the actor Douglas Fairbanks in *The Dawn Patrol*.[28]

Her gumption and irreverence tickled Halliburton. The stocky woman with short black hair enjoyed nothing more than spending time at Rogers Field and the drinking and smoking that went along with the life of a pilot; the ever-rambunctious Barnes preferred this life to the high society in which she had been born.[29] Barnes threw magnificent parties at her San Marino mansion, and during the Prohibition Era she ferried liquor into California from Mexico hidden in her airplane.[30] Celebrities, writers, and aviators flocked to Barnes's house, always looking forward to a night of knocking back drinks and trading flying stories.

The silent film star Ramon Novarro was among her frequent guests. Warm and attentive, the man MGM promoted as a "Latin Lover" cast a spell on Barnes. Though married, she grew ever more infatuated with the leading man. She soon discovered his romantic attentions were solely reserved for men.[31] The aviator shrugged it off and the two became fast friends, partying in Laguna Beach, bar hopping in Los Angeles.

While in Los Angles, Halliburton also sipped cocktails with Hollywood elite, including "America's Sweetheart" Mary Pickford and her husband Douglas Fairbanks. As the first actress to earn more than $1 million a year, Pickford carried a lot of weight in Hollywood.[32] Divorced from Owen Moore, Pickford met Fairbanks in 1914. They married and went on to reign as business and social leaders of the movie world.

Halliburton admired the way Fairbanks dueled his way across the screen. To Halliburton, Fairbanks was the quintessential all-American male incarnate, seeming to live the cliché of always coming out on top no matter the odds. He epitomized the optimism of the post–World War I era, and that attracted Halliburton, who looked to do the same with his books and lectures.[33]

In 1919 Pickford, Fairbanks, Charlie Chaplin, and D. W. Griffith launched United Artists, which let artists produce and distribute their own work and protected their creative autonomy.[34] Despite his friendship with Pickford, Halliburton never approached her about adapting his books into a screenplay; theirs was a strictly personal relationship. He was often a guest at Pickfair, the mansion in San Ysidro Canyon that Fairbanks bought and renovated for his wife in 1919. Luxurious touches like parquet flooring and a sweeping staircase filled the four-story, twenty-five-room Tudor revival mansion. Stables, servants' quarters, and tennis courts dotted the property, which was a focal point for Hollywood society.

The leading couple hosted legendary dinners under the mansion's frescoed ceiling. To be invited to Pickfair was to have arrived.[35] Guests included Amelia Earhart, F. Scott Fitzgerald, Charles Lindbergh, the Duke and Duchess of Windsor, Franklin Delano Roosevelt, and Helen Keller. It was at one of those gin-infused parties that Halliburton met the silent film star Novarro. The star of *Ben-Hur* had recently starred opposite Joan Crawford in *Across to Singapore*. Appearing in a string of heroic roles, the actor boasted looks and allure to rival Rudolph Valentino. Women fawned over Novarro's soft brown eyes and thick black hair. In Hollywood, he represented a new era, where sexual ambiguity suggested culture; culture inspired success; and success was considered sexy.[36] With his matinee idol looks—suave and self-consciously handsome—Halliburton too fit the mold of the ideal man.

Through the 1920s, the film industry was known for sexual permissiveness and tolerance. But by the 1930s, America was undergoing a moral clampdown. Consequently, while some in their inner circle likely caught the furtive glances between Halliburton and Novarro, whose sexuality was an open secret in the industry, the pair took great pains to hide their brief affair. Any publicity that Halliburton and Novarro were romantically entangled had the potential to damn both their careers.[37]

When Halliburton went to Hollywood for dinner or to meet with movie executives, he had to fit the mold of the adventure hero, and that meant he had to pass as heterosexual. He needed to create a coherent, plausible narrative to account for his actions—hence the insertion of lovers in his stories, like the Spanish maiden in *The Royal Road to Romance*. He rarely mentioned other men in his life unless they were his old Lawrenceville and Princeton friends, or various traveling companions. Thus, through all the teas, luncheons, lectures, and autograph parties, Halliburton kept his love life locked in a basement of secrets. He became a master of deflection, forever insisting his lifestyle had no room for marriage. "When a man marries . . . he becomes domesticated, interested in making money and he likes the smugness of his home. His wife in 9 cases out of 10 is arresting and irresistible to other men and he is afraid to travel without her. It would be unwise for me to ever marry."[38]

At some point during Halliburton's extended California stay, he met Paul Mooney, a friend of Ramon Novarro's and a longtime Halliburton fan. Although it's not known exactly when or where they first met, those who knew the pair agreed the men's chemistry was palpable.[39] The two soon became longtime partners, professionally and romantically.

Mooney, the oldest of five children, was born in 1904 to James and Ione Lee Mooney. An aspiring writer when he met Halliburton, he eventually worked with the ex-Nazi Kurt Ludecke on his 833-page book *I Knew Hitler*, published in 1937 by Charles Scribner's Sons. In time the trim man with the mischievous smile would replace Wesley as Halliburton's editor and sounding board of choice.

After a weekend spent carousing with Barnes, keeping company with Mooney, or meeting up with visiting New York City friends, Halliburton returned to the grind of Hollywood. He took meeting after meeting with executives at Fox and Universal. Always it seemed they went in circles. He wanted more money than they would give, more control over the project than they would cede. Still, he wasn't ready to abandon the prospect of seeing one of his books adapted for film. His parents wondered why it was taking so long to clinch a deal. He reminded them of how long it had taken to land a lecture manager and a publisher; perseverance was the name of the game.

"I can't expect to walk into the movies without more battles. Fox and Universal seem to favor a series of 2-reelers specialties, featuring me in them. Metro-Goldwyn-Mayer like the idea of a feature story on Yucatán alone," he wrote. But he also harbored anti-Semitic attitudes toward the industry: "The people [word unclear] works with are impossible—Hebrews of the most trying order. It's always humiliating, but I'm going to see it through to the bitter end—as I've done not a few other situations before."[40] At one point the *New York Times* announced that Fox Studios would turn *The Royal Road to Romance* into a movie. Apparently photoplays were all the rage, for in that same article it was announced that Marlene Dietrich and Gary Cooper were going to star in *Morocco*, a Josef von Sternberg photoplay.[41] Whereas Halliburton's movie never left the drawer—he felt the offer wasn't enough—Dietrich and Cooper's photoplay turned into a romance movie.

As the months passed, a growing restiveness gripped Halliburton. While the public saw an energetic and endlessly charming man, his letters, of which he wrote more than a thousand, revealed a more than occasional bout of melancholy. Fame seemed to bewilder him. Once inured to negative reviews, he tired of the critics, particularly those writing in the *New Yorker*, which alternated between ridicule and thinly veiled accusations of plagiarism.

A *New Yorker* Talk of the Town piece mentioned that Halliburton "startled an audience in California by saying that he had been all over the world and that there was but one place he really wanted to live when he settled down: Chattanooga, Tennessee." The piece went on to say that Joe Cook, a comedian, had recently said the same thing in a speech at a book-publishers' convention, a speech Halliburton attended.

According to the article, Cook said he too had crossed the world and the only place for him was Evansville, Indiana. "The fact that Halliburton was present, as a fellow-speaker, at that convention is just one of those literary coincidences," according to the article, using literary coincidence as a genteel way of accusing Halliburton of plagiarism.[42]

Moreover, the May issue of *Vanity Fair* bestowed him with a rather dubious honor. They put him on the "We Nominate to Oblivion" page alongside Bernarr Macfadden, a publisher of "racey and cheap magazines," and Smith W. Brookhart, "Senator, snitch, boor." As for Halliburton, the magazine said they put him on the page "because Richard Halliburton has made a glorious racket out of Dauntless Youth, because his books are marvelously readable, transparently bogus, extremely popular, and have made their author a millionaire."[43]

"That made me sick at first, but as often before I get over it," he wrote.[44]

Ernest Hemingway and F. Scott Fitzgerald lobbed yet another heap of scorn on the adventure writer. Taking a jab at Halliburton, Hemingway sent Fitzgerald a photo of himself with a note scrawled across that read, "To Scott from his old bedfellow Richard Halliburton."[45] Many years hence, after Halliburton died, Hemingway would refer to him as the "deceased *Ladies' Home Journal* adventurer."[46]

Lastly, there were the repeated accusations from critics that he fabricated his stories, namely his moonlight swim at the Taj Mahal. These charges started long before Halliburton faked his death in the Hellespont and so had more to do with their contempt for the adventure writer. Save for "a stray shot or two from the lecture platform,"[47] Halliburton never directly answered these accusations—except once when he penned a three-thousand-word response to a nineteen-year-old who, in his own letter, pleaded with the adventurer-author to vouch for his exploits. In the letter, Halliburton declared that people would someday remember him by two things, neither of which was true: "One, is that I am a tea party lecturer, which I'm not. And the other is that I took a high dive into the pool of the Taj Mahal. Since it's only three inches deep in most places you can see how true that was."[48]

·····

In the spring of 1930, workers completed the 1,046-foot-high Art Deco Chrysler Building. Its stainless steel crown now sparkled over Manhattan's skyline. Like the skyscraper, Halliburton wanted to once again soar. He needed to push his limits, and his editors were impatient for another book. He couldn't put Hollywood behind him fast enough. "Don't worry about Hollywood demoralizing me," he wrote home. "It's no worse than any other place, but I must admit I'd rather be writing a nice book than messing with these lousy movies."[49]

As always, travel remained his addiction and his tonic. Keen to embark on a new odyssey, he fell for the business proposition of one Captain John McGuire of the Royal Air Force. McGuire was working in Hollywood as a technical advisor on several movies. He met Halliburton through Pancho Barnes soon before his scheduled return to England. McGuire told Halliburton he had neither the money nor a plane and he needed both to make the trip home. Nothing about this struck Halliburton as odd. In fact, it was just the opposite. Taken in by the captain's crisp voice and flawlessly waxed mustache, Halliburton gave McGuire $500, and that was the last Halliburton heard from McGuire. This childlike tendency to trust was typical for Halliburton, a trait his Princeton friends like Mike Hockaday were well aware of.[50]

McGuire may have conned him out of money, but Halliburton wasn't angry. Instead, the incident inspired him. He would fly around the world. Like much of the nation and the world, he too had closely followed Charles Lindbergh's solo flight across the Atlantic in 1927.[51] At twenty-five, the handsome pilot became an instant icon and *Time* magazine's first Man of the Year. Aviation was the thing, Halliburton knew, and he would play his part.

For some time, art had celebrated aviation. Georges Braques was building model airplanes, and back in 1912 Pablo Picasso painted *Still Life: Our Future Is in the Air*. Airplanes were everywhere; they adorned clocks and pencil boxes, cigarette cases and plates. Children played with model aircraft and aviator dolls. Aeronautical games and puzzles flew off toy store shelves.[52] As the sculptor Gutzon Borglum predicted, the airplane would erase the world's borders.[53] For Halliburton, flying around the world was synonymous with progress and freedom. He was nostalgic for his 1919 flight in an open-cockpit aircraft across the English Channel and above the Amiens trenches. Halliburton instinctively knew any book starring him and an airplane would grab people's attention like nothing he had ever done before.

Perhaps the battle to sell the movie rights to his work, and prolonged exposure to the stultifying atmosphere of Hollywood, had been a good thing, he thought. It reminded him of his true calling—to find and seek adventure. Back in January he'd told a reporter, "It is a trite but true saying that wherever you go, you find only what you take with you. Adventure does not and cannot mean travel to everyone. It does not require exploring strange lands or living among strange peoples. It simply means satisfying the imagination in whatever you are doing."[54]

Of course, for Halliburton the sooner he could go explore strange lands and live among strange peoples, the better.

7

The *Flying Carpet*

THE PHONE RANG IN twenty-four-year-old Moye Stephens's kitchen. "I'm Richard Halliburton and I'm contemplating a vagabond journey around the world by air and I want you to be my pilot."[1]

Of course Stephens knew who Halliburton was; the adventurer was as famous as Amelia Earhart, Charles Lindbergh, and Howard Hughes—the business tycoon and film director for whose movies Stephens flew stunts. Hughes was so impressed he took a few flying lessons with the young pilot.

Halliburton and Stephens chatted, and before hanging up the phone, Stephens agreed to meet at the Hollywood Roosevelt Hotel to further explore the idea. What followed was a long discussion in the hotel's wood-paneled bar that gave Stephens a lot to think about. No doubt the thirty-year-old Halliburton knew just what chords to strike to convince the pilot to come along on the aeronautical expedition. Stephens had already worked as a commercial pilot for four years; joining Halliburton would mean walking away from his promised annual salary of $12,000 with the Transcontinental Flying Company. If he went with Halliburton, he would earn only $1,200.[2] Leaving the money was relatively easy: adventure beckoned.

Born in 1905 to Moye Wicks Stephens and Mary "Brickie" Hendricks, Moye Jr. grew up in Los Angeles. A member of the Hollywood High School swim and football teams, the tall youth also participated in rifle competitions. Yet it wasn't until he went to Roger's Airfield and felt the hot sun on the tarmac and smelled the airplane fuel that he discovered his calling. Everything happened at the airfield. Pilots practiced new stunts, film directors like Howard Hughes scouted for stunt pilots, and air shows thrilled crowds on the weekends. The action intoxicated Stephens.

The California native flew for the first time when he was seventeen years old. He was hooked the moment the plane taxied down the runway. From then on, he contrived any excuse to go to the airfield. He traded work for lessons, sweeping out hangars and running errands for pilots. He joined a flying club, a convenient way to get inexpensive flight instruction and, for those who didn't own a plane, a way for pilots to share the cost of airplane ownership and maintenance. To Stephens, pilots were demigods, and he was determined to join the flying elite.

Stephens's parents fervently hoped it was a passing fancy. They saw their son practicing law; he saw himself taking to the skies. Nevertheless, he enrolled in Stanford University School of Law to appease them. He even applied himself to his studies, although in truth, Stephens never seriously considered a law career.[3] He had one goal: to fly professionally. He soloed after eight hours of flying time and earned his pilot's license on September 12, 1924. Two years later, during the hot summer of 1926, the mild-mannered twenty-one-year-old debuted his skills in Hughes's epic World War I film *Hell's Angels*. Stephens also flew in several Cecil B. DeMille productions. Along the way Stephens met Amelia Earhart and, from seeing her around California's many airfields, he developed a strong friendship with Pancho Barnes, one of Halliburton's closest friends.

In January 1929 Stephens graduated from Stanford with a law degree. However, he had not graduated from his desire to fly full-time. Like Halliburton, Stephens didn't share his father's notion of what constituted a respectable career path. Instead of hanging out his shingle, Stephens took a job with Maddux Air Lines. Shortly after that, he signed with Transcontinental Airlines and was assigned to the dangerous western leg of Transcontinental Air Transport's coast-to-coast route.[4] He had the skills and temperament to circumnavigate the globe.

So Stephens was primed when Halliburton invited him to the Hollywood Roosevelt Hotel that morning. With no wife, no mortgage, and nothing else holding him to Los Angeles, he didn't mull the offer over long. If he joined Halliburton, he'd get a chance to partake in something extraordinary.

Halliburton had his pilot, but for want of an airplane, the adventure was at risk.

The men needed financing to make this flight around the world work, and while his editors at Bobbs-Merrill loved the idea, they would not contribute one cent. Similarly, Loring Schuler, his editor at *Ladies' Home Journal*, was clear about not helping with expenses. Schuler even wrote to Halliburton's father, Wesley, telling him that he wasn't being frugal so much as cautious. He found the idea of flying around the world—even though his son planned to ship the plane across the Atlantic and later the Pacific Oceans—positively risky. Indeed, when Halliburton visited Schuler in Maine over the summer of 1930, Schuler tried in vain to discourage the trip.[5]

The adventurer considered a new sponsor: his distant cousin Erle Halliburton. Erle had left Henning, Tennessee, in 1910 with five dollars in his pocket. He spent several years as a laborer in the oil fields of Oklahoma and Texas. In 1922 he invented a device for capping oil wells and earned his fortune; by the mid-1950s he would boast at least thirty-eight patents for oil-related tools.[6] The oilman quickly expanded his business ventures to include S.A.F.E. Way Air Lines based in Oklahoma.

Halliburton hesitated before calling on Erle. He liked his cousin and his wife well enough, even if they were a bit too staid for his tastes. On the other hand, Halliburton was a bit too wild for their tastes. However, Erle's daughters Vida and Zola adored their older cousin. He had an endless supply of fantastic stories and frequently took them riding in his car. They giggled at the way he showed up to their mother's formal dinner parties in flannel slacks and tennis sneakers and sat with one leg draped over the armrest.[7]

Thus, Halliburton got behind the wheel of his Buick and drove non-stop to his cousin's Pasadena ranch to try to sell him on the idea. After a few drinks, the oilman offered Halliburton and Stephens a Lockheed Vega for free. The plane carried four passengers and "is the last word in speed and smartness," Halliburton noted.[8] It was an enticing offer, because a free plane would save Halliburton several thousand dollars. Stephens advised Halliburton to resist temptation and turn down the offer. That the Lockheed Vega could reach speeds of 220 miles per hour in the air and land at 60 miles per hour was not a selling point in their case, Stephens explained. Too often they would have to land in places unable to accommodate such speeds. Instead, the pilot suggested they travel to Wichita, Kansas, and check out the Stearman Aircraft Corporation.

Stephens had his eye on a Stearman C-3B with a J-5 Wright "Whirlwind" engine. Possessing only the most basic knowledge about airplanes, Halliburton trusted Stephens implicitly. "So, after a lot of 'talk, talk, talk!' Bids and bargaining," he bought a Stearman for $8,000, telling his parents it was "exactly the ship after all for my purpose."[9]

The C-3, a three-seat, open-cockpit plane, would gain worldwide recognition in 1932 when the American Ross Hadley flew one around the world. Known for their stability, cinematographers often used the planes as camera ships during movie shoots. The Stearman had little room for baggage and it landed slowly, but it was sturdily built and its engine was similar to the one in the *Spirit of St. Louis*, the plane Charles Lindbergh flew across the Atlantic.[10]

Halliburton took one look at the plane when he picked it up from a Los Angeles dealer and decided it desperately needed a makeover. He would leave the wings gold, but the dark maroon, almost muddy brown, body looked dull. It was short on pizzazz. Halliburton repainted the body a bright scarlet and gave the struts several new coats of glossy black paint. Stephens supervised the fine-tuning and dictated several modifications including extra gas tanks and larger wheels. Halliburton called his new airplane the *Flying Carpet*.

This was undoubtedly going to be Halliburton's most dangerous expedition yet, in spite of the many safety improvements made to aircraft in the past years, including cockpit instruments, better altimeters, rate-of-climb indicators, and compasses. However, at times they would be flying over volatile regions and at other times they would be crossing poorly mapped territory. Even so, Halliburton had faith. He assured his parents that Stephens had shown himself to be a clear and cautious flyer.[11]

While Stephens concentrated on the mechanical aspects of the trip, Halliburton attended to the itinerary, visas, publicity, and fuel. He hoped to land a sponsor because at four dollars per gallon, fuel would account for a huge percentage of the budget.[12] To that end he and Stephens stopped in St. Louis to sign a fuel contract with Shell Oil. Halliburton trusted he could convince the company to sponsor his expedition. Sponsorship was gaining popularity; many pilots represented oil companies at air races. Shell sponsored Jimmy Doolittle, who would lead the Tokyo Raiders during World War II. Gilmore sponsored Roscoe Turner and Standard Oil sponsored Edwin Arnold.[13] Though intrigued with the idea, the Shell executives decided against giving Halliburton free fuel. Instead, they agreed to arrange for chits for gas, maps, and suggested routes.[14]

His passion for adventure reignited, Halliburton hoped to parlay this fourth book into a new phase in his career. He still wanted to pursue his Rupert Brooke biography. "We must up stakes and strike out for fresh fields. This flying idea will establish me beyond all criticism, and I'll be able to abandon travel books with a proud gesture instead of feeling it's been forced upon me by malicious critics and a cooling public," he wrote home.[15]

In late December, Stephens pointed the *Flying Carpet* east. He and Halliburton were on their way to spend Christmas in Memphis, but the weather conspired against them. Fog delayed their flight and the two didn't arrive until December 26. As they made their final approach into the city, they spotted Wesley's office building, one of the tallest in the city. A short while later, inside the Halliburtons' home, the author and pilot tucked into their holiday dinner a day late.

After getting a full battery of inoculations against tropical diseases, the two took off for Indianapolis. Halliburton needed to stop by the Bobbs-Merrill headquarters and review the book's concept with David Laurance Chambers. Next they went to Philadelphia so Halliburton could meet with newspaper publishers to hash out ideas for a proposed series based on the trip. Halliburton would bank on magazine and newspaper royalties to help finance his round-the-world jaunt. Still, to make sure he had enough funds to cover expenses, he also sold part of his remaining stock portfolio, which included General Motors, General Electric, and US Steel.[16]

In January the *Flying Carpet* landed on the outskirts of Washington, DC. Halliburton and Stephens's itinerary called for them to fly over politically sensitive areas, and they needed to secure government permission to cross certain airspace, including India and North Africa. The pair met with officials from the US Department of Commerce and the US State Department. Following the meeting, Secretary of State Henry L. Stimson furnished Halliburton with a letter asking that consular officials in the various countries they wished to visit welcome the writer and the pilot.[17]

Then it was back to the big brick city of New York. The *Flying Carpet* touched down on Roosevelt Field on Long Island. Halliburton and Stephens almost couldn't see the landing strip for the crowds gathered at the historic airfield hoping to catch a glimpse of the adventure writer.[18]

After ensuring the plane was safely on its way to a hangar in Newark, New Jersey, Halliburton and Stephens checked into the Duane Hotel. The author had tea with the novelist and playwright Edna Ferber and dinner with America's Sweetheart, his movie star friend Mary Pickford. He also caught up with old friends, including his *New Worlds to Conquer* companion Fred Healy, who "was distressed almost to tears over not going on this new adventure with me, but of course such a thing would have been utterly unwise."[19] Healy wouldn't have been able to take the time away from his job at Putnam and Sons and as dear a friend as he was, this adventure called for a pilot, not a friend.

At the end of January, Halliburton and Stephens drove to Newark, where the plane remained in storage. The two men wanted to personally watch the *Flying Carpet* loaded onto the truck that would carry it to New York Harbor. They followed the truck back to New York City to where the cruise liner the *Majestic* was docked. The White Star Line charged Halliburton $450 to ship the plane across the ocean. He and Stephens paid $270 each for passage.[20] Down at the dock, Halliburton nervously watched as the dockworkers lowered the scarlet-and-gold plane onto the deck. "Though everybody did it clumsily it being the first time for the boat as well as for us. I just about had nervous prostration during the few tense minutes when our ship was suspended in the air," he wrote home.[21] Stephens supervised the removal of the plane's wings and watched workers stow them below deck. He returned topside to ensure workers properly tied down the aircraft. A tarpaulin covered the scarlet body.

Once the plane was attended to, Halliburton and Stephens noticed a battalion of photographers snapping away. Flash bulbs popped. Stephens quietly stepped back, leaving Halliburton to star alone in the pictures. Halliburton also sat down for the first of several interviews aboard the *Majestic*.[22] He knew this trip troubled his parents, and in a quiet moment he wrote them a letter vowing that once he came home he would "never subject you again to the anxiety you've suffered over me for ten years. I'm through."[23] In a paragraph which his father ultimately deleted for public consumption, Richard promised he would never do anything "hazardous or indiscreet. . . . My whole scheme of life is to try and run my affairs as diplomatically as possible in their relationship to the people I love and associate with. No one, not even my family can possibly appreciate how complicated my life is. But I trust to have the self-control to keep it on track."[24]

On January 31, 1931, the *Majestic* sailed for England. Cold rain pelted the ship when it docked more than ten days later. Fierce winds lashed the passengers as they disembarked. After unloading the aircraft, Halliburton and Stephens spent three days at the airdrome repairing and reassembling the *Flying Carpet* like a jigsaw puzzle. On the fourth day the weather had still not abated. On the fifth day the two went to London.

Inside, their hotel rooms were barely heated; outside, the weather stormed. Fog, drizzle, bitter cold, and slush chilled Halliburton to the bone. Where their hotel accommodations were lacking, the airdrome was most efficient and helpful. Meticulous in his preparation, Stephens tested chutes and checked the instruments once, twice, and three times more.

While Stephens dealt with the airplane, Halliburton met with government officials to ensure they had the proper visas for Africa and Asia. There was "endless red tape and silly regulations." He was delighted, however, to enlist Edward Stanford Ltd., the cartographer to the King of England.[25] "Our maps glitter before us (to Morocco and back up and over to Alps to Italy) they are perfect and we can't possibly get lost. We've seen the Soviet officials about flying in Russia and for France and for Spain. We have a stack of official papers a foot thick. We've been movie-toned and photographed to death."[26]

In between piecing together the paperwork, he spent a weekend in a sixteenth-century castle and "ate on King James table and slept in Queen Elizabeth's bed—all very cold and dreary. . . . I'll have died of flu a dozen times, after California, except that I've had my usual bronchial inflammation for 2 months and so was immune from any more."[27]

Sixteen days later, the adventure writer and his pilot zoomed off to Paris. Stephens noticed an odd vibration as they crossed over the English Channel. Apparently the workers had installed the aileron controls upside down when assembling the plane back in California. It took three weeks to fix. In any other circumstance Halliburton would have found being stuck in Paris a delight, but waiting for repairs was tedious, even with visits to the walled port city of Saint-Malo and the island monastery Mont Saint-Michel.[28] Numerous cocktail parties and dinner invitations filled his evenings, and Halliburton made sure the hosts always included Stephens.

And then it was wheels up. The *Flying Carpet* flew south, skimming the sandy coast of Spain. They covered nearly six hundred miles over Cartagena, Alicante, and Valencia. The sunlight reflected off the topaz waters of the Mediterranean. When Gibraltar came into view, Halliburton felt pulled back in time.

"I'd had such memorable adventures there in 1921—the ecstasies and escapades—and now 10 years had passed. The Rock had not changed by so much as a tree or bush—but I'd changed," he wrote home. "Muted? I'd ceased to be the person I was on my first encounter with Gibraltar. I was not 10 but 100 years older. Gibraltar typified my youth—that's gone, but the fact that I should again visit the place in so adventurous a vehicle as an airplane . . . assured me that I had not yet begun to fossilize."[29]

His Wedgwood-blue eyes watched until Gibraltar faded in the distance. Halliburton leaned out the window, trying to follow the coastline as the *Flying Carpet* flew on to Africa. "He'd get interested in something and he'd start looking. The wing would go down and the first thing you know we were in sort of a spiral," Stephens remembered decades later in an interview.[30] Halliburton's aversion to safety belts drove the pilot to distraction.

When they landed in Rabat, Morocco, French military officers greeted the two, who then waited eleven days for permission to cross the Sahara Desert. The French were reluctant to allow the flight. They didn't want to have to rescue the globetrotters should they fail to reach the other side of the sandy sea.[31] Fortunately for Halliburton, French Prime Minister Pierre Laval intervened. Laval, who later faced a firing squad for his role as head of government in the Vichy regime, fired off a cable to officials in Arem granting the *Flying Carpet* permission to land.[32] Just before they left, Stephens discovered a cactus needle, or something equally sharp, had punctured a tire. They had to wait one more day until it could be patched. "By this time Dick was frantic. You know he was very high strung, and nervous, and being held up was just more than he could stand," Stephens said.[33]

Finally, with fuel tanks overflowing and enough food and water for two weeks, the plane struggled to take off. Once airborne, the sunlight glinted off its golden wings. With the French Foreign Legion fighting the Berbers throughout Algeria and Morocco, Halliburton hoped the American flag on the tail would deter North African nomads from shooting at them as they did on French military aircraft.

They headed toward Gao, a French Foreign Legion outpost located on the Niger River. From the air they followed the same thirteen-hundred-mile journey that a military car patrolled every four days. Should they be forced down, help would come—eventually.

Even with extra fuel tanks, the plane carried only enough gasoline for six hours of flying, or about 540 miles in ideal flying conditions; a headwind meant burning through the gas much more quickly. Fortunately, Halliburton and Stephens were permitted to draw from two Shell Oil–maintained fuel dumps. There was one about 400 miles south of Colomb-Béchar at the Adrar oasis, the largest oasis in the Sahara. The second one lay about 500 miles farther south.[34]

Stephens couldn't locate the first fuel dump. Blowing and stinging sand cut visibility to zero and interfered with his magnetic compass. Below lay the parched earth. "The first 400 miles, we saw several oases to break the monotony of wilderness. But the rest 800 miles was the real thing—not a rise of 100 feet—not a blade of grass, or a human being. This part of the Sahara is hard ground—a burned crust of gravel and sand without a dip or a crack," Halliburton wrote home.[35]

Stephens circled around several times, eyes shifting between fuel gauge, the compass, and the window. He looked this way. Then that way. At long last he found his target. The wind had blown the sand into drifts until it covered the fuel tanks. After digging them out, the two men transferred the life-saving gas a gallon at a time. Halliburton crammed a receipt for one hundred gallons near the tank. Perhaps Shell Oil would cancel his debt after his return.

The fuel tanks were filled, but it was now too late to leave. Above the stars winked. Halliburton and Stephens ate canned beef and slept on parachutes spread out on the ground under the plane's wings. A windup phonograph provided the evening's entertainment.[36] They awoke before the sun slid over the horizon, their bodies cold to the core. The temperature had plummeted 75 degrees during the night, to just below freezing.

By the time the *Flying Carpet* landed in Gao, fine sand caked the engine. It filled just about every possible crevice in the plane. After cleaning the plane, they flew over fields of poppies and stands of poplar trees on their way to Timbuktu, on the edge of the Sahara. A decaying jumble of centuries-old mud-brick houses dotted the sweep of the hillside.[37] Halliburton and Stephens were shown sleeping quarters in a mud-walled rest house thick with flies. It smelled of age-old earth and travelers past. They supped with French army officers. Stephens spent the rest of the night drinking and singing with his newfound comrades while Halliburton walked the town, such as it was.

Later, after an hour or two of tossing and turning in the stuffy house, they went to the roof, shoved blankets under their heads, and fell asleep, despite the bats and nesting storks. They couldn't get out of Timbuktu fast enough.[38]

They flew back to Colomb-Béchar, the French Foreign Legion's training headquarters. Meeting the storied and notorious legionnaires, who were marking their one hundredth anniversary, was a highpoint for Halliburton, who planned on writing an article about them for the *Ladies' Home Journal*. Like children in a school play, both Halliburton and Stephens donned uniforms and posed for photographs with the legionnaires.

During their two-week stay with the legion, Halliburton met men from nearly thirty nations. He went into the story thinking he'd find a bunch of drunken louts. What he found was quite the opposite. Yes, they were rootless, but he found them imbued with a sense of purpose and highly disciplined, willing to fight and die in the scorching desert for what amounted to a few centimes a day. He was surprised to find good food and clean barracks. Halliburton's story would be a scoop, but perhaps not exactly the scoop *Ladies' Home Journal* had anticipated. His piece was an honest portrait that held none of the public's prejudices.

By now more than a year had passed since Halliburton first met Stephens at the Hollywood Roosevelt Hotel. Predictably, fissures started appearing in their camaraderie. There was a great deal of mutual respect and overall the two still got along, but there were times when Stephens's "complete willingness to sit tight in a café for hours [and sip liqueurs] and his utter lack of adventurous spirit" grated on the author.[39]

During Richard Halliburton's flight around the world, he and his pilot Moye Stephens Jr. stopped in Colomb-Béchar and spent time with French legionnaires. This photo appeared in the book *The Flying Carpet*. *Author's collection*

Likewise, Halliburton could aggravate Stephens. Open-minded about Halliburton's homosexuality, the pilot thoroughly respected Halliburton and the lengths to which he went to safeguard his private life.[40] He appreciated that, as a public commodity, Halliburton couldn't shatter the image of the swashbuckling writer with a woman in every port. "He didn't discuss his partners at all. During the trip I met some people, some homosexual people that he met along the line," he said.[41] Rather, Stephens's issues with Halliburton had to do with the way the author tended to put story above safety and his tendency to veer toward impatience and, sometimes, depression when things started slipping beyond his control,like when they waited to fix the ailerons or if too long a time passed before hearing from his editor.

However, knowing they had many more miles to fly and many more places to go, Halliburton learned to steer around Stephens when he was irritated with the pilot, likewise Stephens learned to steer clear of Halliburton. Thus the pair avoided any serious and lasting clashes.[42]

When they arrived in Fez, the French military treated Stephens to a parade and bouquets of flowers. He was a regular local Lindbergh. The acrobatic French flier Michel Detroyat also happened to be there and he invited Stephens to perform in the city's very first air show.

Halliburton adored the ancient city; it was the North Africa of his dreams. A riot of color by day, it held just enough mystery by night. Halliburton set about finding a house to rent so he could write; he needed to continue working on his legionnaire experience, hoping to whittle it down to fifteen thousand words.

By June, the *Flying Carpet* desperately needed a complete overhaul. The sand, filth, and general wear and tear had taken their toll on the mechanics. Stephens flew them to Paris. Whenever the scarlet-and-gold plane landed, people wined and dined the pilot and the author. People knew Halliburton; his first three books had been translated into nine languages and the British editions were available throughout the Middle East. From his room at the Wagram Hotel in the 17th arrondissement,

Halliburton continued working on his French Foreign Legion story, while Stephens supervised the work on the plane.

Halliburton also sat down for interviews with several reporters. Over drinks at the Wagram Hotel's bar, Halliburton told Don Brown, a reporter with the *Chicago Daily Tribune*, a strange and fantastic story. He was, he said, surprised to learn slavery in French Equatorial Africa was alive and well. When the *Flying Carpet* touched down "the natives went wild over the brilliant color scheme of our plane, we decided that it would be a good thing to buy a couple of slaves to help take care of our personal needs while we were there," Halliburton said. He described riding swaying camels out of town to make the purchase from the Taureg tribe. "It was on the bootleg system, like driving out of Memphis to find a roadhouse," Halliburton said. "After much argument they sold us a boy and a girl. They brought them out stark naked and extolled their physical virtues to the skies. We paid $5 a piece. They were black as ink. I put the girl on the camel behind me and Moye took the boy on his camel."[43]

Stephens remembered the episode quite differently. There were slaves in that part of Africa, Stephens later said, but "we didn't buy any. I don't think they would have regarded the purchase of slaves as being quite the right thing to do."[44]

The discrepancy in their accounts reveals two things. First, it shows how Halliburton was at times an unreliable narrator, prone to exaggeration. To be sure, he never made claims to the contrary, even admitting to occasionally adding "buckets of fanciful bright paint flung over it" to liven up his stories.[45] Second, Stephens's recollection many years later shows his desire to protect Halliburton's name. Though the truth may never be known, the account became part of the author's story chest, something readers took out and read with equal parts incredulity and fascination.

From Paris it was a quick hop to Venice. Never one to forgo a swim, Halliburton decided to take a dip in the Grand Canal. Standing in swim trunks at the edge of the water, he braced himself to dive into the rot stink of the canal. One and a half miles separated the Rialto

Bridge and St. Marks Square. Stephens sat comfortably in a gondola, happy to watch his friend's shenanigans. Halliburton dove into the water, not realizing he was just across from a police station. An officer spotted the writer the moment he pushed off the edge. He gave chase, shouting at Halliburton to get out of the water this instant! The officer admonished the Tennessean—it was forbidden to swim the Grand Canal—and fined him ten lire.

"The water was so dirty I was about glad something made me get out of it. As yet I've not developed any Italian diseases," Halliburton said, laughing it off. Afterward, Halliburton, Stephens, and the policeman went out for a round of beers. Naturally the story made the local papers.[46]

Because it was Halliburton, the story didn't stay local and the *New Yorker* pounced on a chance to make fun. "Our dear Richard had been touring the world in an airplane . . . and with a companion (known as Whoopee, by the way) plunged into the Grand Canal and started swimming. Even as he swam, however, the instincts of a travel-book writer didn't desert him; if you'll believe me, he paused now and again to view the points of interest along the way. . . . So on they went, splashing and staring, until they reached the Rialto bridge . . . there a policeman, unused to the Halliburton ebullience, nabbed them. But isn't our Dick a card, though? Think of thinking of poetry at a time like that."[47]

Next the *Flying Carpet* alit in Constantinople, where US Ambassador Joseph Grew and his wife, Alice Perry Grew, invited Halliburton and Stephens to a chic dinner at their residence. The next morning the pilot and the author flew straight up the Bosporus to the Black Sea and onward to Aleppo, Syria. In all his writing he never mentioned the Armenian Genocide, when more than a million Armenians perished at the hands of the Turkish military and paramilitary forces. The omission of the 1915 atrocity was entirely in keeping with Halliburton's works to date. He paid attention to texture, sounds, and color. He expounded on ancient history. Yet, he had little to no interest in writing about recent history or political turmoil.

Aleppo was but a brief interlude before they flew on to Jerusalem. Halliburton found Palestine a history lover's paradise but warned anyone with a love of religion to stay far away: "The hatred, the fighting, the religious fools, sicken one away from any Christian feeling about the place."[48]

Stephens flew on ahead to Damascus, while Halliburton once again felt the draw of the local waters. On September 8, at nine in the morning, he wriggled his toes in the sandy shores of the Sea of Galilee. Steep olive-green mountains rose in the background. Thinking he would be underwater the whole time, he ignored Stephens's advice to smear on the paste-like "sunburn cream," though in all likelihood, the petroleum jelly–based ointment available in the 1930s would have offered him little protection. In he went.[49] A fisherman followed closely in his boat. Halliburton swam nonstop for several hours. By the seventh mile, he felt so invigorated he wanted to swim the seven miles back. Alas, the wind turned against him and the sun seemed to be shooting flames into his skin. He rested on the eastern shore until sunset.[50]

It wasn't until evening when he looked in the mirror that Halliburton realized the extent of his sunburn. His neck and back burned scarlet. He took to bed for two days, unable to put on a stitch of clothing over his scaly, flaking skin.[51]

"He was not physically robust, but his nervous energy and his determination was what carried him through these adventures of his, I mean swimming through the Panama Canal and swimming the Hellespont and things of that sort," Moye Stephens said. "It was sheer nervous energy that carried him through those things. And, swimming across the Sea of Galilee and getting himself blistered to where he looked like a boiled lobster in the process."[52]

Though not fully recovered, Halliburton let Stephens drive him to Damascus to retrieve the *Flying Carpet*. "He got into the back seat and he held on to the straps. Of course, where he was sitting was sunburned, too. There was never a peep out of him through that long drive on a rough road all the way back to Damascus. He had guts," Stephens said.[53]

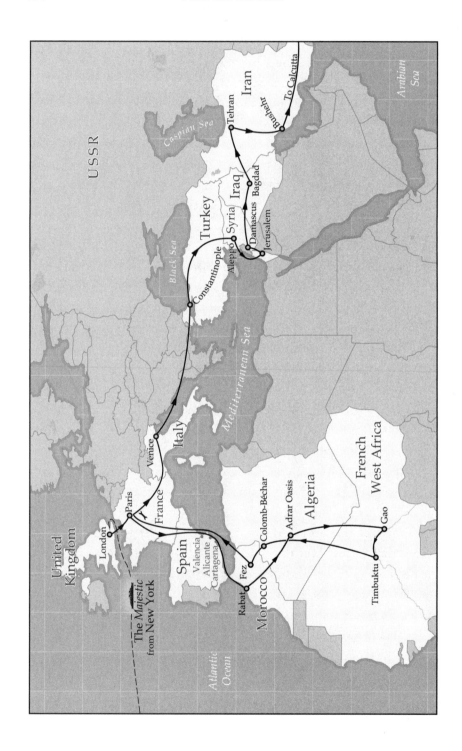

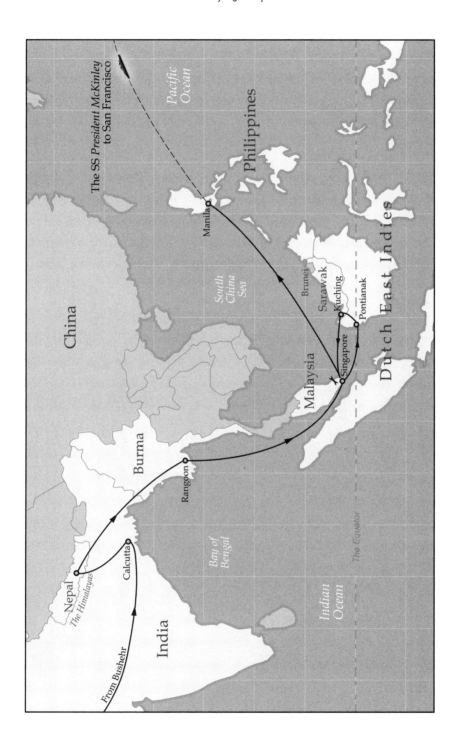

"Bagdad!"[54] That one-word telegram conveyed all to Wesley and Nelle Halliburton: their son was safe. Halliburton and Stephens had crossed the Euphrates at sunset; the domes of Bagdad glowed red and gold against the dying sun.

The two Americans enjoyed a delightful tea with Crown Prince Ghazi of Iraq. Teacups and saucers cleared, Halliburton persuaded the seventeen-year-old prince to come fly with them. The prince jumped from excitement. Two Royal Air Force fighters escorted the *Flying Carpet* as it flew seventy-five miles up the Tigris River to Samarra for lunch. Ghazi's uncle and a photographer flew alongside in the escort planes. At Halliburton's behest, Stephens treated the prince to a few slow rolls and a loop or two through the chilled air.

Richard Halliburton and Moye Stephens Jr. treated Prince Ghazi of Iraq to his first airplane ride. This picture appeared in *The Flying Carpet. Author's collection*

Halliburton lectured at the city's American school, where a sincere pupil presented him with two small rugs, or "flying carpets." He sent one of the cream-, navy-, and beet-colored rugs home to his parents and kept the other under his feet inside the other *Flying Carpet*.

In December, Halliburton and Stephens flew into Tehran wrapped in thick sheepskin overcoats, the crystal sky as frozen as their fingers and noses. It had taken them five hours to cross the region's wild and arid mountains, some of which rose twelve thousand feet.

The city's bazaars enticed Halliburton. He wanted one of everything he saw. On a whim, he bought a nightingale. "He's hanging in his cage in my hotel room and has bursts of song when he's warm and well fed. When we fly on south I'm taking him abroad. The first nightingale ever to ride on an airplane I'm sure," he wrote home.[55] The nightingale did not survive the trip.

While in Persia the two men met the celebrated German aviator Elly Beinhorn. Actually, Stephens met her first, having flown ahead from Tehran to Bushehr while Halliburton traveled over land via Isfahan and Shiraz. Beinhorn's arrival was nothing short of dramatic; engine failure had forced her down one hundred miles from the city, and so she had to hitch a ride on a truck. After learning of her predicament, the ever-gallant Stephens took her back to her aircraft, which still sat in the desert. He also helped Beinhorn fix the plane's engine.

"These boys would be very useful to me in case of need—and it would be dandy to be with them again," Beinhorn recounted in a newspaper interview with the *New York Times*.[56] The three got along quite well and decided to travel together for a spell. The trio said yes to an invitation from the Calcutta Flying Club to participate in a private air show for the maharaja of Nepal.

While they were in Calcutta, Halliburton heard that Mary Pickford's husband, Douglas Fairbanks, intended to fly around the world in a plane called the *Magic Carpet*. Alarmed, he dashed a letter off to the movie star. "If this story is only a newspaper rumour, and if your plans have been changed—this letter will be pointless," Halliburton wrote. "If the story is fact, I think the following information should be respectfully brought to your attention. . . . There is an around-the-world flying expedition called *Flying Carpet* now under way . . . it happens to be my own plane and my own expedition."[57] Fairbanks immediately sent word telling Halliburton the rumor was unfounded. In fact, Fairbanks was at that very moment traveling to the South Seas to film a dramatic story and hunting travelogue.[58]

Halliburton was about to encounter his own dramatic story: Mount Everest. He decided he wanted to fly over the twenty-nine-thousand-foot-high mountain, even though the nominal altitude ceiling of the Stearman was sixteen thousand feet. In 1924 the British flier Alan Cobham had tried to fly over the summit, and failed. The Nepalese government rejected Halliburton's request to soar over the mountaintop, as the presence of Europeans in and about Nepal was often met with suspicion.[59] Well, at least they could fly near enough to capture the stone giant on film, thought Halliburton.

Not for the first time, Stephens reminded Halliburton to buckle his safety belt. Gingerly, Stephens pushed the throttle forward. "By leaving out everything: our parachutes, tools, everything, just stripping it down, and not even taking a full load of gas, I was able to waft it up to 18,000 by taking advantage of updrafts," Stephens recalled.[60] The tachometer nearly redlined as he struggled to gain altitude in the thin air. The plane shook violently. The rivets threatened to pop.

Stephens turned the aircraft away from a ridge until Everest appeared directly in front of them. Unbeknownst to Stephens, Halliburton had unbuckled his safety belt and stood in the cockpit. He raised his camera to his eye, poised to take the once in a lifetime shot. The drag from his upright body caused the *Flying Carpet* to stall. The plane dropped a thousand feet nose first. The force nearly threw Halliburton from the plane. He scrambled into his seat as the ground rushed toward them. Stephens pushed the stick forward with all his strength. The plane steadied. Death averted, Halliburton now possessed the world's first-ever aerial photographs of Mount Everest.[61]

Upon landing, Halliburton told Stephens they could try for another photo again in the morning. "You and who else?" Stephens asked him, feeling angry and alarmed about what had just happened.[62] First, there was no place in the high altitude where the *Flying Carpet* had a prayer of landing. Second, they'd left their parachutes behind the first time to conserve weight and space.[63] Once again, Stephens's conviction that Halliburton courted danger and death was confirmed.

During a mid-January stop in Singapore to attach pontoons to the plane, Halliburton felt his enthusiasm for the trip wane considerably. Like the peeling paint on the *Flying Carpet*, most of the gloss had disappeared. Trying to buck himself up, he remembered they would soon be in Borneo. He packed bathing suits and sunburn cream.[64]

While waiting in Singapore, the adventure writer started thinking about what life would be like once he returned to the States. From his father's newsy letters Halliburton knew the economy back home remained quite grim and that campaign season had opened; Franklin Delano Roosevelt hoped to dislodge President Herbert Hoover from the White House. But aside from working on the *Flying Carpet* book, the only thing he knew was he wanted Paul Mooney to be a big part of his life going forward. Of this he was certain. So much so, he wrote his parents about his plans.

He informed his parents that while he would absolutely share every dinner with them, he would no longer stay in his boyhood room. Instead, he planned to rent a small apartment in town. He explained he meant to invite one of his old writer friends from California to "occupy with me whatever quarters I occupy. He is one of the most intelligent, and pertinent, critics I know, and very capable in a secretarial way. . . . I would pay him a small salary, but treat him entirely as my friend and guest. We were much together in California, and got along famously."[65] He folded the letter to his parents, planning to mail it later. For now, the task at hand needed his full attention.

Attaching the pontoons required precision and patience. First Stephens suspended the plane on cables and removed the landing gear.

Next he positioned the pontoons with their centers of gravity precisely under the plane. Finding the pontoons' center of gravity was easy; he simply balanced them on a sawhorse. Pinpointing the plane's center of gravity was another matter. After many unsuccessful attempts, Stephens cabled the Stearman factory in Wichita, Kansas. An engineer mailed back drawings. What Halliburton and Stephens thought would take only two or three weeks turned into nine.

Meanwhile, Halliburton, frustrated with Stephens for his seeming to be oblivious about time and money pressures, started working on his manuscript. He also spoke twice to the local Rotary Club and, smartly turned out in a pressed suit, attended several cocktail parties and teas.[66]

Whether it was from travel fatigue on the part of the pilots, or mechanical fatigue on the part of the *Flying Carpet*, troubles started piling up when the two men reached Dutch Borneo. Landing and taking off in the tidal rivers, with the current rushing past and logs everywhere, quickly lost its novelty. A sunken log pierced a pontoon when Stephens attempted a water landing.

Then their first truly dangerous accident happened. Several onlookers pressed together onshore, gaping at the sky as the scarlet-and-gold aircraft buzzed into view. Stephens landed the plane in the middle of a tidal river. Halliburton climbed out, and while standing on the pontoon, he wound the anchor line around his arm. Suddenly he lost his footing. The line caught on the propeller and whipped the rope from Halliburton's arm, lashing his fair skin. The momentum of the rope uprooted the forty-pound anchor. Like a mace, it whizzed through the air. Halliburton ducked. "It couldn't have missed him by that far, and boy, if it had hit him it would probably have killed him. If it had hit him in the head it definitely would have killed him," Stephens recalled decades later.[67]

The propeller was bent double and the anchor rope torn to shreds. Once he caught his breath, Halliburton realized he'd already shipped their spare propeller home. For a moment it seemed the trip was doomed to end right there. Fortunately, a local blacksmith bent it straight again—or straight enough.[68]

The local paper jumped on the story: "We, spectators, had the jump of our lifes [sic] to see Mr. Halliburton having such a narrow escape! Before I could get across the river I saw you straitening [sic] and I was very glad you obviously had'nt [sic] had much serious damage. Though I regretted much not to be able to shake hands and tell you a proper goodbye . . . I believe Mr. Halliburton understands our language enough to grasp the meaning; if not, you surely can find someone who can translate it for you. Don't be too famous to forget us all; you gave us some very pleasant days, and we really regretted very much to must let you go so soon."[69]

His arm bandaged, Halliburton and Stephens took off for Kuching, the capital of Sarawak. Charles Vyner Brooke and his wife Sylvia Brett Brooke ruled the small realm, which would be ceded to Malaysia in 1963. Hailing from an ancient English family, the Brookes, who had three daughters, were the only English family to occupy an Asian throne. They had their own flag, money, and postage stamps. Known as the White Rajahs, the dynastic monarchy ruled over the Chinese and a Dayak tribe. Protocol dictated Sylvia walk four paces behind her husband in public and in any official capacity. The Dayak people considered her a slave.

The White Rajahs ruled over a land where roads were few but jungles were plenty. It was a lush land where houses were built on riverbanks and where tangles of scarlet rhododendron, golden allamanda, and pitcher plants grew.

The *Flying Carpet* landed across from Astana House, the official residence, just as Sylvia Brooke, the forty-seven-year-old rani, was betting on horses at the racetrack. When she returned, she saw to it that Halliburton and Stephens were comfortably lodged at Astana. With its verandahs, potted palms, and high ceilings, Astana was the epitome of tropical colonialism. That same evening, Halliburton and Stephens attended the Grand Prix Ball. Wearing their flying clothes, Halliburton and Stephens made a grand entrance. They stood out considering that "every woman present was jeweled . . . every man resplendent in military or civil uniform." Dressed in loincloths, the local headhunters stood on the manicured lawn, watching the grandeur unfold.[70]

Inside, Halliburton waltzed across the polished dance floor with the rani, whom he declared the best dancer at the party. He proposed she join them aboard the *Flying Carpet*.

"Had I said to an Englishman—want to fly he would've told me no way. But not so America. I had hardly finished the sentence before Dick Halliburton had whisked out his note book and was go-getting me into that plane. 'Fly' he said 'Gee girl, that's easy—Monday stone steps . . . nine o'clock . . . we'll take you up.' I hadn't time to protest. I hadn't time to be alarmed. That's America!"[71] The government officials balked, worried about what they would tell Charles should something horrible happen. But the always gutsy rani would have her way. She thrilled at the idea that the man who had taken part in *Hell's Angels* was going to take her for a ride. And so, with the rajah away in England, the rani and two of her daughters took flight.

With a roar, the *Flying Carpet* streaked through the water and soared above the web of rivers threading in and out of the green jungle like veins. They tried shooting ducks from the plane but missed every time. Brooke drew the line at photos. "Though if he could have taken an X-ray impression of me it might have been different. It might have been interesting to see all my bones leaning together in fear," she recalled.[72]

Brooke wasn't the only one to make her flying debut over the lush island. Chief Koh, the Dayak chief of the headhunters, also took to the skies. To find him, Halliburton and Stephens followed the Rajang River into the very heart of Borneo. Few white men had ever reached the headwaters. Hiking through the rain forest with headhunters, Halliburton and Stephens couldn't slap the mosquitoes away fast enough. The dense canopy diffused the light, and in the thick humidity the sunlight looked like beads on the climbing foliage. The vines and trees hemmed them in, and Halliburton felt all sorts of eyes upon them.

Chief Koh of the Dayak became the first in his tribe to fly when he went for a ride on the *Flying Carpet*. This photo appeared in Halliburton's book *The Flying Carpet*. *Author's collection*

Hours later, they reached the house where Koh waited. Under the thatched roof they sat on the floor next to the tattoo-covered chief.[73] Before eating, the Dayak men threw a bit of their food out the window as an offering to their gods. In between courses, Stephens stepped outside onto a bamboo balcony. He glanced upward and saw clusters of heads hung from the ceiling. "I kept banging my head on them because I'm taller than most of the Dayak," he recounted.[74]

According to Halliburton's articles and letters, he and Stephens even learned how to shoot blowpipes. He also wrote about keeping twelve shrunken heads, a gift from Chief Koh, until Stephens tossed the stinking heads out of the airplane. However, according to Stephens, that never happened. One, the Dayaks would never give away one head, let alone twelve heads, as they consider the heads among their prized possessions. Two, "as far as putting ten or more heads in the airplane, boy, we had it loaded down where we barely got off the water as it was." Stephens hardly minded the tale. He knew Halliburton added little nuggets like that to liven up the story.[75]

The end of the trip neared. They had exchanged Sarawak—where they narrowly missed a deadly typhoon by forty-eight hours—for another stop in Singapore.

While at the Raffles Hotel, Halliburton met Canadian journalist Gordon Sinclair. With cold drink in hand, Sinclair sat on the porch of the famed hotel with the animal trainer Frank "Bring 'Em Back Alive" Buck and Col. Theodore Roosevelt, who was governor of the Philippines at the time. Buck aimed to catch a giant python to bring back to America.

"As we sat sipping a drink we were joined by another man, a tall, good-looking chap who seemed to know all the others. He talked about Borneo, whence he had just come, and then, belatedly as an afterthought, was introduced to me. This was my first glimpse of Richard Halliburton, but the actual introduction was muffed. It was one of those times when you don't catch the name properly but rather than raise the point you let it go. The next day this slim adventurer was back and I learned just who he was," Sinclair recalled.[76]

Sinclair knew Halliburton's earlier works. His newspaper stories were a bit too flowery for Sinclair's early literary tastes; however, the Canadian felt once properly edited and arranged, the stories provided the base for some of the most entertaining travel books he'd ever read, especially *The Royal Road to Romance*.[77]

At last, Halliburton and Stephens reached their last stop before their homecoming. In the Philippines, after a swarm of locusts nearly brought down the plane, Governor-General Theodore "One Shot Teddy" Roosevelt III and his wife invited the Americans to lunch. American naval aviators treated the famous crew of the *Flying Carpet* to endless parties. By now Halliburton had traveled forty thousand miles and spent $50,000 on the trip. His account was now $2,000 overdrawn. Fortunately for Halliburton, *The Flying Carpet* would net more than $100,000 in the first year of its publication.

But for now, as he sailed for home aboard the SS *President McKinley*, Halliburton took time to reflect on what it meant to fly around the world. Ultimately, he decided flying was at once liberating and enchaining: The airplane allowed him to visit the remote outposts of the world, it was fast, and it literally took him to new heights. Yet, he despised the constant maintenance and fine-tuning the machine needed.

"My sole obsession now is to retrench, retrench . . . and get clear of everything but peace of mind to work on my stories," he wrote home. "Tomorrow we land—on Wesley's birthday. A glad and sad coincidence."[78]

8

Interview with an Assassin

O NCE AGAIN BACK IN Memphis, Richard Halliburton found himself
navigating the complicated waters of his personal life. His parents
knew he intended to live with Paul Mooney upon his return; his frank
letter had made sure of that.[1] Halliburton tried to clothe his rationale
in the fabric of practicality; Mooney was key to the book process,
but Richard couldn't resist gushing about him all the same. "More
than ever I'll need Mooney in Memphis. His literary eye and ear are
extraordinarily fine—and his cooperation invaluable," he wrote. "He
is a most attractive broken-nose Irishman who has a more tonic effect
upon my spirits than anyone I know—and he will have on yours. It
will be great fun having him with us. You needn't have any uneasiness
about him whatsoever."[2]

His parents weren't merely troubled with the relationship, they
absolutely frowned on it. They disliked Mooney personally and what
they perceived as his editorial intrusion into their son's life. In later
years, Wesley and Nelle Halliburton went to great lengths to hide their
son's relationship with Mooney. Richard's father would delete nearly
every reference his son made to Mooney in his correspondence—be it
personal or professional.

Some of the many foreign stamps from Richard Halliburton's letters. His father, Wesley Sr., carefully pasted them to pages in a scrapbook. *Courtesy of the Halliburton Archives, Barrett Library, Rhodes College, Memphis, TN*

As such, Halliburton and Mooney left Memphis after a short while. In September 1932 Halliburton and Mooney took rooms at the Standish Arms in Brooklyn, New York. Other writers, including Walt Whitman and Truman Capote, had once lived and worked in the Beaux-Arts style building. Halliburton spent long days hunched over his desk, putting the finishing touches on *The Flying Carpet* and selecting photographs for the book—he had hundreds from which to choose. In the evenings, he watched the lights flicker across the harbor from the window in his simple, comfortably furnished living room.[3]

He would not call Brooklyn home for long. California beckoned.

September yielded to October as Mooney dished out editorial advice regarding *The Flying Carpet* and worked on the copy for the dust jacket and inside flap. Halliburton had already chosen the book's cover. The cloth cover would be elegant, black with gold lettering; the dust jacket would picture his scarlet-and-gold plane flying over the Taj Mahal in the early morning light.

Halliburton and Mooney easily settled into a measure of domesticity. After they moved to Hollywood from New York City, they found a "grand little house . . . with a big living room, dining room, complete kitchen, 1 bedroom—and a bath—a rose garden and patio a rented Ford roadster and a Negro man cook."[4] Later, Wesley edited the reference to one bedroom to read as two bedrooms and changed "we saw" to "I saw the house was for rent—looked at it—loved it—moved in." Halliburton and Mooney swam daily, and Halliburton happily reported home how his regular exercise allowed for a deep tan.

Living more than a thousand miles from Memphis emboldened Halliburton in regard to his relationship with Mooney. In yet another letter home, he offered his parents a further glimpse into his attraction to Mooney. "We've gotten so we play an idea back and forth between us like a tennis ball, and it develops sharply and rapidly. The idea remains static if only one of us tries to force it."[5]

Halliburton had come home to a nation mired in the Great Depression. As Halliburton wrote home, not one part of the economy was safe from its effects: "There is no book business whatsoever. The bookstores are doing 10 percent of their 1929 trade. We must expect our profit from magazines and radio to get out of debt."[6]

Book sales may have lagged, but seven years after he first arrived on the literary scene Halliburton remained very much in demand. He dashed for trains at all hours of the night, his itinerary resembling a game of connect the dots. Whether it was speaking to 450 people at the Catholic Actors Guild monthly meeting in New York's Hotel Astor, or spellbinding students with tales of flying over the jungles of Borneo at a school in New Jersey, Halliburton's lecture calendar barely allowed time for lunch.[7] Sometimes he would arrive somewhere without a change of clothes or a razor to shave. And so it was that he stood before a bevy of teachers in borrowed clothes, more than a hint of stubble on his chin.[8]

It was mid-November and he had traveled from Lawrence, Kansas, to Kansas City, Missouri. Not for the first time, he hadn't a moment to change out of his wrinkled trousers and shirt. He rang up his old Princeton classmate Mike Hockaday, who came to the rescue with a freshly pressed suit. Halliburton's audience didn't notice that it ran a touch large, nor did they pay any mind to the black smudges of fatigue under his eyes. They simply sat in rapt attention. The room held its breath while he spoke. Not one shoe scraped, not one tissue rustled. Halliburton enthralled; he drew listeners in, keeping his voice steady and low. At the end of his talk, the room exploded in applause. "He obviously succeeded in his mission of getting the teachers far, far from Kansas and their social norms," wrote one Kansas-based reporter after the event.[9]

Halliburton took a break from work for the long Thanksgiving weekend and went back to California. The holiday "was curious for Paul and me. We drove 'Pancho' Barnes 50 miles down the coast to her summer home—took off our clothes and pulled clams from the rocks [all day] then put the clams in a big stew pot to steam and made that for our Thanksgiving dinner," Halliburton wrote home.[10] His father later excised any mention of Mooney and skinny-dipping from the letter.

In December 1932, for only the second time in history, a pin-straight pine tree stood in the still-unfinished Rockefeller Center. A chorus of rosy-cheeked angels floated across the cover of the *New Yorker*, and *The Flying Carpet* landed in bookstores. The book catapulted onto bestseller lists nationwide. Readers' stomachs lurched when Halliburton nearly fell from his plane as it flew through the thin air of Mount Everest, and they sweated alongside the writer as he hiked through the jungles of Borneo.

"It has given me a great deal of pleasure to read your book 'The Flying Carpet' and I think it is the best of all your immortal works. I feel a personal obligation for the pleasure it has given me, and I don't have such a lot of pleasure either," wrote F. N. Doubleday, the founder of Doubleday Publishing, from his Oyster Bay, New York, home.[11] Children like Maggie DeVault of Tennessee remembered her eighth grade teacher reading aloud from the book: "I was hooked."[12]

By and large reviewers heaped praise on the book. Some said Halliburton wrote with a compelling poetic insight, others commended his more mature and authoritative voice. This time the *New York Times* said, "He has a sense of humor that makes many of his descriptions and tales amusing and he is always quickly responsive to beauty. His book is a fresh, unhackneyed, happy performance that gives to the reader something of the sensation of magic implied in its title."[13] *Time*'s review on the other hand was a backhanded compliment: "For vicarious thrills of thoroughly professional daring, *The Flying Carpet* can safely be recommended to ladies' social circles."[14]

The Flying Carpet even won over one of Halliburton's harshest reviewers. His most "pungent critic," Corey Ford, wrote Halliburton a long and somewhat apologetic letter.[15] Ford opened his letter by saying he never intended to parody Halliburton. On the contrary, he had merely poked fun of the way Halliburton turned adventure into a business. In turn, he, Ford, simply made a business parodying Halliburton.

An example of suggested advertising booksellers would use to promote Richard Halliburton's books. *Princeton University Library*

Ford also mentioned he had ordered a copy of the new book from Bobbs-Merrill because "I thought I might enjoy it, and as a matter of fact, I did enjoy it a good deal. It is much the best book you have done; and the—if you will pardon me—hokum quality of impetuous youth which I regretted in your other works seems to be lacking here. You appear to have written this book with genuine spirit. . . . So you may rest assured that you are henceforth immune from the attacks of this particular pop-gun. I had decided that, before your letter arrived. If for no other reason than that, in these perilous times, I should not wish to take the bread-and-butter from under anyone's feet."[16]

From the contents of Ford's letter, it appears Halliburton initiated the correspondence, proposing the two writers make amends. Not necessary, Ford said, because in his view there were "no hatchets to be buried. You may not believe me, but I have never consciously 'made war' and I truly did not intend the parodies of your books to be personal or malicious. I'd enjoy having a drink with you, and matching stories about Borneo, where I learned to hunt heads myself."[17]

Sandwiched between supper with Lowell Thomas and dinner with Corey Ford, Halliburton took the train to Toronto and spoke about both Rupert Brooke and his round-the-world flight.

Not an empty seat remained in the Canadian venue; several fans pressed against the auditorium's back wall. As Halliburton walked on the stage, the room erupted in cheers. The man needed no introduction. "The girls would shriek just like they used to for Sinatra," said John Nicholls Booth, describing what it was like to hear Halliburton speak for the first time. "He brought out a dimension to travel no one had thought about before—involving oneself in travel, really becoming a part of the place."[18]

Several weeks earlier Booth sent Halliburton a fan letter. In it he enclosed a snapshot of him standing, with arms akimbo, atop a Native American totem pole somewhere in Washington State. Now hoping to meet his idol, Booth elbowed his way backstage after the talk; at least ten people already stood in line. Booth waited his turn, fidgeting with nervous energy. Halliburton stepped out of the dressing room and greeted his fans. When Booth's turn came, he stuck out his hand. He pinched himself; he was actually shaking the hand of the man who had swum the Panama Canal and climbed Mount Fuji. When the famous author invited Booth to share a late-night bite at a nearby diner, he nearly fainted from surprise.

After a quick glance at the menu, they ordered. Booth noticed Halliburton carried a bundle of fan letters with him and flipped through them while they ate and spoke. Just as Halliburton was about to reach for his glass, he looked at the letter in his hand, glanced up at Booth, and then back at the letter. Coincidentally, it was Booth's letter and photo. After coffee and dessert, Halliburton collected the check. Noting the late hour, he asked Booth where he was staying. Booth told him he planned to catch the next available train. Nonsense, Halliburton said. He had an extra bed in his hotel room, so why not spend the night. There was no need to hurry to the station.[19] Whether the two had a tryst is unknown. Booth never said anything and, unsurprisingly, Halliburton remained mum.

In any event, the next morning Booth went downstairs to the hotel gift shop to buy *The Flying Carpet*, which was on sale for one dollar a copy. A hefty sum in 1932 but worth the splurge, especially since Halliburton signed his copy, Booth said.

Over the next ten years, the two corresponded and occasionally saw each other. Booth became a successful magician and performed in nightclubs across the United States. An avid traveler, Booth repeated some of Halliburton's adventures and even published his own book in 1950, *Fabulous Destinations*. "I scaled the mountain Popo and admired his determination to do that," Booth said. "He climbed it, not once, but he did it twice so he could have a good photo. Imagine, climbing 17,870 feet in order to get that photograph."[20]

As people toasted the arrival of 1933 with Hoffman's Pale Dry ginger ale[21]—Prohibition still had another twelve months to go—Wesley and Nelle Halliburton planned a February party to honor their son. Richard flew back to Memphis from California. The Halliburtons hosted the elegant soiree at the storied Peabody Hotel, the stained glass panels set in the burnished wood ceiling and the crystal chandeliers bathing the lobby and the guests in warm light. On the eve of the party, Wesley presented his son with a slim gold pocket watch. A sprinkle of rubies adorned the inside, which was simply engraved: RICHARD HALLIBURTON 1933.[22]

During his time home, Halliburton sat for an interview with the *Nashville Banner*. He told the reporter he thought *The Flying Carpet* was his last romantic travel story.[23] "I don't want to keep on writing these books until someone says 'I wish I had not written this,'" he said. The more Halliburton succeeded, the more terrified he became of failing—even if a small part of him wanted to stop writing adventure books and delve into something else.

That something else was, of course, the Rupert Brooke biography. Halliburton had been fixated on the idea of writing the English poet's story for years. He had amassed quite a collection of notes, letters, and books on Brooke and had already begun composing the biography in his head. Yet, every time he broached the idea of experimenting with a new genre, Bobbs-Merrill pulled him back. They wanted a new book, they just didn't want a Brooke book.

The calendar flipped ahead; 1934 found Halliburton thirty-four years old and restless. He had ironed out a deal with the Bell Newspaper Syndicate to write twenty-five hundred words a week for $200 a week. He spoke at the Women's Press Club in New York City and then hopped a train to Boston where he spent time with "a group of fabulously rich people," including the Huttons, the Woolworths, and the Biddles.[24] It wasn't enough. Mooney urged his lover to find a new project. His parents urged him to find a new project. David Laurance Chambers, his trusted editor at Bobbs-Merrill, urged him to find a new project. After the success of *The Flying Carpet*, he and the rest of the publishing team were impatient for their star author to set to work on something fresh.

But if Halliburton couldn't write about Brooke, he didn't know what he wanted to do next. Inspiration would come, as it always did—but he knew he couldn't force an undertaking. At last an idea came: he would hop from continent to continent, from sea to sea, writing about the unknown, the forgotten, and the underappreciated. He would go to the Soviet Union and find an elephant and ride it across the Alps. And so he upped the stakes further for this next book.

He chose Mexico as his first stop. He had heard about the Seri Indians, a semi-nomadic people living on Tiburón Island in the Gulf of California. His friend Pancho Barnes offered to fly him south. He knew Barnes would make a marvelous companion and perhaps lend color to his story.[25] On July 13 they dipped into Mexico, arriving in Hermosillo, a city in the northwestern part of the country. Halliburton hired a guide who knew the Seri Indians and spoke their language. Leaving the smoky green hills, they drove one hundred miles right across the open desert to the coast.

Fierce warriors, the Seri are said to have inhabited the island for more than five hundred years. They retained their language and culture first in the face of the Spanish conquest and then under Mexican subjugation. In a letter home, Halliburton described the reclusive tribe as "no longer dangerous—just dirty and slovenly. But it's still extraordinary that such a primitive race should live so close to Hollywood. They have no houses—no arts and crafts—no religion—no villages—just gypsies and scavengers—living on raw fish and always in motion."[26] If the Indians underwhelmed Halliburton, the variety of animal life tickled his fancy. He saw egrets, pelicans, pink flamingoes, sharks, and whales. He hunted turtles one morning, and one night, club in hand, he hunted pelicans.

Halliburton envisioned this next project as a means to bring American citizens closer to their history. With that in mind, he sailed across the Straits of Florida to the Dry Tortugas. Fort Jefferson, a mountain of solid brick, emerged from the turquoise waters. The "colossal folly" as Halliburton called it, was the "largest mass of unreinforced masonry ever raised by Americans."[27] A solitary figure on the ramparts, Halliburton ruminated on the events that led to Dr. Samuel Mudd's imprisonment in 1865 on what he called America's own Devil's Island. The southern doctor achieved notoriety for setting the leg of John

Wilkes Booth, President Abraham Lincoln's assassin. He broke it after leaping from a balcony at Ford's Theatre. A court convicted Mudd as a conspirator and sentenced him to life imprisonment in Fort Jefferson. President Andrew Johnson pardoned the doctor in 1869. Halliburton's next book, *Seven League Boots*, would devote a chapter to his time on Fort Jefferson.

When Bobbs-Merrill released *Boots* in 1935, Halliburton would receive a note from a Mrs. Albert S. Glover of Newton, Massachusetts. The eighty-one-year-old had lived at Fort Jefferson during Dr. Mudd's imprisonment and was impressed with the way Halliburton captured the ambience of the island fortress. "I do not believe there are many people alive who could write of Fort Jefferson as it was at that time," she wrote Halliburton.[28]

Next, Halliburton skimmed across the Caribbean Sea under a scorching August sun to Cuba. He wanted to see the wrecked battleships of the Spanish-American War. It was an exhausting bus ride from Havana to the eastern side of the island. Of the six ships sunk in the Battle of Santiago, only two were visible from the surface. Lifting his new Leica camera to his eye, Halliburton focused on the ships' gun turrets and snapped several photos. He spotted the *Merrimac*, which now lay submerged in about forty feet of water, its hull split in two. He wanted aerial photos, so he persuaded a local air company to lend him a plane and pilot. This slice of history called for a chapter in his book, and of course a feature story, but he would postpone writing it until he could interview the ship's commander, Admiral Richmond Pearson Hobson, who now lived in New York City.

Six days later Halliburton traded the "gloriously beautiful" island of Cuba for Haiti.[29] Sitting outside his hotel one evening, reviewing his notes on the trip, he watched as the trees took on hazy shapes in the violet and peach light. It was a splendid moment. Still, Halliburton spurned Haiti as "merely the western half of a backward island in the West Indies population by primitive Africans addicted to voodoo worship."[30] Aside from the three-thousand-foot high Bonnet-à-l'Eveque, or Bishop's Bonnet, which he thoroughly enjoyed climbing, Halliburton was "less hopeful that there could be anything beautiful in such a decayed and backward country."[31] Racist condescension and stereotyping polluted Halliburton's account, particularly in his retelling of the story of Henri Christophe, King of Haiti. And yet in his mind such racist pronouncements were not inconsistent with his love for exploration and interest in other cultures.

From Haiti, Halliburton crossed the border to the Dominican Republic in search of Christopher Columbus's bones. The island's government offered Halliburton a chance to view the bones, feeling it a small gesture compared with the way Halliburton's article and book would both publicize the island country and the new Pan-American Columbus Lighthouse proposal, which was to be a symbol of regional fellowship.[32] The lead casket containing said bones was opened for the first time since 1891.

At the end of August, Halliburton popped back to Laguna Beach to spend time with Mooney before leaving for Europe. He would sail from New York City on September 21, and needed enough time to visit the Library of Congress in Washington, DC, to research his *Merrimac* article and interview Admiral Hobson. Because he had built in extra time, he took a detour to the casino in Asbury Park, New Jersey. And that's how on September 10 he found himself standing on the boardwalk in Asbury Park, watching as flames consumed the luxury liner SS *Morro Castle*. The ship burned furiously for three days and nights. The steel plates buckled and the superstructure twisted. It was, Halliburton wrote home, "the most terrible sight I've ever seen. There were still 50 bodies in the staterooms which were too hot to be entered."[33] The fire started in the ship's storage room. Within twenty minutes it spread through the ship's main electrical cables. Because the ship was constructed with highly flammable materials, as well as a lack of safety measures, many passengers had to either "jump or burn."

However, Halliburton wasn't going to report on the story. One, there were too many other reporters on the scene. Two, he had never before reported a straight news story. But the immediacy of the event gripped Halliburton and he realized he had a taste for breaking news.

On the last day of summer, Halliburton sauntered up the ramp of the *Champlain* and sequestered himself in his cabin, leaving only for meals. He worked furiously on "Seven Volunteers for Death," his story about Admiral Hobson and the *Merrimac*.[34] Ten days later he arrived in Le Havre, France, and rather than continue to Paris, stayed in the port city for a few days to finish another article. Once he had wrapped up his story, he took the train to Paris and spent a few days playing tourist while trying to find an elephant for his Hannibal venture.

After climbing 1,710 steel steps to the top of the Eiffel Tower and ordering drinks in a nightclub with George Vanderbilt's now married daughter, Halliburton found Elysabethe "Dally" Dalrymple, an elephant upon which to ride so he could reenact a fraction of Hannibal's march over the Pyrenees and the Alps at the start of the Second Punic War. He could have the pachyderm for $1,500—a tidy sum, but Halliburton figured he would make up the difference writing three Sunday stories for $480 apiece. "By next Tuesday night Dally and I expect to leave for Switzerland. Dally is not my new girl. She's my new elephant. I've had to labor 10 hours a day for two weeks to get her, as such a project as mine is unheard of," he wrote home.[35] To him the elephant stunt was a sound investment in publicity. Fox Studios sent the "Movietone people" to cover the event for newsreels and the Associated Press also planned coverage.

On paper, Halliburton's plan looked faultless. Depending on the elephant's mood, the author would start at Montreux, on the shores of Lake Geneva. He planned to walk, and occasionally ride, the elephant until he reached the start of the St. Bernard Pass. He calculated it would take two days, perhaps three, to cover the forty-five miles to the top of the pass. Once there, he would shelter and eat with the St. Bernard dogs and monks.[36] The long and steep ascent is an impressive stretch of mountain road even in summer, even in an automobile.

Unfortunately for Halliburton, cooperation wasn't in the elephant's nature. "I went to the zoo, and all seemed well. I paid my money and away we went—as far as the street," Halliburton said. Honking automobiles terrified the animal. She panicked and fled a half-mile down the boulevard. "Fortunately nobody but the mahout was aboard."[37] It turned out Dally happily allowed people to ride her in the leafy embrace of the park. Out on the boulevards it was another story. There the noise, traffic, and people proved too much. Reluctantly, Halliburton shelved the elephant idea and left for Berlin.

Germany was a changed country since Halliburton's visit thirteen years before with Mike Hockaday. Adolf Hitler was now chancellor. The Nuremberg Laws had yet to be enacted and many still viewed Hitler and his brown shirts as the lunatic fringe, but even so there were signs of the terror to come. Bands of Hitler Youth roamed the sidewalks, arms thrust outward in Heil Hitler salutes, and the red, black, and white colors of Nazi Germany had invaded many a public and private space. "Superficially I don't see any great difference between now and 1921 when I was here last. Uniforms are everywhere. The older people seem to be very cool about Hitler, but the kids are all maniacs on the subject—and they will be in command in a few years," he said, ending his letter on a note of caution.[38] Two days later Halliburton left the swastikas and jackboots of the Third Reich for the Soviet Union.

Halliburton snuck in over the border at Vladivostok and arrived in Moscow on a gust of bitter cold. He checked into the Hotel Metropole, the bastion of foreign correspondents. Relaxing in the bar in the evening with other writers and reporters, Halliburton picked up the kind of tradecraft needed to successfully report in the Soviet Union. For starters, Halliburton learned the best way to get around the country was to hitchhike, forking over rubles for rides.

The apparent explosion of energy in Moscow surprised Halliburton. Coming from the United States, where unemployment had reached nearly 22 percent, the frenetic pace of the country's factories and never-ending construction projects astounded the Tennessee native. Having all but cut off foreign trade, the communist regime had to supply more than 160 million people with everything, Halliburton wrote.[39] All of this made the Soviet Union "the most interesting story on earth."[40]

In October, Moscow marked the seventeenth anniversary of the Communist Revolution. Halliburton waded into Red Square and marveled as one hundred thousand soldiers, a thousand tanks and two thousand airplanes, and one million workers paraded past Stalin's review stand. "The dictators here sit on high with half closed eyes and consider the 160,000,000 Russians are guinea pigs. These pigs are injected with this, deprived of that—millions may die from a bad experiment. The dictators are not conscious of the fact."[41]

To the son of a real estate agent and schoolteacher, the parade was an obscene display of power. He felt privileged to watch from the sidelines, but "to be subjected to it would be fatal for a liberty-lover like me," he wrote home. Seeing that Moscow was "full of American Reds, shouting their heads off for the Soviets" amused him, because he knew they were going back to America almost as quickly as they had come.[42]

Halliburton was in no hurry to return to the United States. He hadn't even begun unraveling the mystery of the Soviet Union. He walked the snow-swept streets talking with people, fountain pen and toothbrush tucked in his pocket.[43] The country was a puzzle; its inconsistencies and hypocrisies both repelled and attracted him. He admired the gains in literacy but decried the living conditions; he appreciated the number of women in the workforce, but disparaged the stifling of opinion. Russian people were among the dirtiest and most poorly dressed people he had ever seen, he wrote home. Yet, he conceded that well-made clothes, sturdy shoes, and other staples most Americans took for granted were nearly impossible to purchase. Russians lived at the mercy of the state: "They live jammed helplessly into living quarters unendurable to Americans. They can not leave Russia—their newspapers, books, movies are nothing but Soviet propaganda, extolling Communism and spilling on all other systems . . . everybody in fact except peasants and factory workers have been killed or exiled."[44]

For a young man accustomed to the freedom to travel, read, entertain, and "enjoy fine things that make life worth living—Russia is a hateful, tyrannical prison cell. For none of these things can one enjoy privately, for one's self."[45]

Then, in the midst of his stay, came the Kirov assassination. On December 1, Sergey Kirov, one of the leaders of the Russian Revolution, was shot to death in his office. Historians believe Josef Stalin instigated the murder. For three days and nights, Kirov's body lay in state across from Halliburton's hotel, and the nation was plunged into "mechanical grief." For three days and nights, Halliburton was confined in his hotel. The police blocked every street leading to the square. On the fourth day, Halliburton pushed through. He hadn't slept an hour. He had lain awake all night; the filling in his molar had fallen out. The pain a particular torment, he took himself to a dentist and, unable to return to his hotel, slept at the US embassy.[46]

His tooth fixed, his brown case packed, Halliburton purchased a ticket for the fabled Trans-Siberian Railway. Jammed with people, the car was dark and cold. He spent two days sitting and sleeping on his suitcase. Although surrounded by people, the normally loquacious American found socializing difficult. He felt claustrophobic from being under constant watch. Here and there, as he rode along the world's longest railway line, Halliburton saw the skeletal remains of churches littering the ground; he learned the authorities ordered them razed and the land be put to other uses, usually farming.[47] Halliburton longed to open the window, breathe in the cold air, as the countryside zipped past. Impossible of course, but in the close quarters the thought itself was refreshing.

After 1,128 miles the train slowed. It pulled into Sverdlovsk, or Yekaterinburg, a snowbound city on the Siberian side of the Urals where winter ruled with a vengeance. Halliburton had never planned on visiting Yekaterinburg, but back in Moscow, William Stoneman, a reporter for the *Chicago Daily News*, tipped him off to a story. Apparently, Pyotr Zacharovitch Ermakov, commissar of Verkh-Isetsk Iron Works, wanted to talk. Ermakov was reportedly part of the team that assassinated Tsar Nicholas II and his family. Actually, Stoneman thought the story a hoax and figured Halliburton was naive enough to bite. Stoneman thought it would be funny to watch Halliburton track the fruitless lead.

Halliburton couldn't have known if it was a hoax or not, but he liked a gamble and the promise of intrigue. And so it was that the writer was now looking for a place to stay, along with Stoneman's interpreter, whose father was killed by anti-Communist forces in 1918. Come morning, he shrugged on his parka, pulled on his hat, and left his warm hotel room. He and his interpreter crunched through the snow on their way to Ermakov's tiny, two-room, Soviet-style apartment. He had called ahead twice before trying to arrange for the interview. The wind bit his cheeks. Warily, Ermakov's wife opened the door. Halliburton barely got a chance to explain why he had come; she nearly slammed the door in his chapped face. Two times Ermakov's wife refused. Halliburton would not be dissuaded, and she finally agreed to speak with the American writer. Ermakov's hacking cough rumbled through the space. He had heard the terse exchange and summoned the writer inside.

Halliburton ventured into the back bedroom, where a feverish Ermakov lay on a low bed under a mound of red quilts. For the first time in his life, Ermakov spoke about the killings. Halliburton sat, rooted to his chair. He wrote so fast and hard that his pen left indentations in his notebook. Sweat poured from the translator's brow, not from the close space, but from nerves.

In a pebbly voice, Ermakov took Halliburton back sixteen years. He recounted how it took thirty-eight pistol shots to kill the seven members of the Romanov family and their four servants in the cellar room in the nighttime hours between July 16 and 17, 1918. He described how upon stripping the fallen bodies, he and his team discovered jewels and gold sewn into the women's gowns. His heavy black hair falling in front of his bloodshot eyes, Ermakov detailed how he and the soldiers burned the royals' bodies and buried the bones.[48] So vivid was Ermakov's description, Halliburton smelled the charred flesh.

After Ermakov finished his grim tale, Halliburton and his translator left the apartment. The cold air smacked them in the face. It felt good to be outside. They walked back to the hotel. The trees threw long shadows on the snow, now tinted blue in the fading light. Once in the hotel, Halliburton tried to slow down his thoughts. Surely this was his most electrifying interview to date.

"The man who murdered the Czar and all his family, the actual assassin who was jailor, executioner, undertaker, cremator, has kept silent for seventeen years. I got him on his sick bed, and heard his story poured out—unguarded, complete and terrifically vivid. . . . I'm still a little weak over the melodramatics of the thing. . . . It was *history* he told me."[49] Halliburton's instincts told him the exclusive was too juicy to file with the syndicated newspapers. He would have preferred to write it for *Liberty* or *Cosmopolitan* and then include it as a standalone chapter in the next book.[50] He would ask $10,000 for the piece, hoping to use the earnings to pay off the remaining mortgage on his parents' house and perhaps treat his father to a new Ford. Nonetheless, he was contractually obligated to file it with the Bell Syndicate.

The trip to Russia changed Halliburton. "Unconcerned heretofore with politics and social problems, I now found myself *very much* for fear that I, and those I cared for, might some day be forced to live under such a regime as I had observed during the past two months."[51] In gaining a new appreciation for the dramatic geopolitical forces at work in the world, he had shed his innocence. His nose for news awoke.

When *Seven League Boots* was published, his chapter "Straight Talk from Russia" proved highly critical of the Soviet Union. He found the despotic regime enthroned in ignorance and bent on persecuting knowledge.[52] In an interview with the *Independent* in Helena, Montana, he told the reporter, "The whole Bolshevik undertaking has been marked by a degree of intolerance, bigotry, individual constraint, and intellectual gagging seldom if ever duplicated in the history of any race."[53]

But for now Halliburton remained in Stalin's country, tired of the arctic weather, the filth, and the food. But more so, he was exasperated with his omnipresent "baby-sitters." He learned his second interpreter—the one who'd gone with him to the interview—was actually a spy. Any time more than two people gathered in his room, anytime someone remained later than midnight, or anytime his phone rang, he got a rap on the door from one of his minders. Packages mailed to New York City containing official Soviet photographs never reached their destination.[54] He felt himself growing mad.

"The censors opened all my letters to my family in which I spoke very violently about conditions in Russia. Telling the truth is considered 'unfair.' I hated the whole place venomously, and was happy to be forced to go someplace else. The deportation order caught me in the Caucuses, but not before I had material for two swell Sunday stories," Halliburton wrote Chambers.[55]

After more than a month, the Soviets and Halliburton had had quite enough of each other. Given just ten days to leave the country, Halliburton made his way to Batum, a Georgian city on the Black Sea.[56] Coincidentally, his visa had expired. The police kept him in his hotel, "the foulest hole you can imagine. The guests, all first-class Russian Communists, had so befouled the toilet that they were using the floor."[57] Finally on December 31, he booked passage on a steamer and, as the clock struck twelve, sailed through Hellespont. The ship's whistle blowing, the night and fog hid the shores.[58]

In Greece he cloistered himself inside a rented whitewashed cottage for ninety days. In the quietude, he worked on both the Romanov story for *Ladies' Home Journal* and tried to put his notes into some semblance of order for his manuscript. He didn't have much time. Bobbs-Merrill expected a fall book.

As a small diversion, Halliburton brainstormed potential titles while he labored over the manuscript. He knew a clever title could mean all the difference when it came to sales. He asked his parents to weigh in with different suggestions. "Speaking of books, I'm less and less satisfied with 'The Islands of Desire' for our next title. It hasn't enough vitality. I've a new enthusiasm (for the moment) for *My Seven-League Boots* or just *Seven-League Boots*. It indicates action—it fits the school public like a glove, and will not discourage our mature audience. It's short and snappy. . . . It covers the wild shifts in geography—Cuba—to Russia—to Greece and Arabia. What do *you* think?"[59]

The mornings were splendid, cornflower-blue skies and azure waters. He swam and sunbathed and wrote long letters to Mooney and his parents. He kept Chambers abreast of his work, Schuler too. It wasn't all smooth writing. Sometimes when he read over his work, the words seemed to stop making sense. The more he delved into the Romanov story, slated to be an eighteen-thousand-word magazine piece, the more he doubted its veracity. Through the grapevine he heard that Ermakov didn't "murder the Czar himself, but was only chief— . . . I had my story all finished, when the truth came out in a number of testimonials I found relative to the murder."[60] He tossed fifteen thousand words in the wastebasket and started anew. Once he was satisfied, he clipped the pages together, put them in an envelope, and mailed them to Chambers at Bobbs-Merrill.

In the end, it turned out Ermakov wasn't a liar, but neither had he told Halliburton the whole truth. He hadn't led the assassination team. Instead, he was the right-hand man of Yakov Yurovsky, the leader of the firing squad, who reportedly acted on Vladimir Lenin's orders.

Since that night in 1918, countless books, articles, and movies have been devoted to the assassination of the Romanovs. For decades both Halliburton's article and subsequent book chapter were outright dismissed. Critics called it misinformed and erroneous. Stoneman himself dismissed Halliburton as "the worst kind of phoney,"[61] a snub some thought was directed at Halliburton's journalistic capability. However, it is more likely Stoneman was referring to how the writer hid his homosexuality. Furthermore, he was jealous of Halliburton's scoop.[62] A recent examination of Halliburton's work calls for its inclusion in the body of work relating to the Romanov assassination.

Halliburton moved on from Greece to Palestine. Violent winds and rough seas conspired to keep him sick all the way across the Mediterranean Sea. The only scenery he noticed was the ship's railing and his bunk. From Haifa, he motored straight on to Jerusalem. While the Holy Sepulcher Church was unrecognizable, hidden as it was under steel scaffolding, he found the Garden of Gethsemane a fragrant delight.[63]

When Halliburton picked up his mail at the American Express Office, he was pleased to find envelopes bearing the Bobbs-Merrill return address. He knew it contained Chambers's feedback on the Romanov article. He refrained from tearing open the envelope right there in the middle of the office. He went back to his hotel room, sat down, and pulled out the letter.

"The three Romanov articles are knockouts—perfectly thrilling. They moved me deeply. What a wonderful scoop, and how well you have handled it all. I do not feel at all convinced of the possibility of Anastasia surviving, but I suppose it is a romantic and popular idea and I must confess I have not read the book about her," Chambers wrote, adding how the office was abuzz with excitement over the "thrilling and astonishing" stories.[64] Relief flooded Halliburton. He had felt it was some of his best work, but until he heard from Chambers, he couldn't be sure.

However, on a more serious note, Chambers sought to temper Halliburton's expectations when it came to the eventual release of *Seven League Boots*. The book business had slowed even more during the past several months. He hoped sales would increase during the summer when people took vacation and looked for summer reading. If that happened, Chambers said the new book would come out at the right time and with decent financial prospects.[65]

While Halliburton traveled hither and yon, Mooney stayed put in California. Though their letters to each other during this period didn't survive, references to each other's adventures and the humdrum of daily life show up in their correspondence with others in their social circle. For instance, Mooney kept in close touch with his sometime lover William "Bill" Alexander Levy, a Laguna Beach, California, architect. "Nothing is as welcome as a note from you," Mooney wrote.[66] William Alexander dropped Levy from his last name to hide his Jewish identity. A few years before his trip to the Soviet Union, Halliburton had met Alexander during a performance of *Salome*, which he attended with a group of gay men. Alexander was Mooney's invited guest and joined Halliburton, bodybuilder Leopold De Sola, and another man named Charles Wolfsohn. After the performance, the group returned to the Barbizon Hotel. "Mooney was the older man and the younger Bill fell madly in love with him and they were nearly inseparable," recalled

Michael E. Blankenship, a friend of Alexander.[67] Halliburton knew Mooney and the architect were still involved. There was little jealousy on Halliburton's part, as the two had never promised monogamy and had "an open relationship and had their own dalliances when they were not together (and sometimes when they were!)." Moreover, Halliburton and Mooney were exploring the idea of building a house in southern California, and if they did, they would likely hire Alexander.

Yet during that spring of 1935, with an ocean and a continent between them, Halliburton felt removed from what was happening back home. He had spent time in Cairo, where he swam in a hot sulfur spring to cure himself of insect bites and visited an oasis 350 miles west of the city. He searched for a eunuchs' club, found it, and artfully worked it into a story about Cairo's morals. "I decided I might have *one* sex-sensation story out of the 50," he wrote.[68] And then it was off to Jedda.

There he did something quintessentially Halliburton: he invited Abdulaziz Ibn Saud, Saudi Arabia's first king, to join him for a spot of tea and conversation under a tent in Jedda, just eight miles from Mecca. The king accepted with pleasure.

Abdulaziz sent a military escort for Halliburton. Dressed in robes and a turban, what he described as the official costume all Mecca pilgrims wear, Halliburton joined the chaperones. Eight miles later, Halliburton arrived at the meeting spot. Colorful carpets covered the sand outside the purple tent. Inside the royal pavilion stood the King of Arabia. At six-foot-six, the fifty-five-year-old ruler cut a magnificent figure. Married 160 times, Abdulaziz had fifty-four children. His entourage included his six oldest sons, slaves, and a security phalanx of two hundred soldiers.[69]

Before greeting Halliburton, the king prayed. His sons lined up behind him, and behind them stood the hundreds of soldiers. They kneeled as one and bowed toward Mecca. "The King acted as leader and quoted from the Koran. And all the sons' soldiers responded Amen . . . this desert prayer meeting made a fine climax to my story," Halliburton said.[70]

Halliburton would not live to see the rest of Abdulaziz's story play out—fifteen years hence the man considered to be the founder of modern Saudi Arabia would preside over the nation's oil industry. But for now, this meeting in the desert gave Halliburton material for three stories: "Where I'll Spend My Honeymoon," "The Road to Mecca," and "The Giant." In turn these articles pulled back the veil on the mysterious desert kingdom for scores of Americans.

From the Arabian Peninsula, Halliburton headed north, crossing back into France. He hadn't abandoned his plan to cross the Alps à la Hannibal. He wanted the zookeepers in the Bois de Boulogne to let him reunite with Dally, the elephant who didn't like cars. He asked them to start getting her accustomed to traffic. They told Halliburton they would try their best, but they could make no promises. Halliburton assured them he would assume all responsibility for the elephant and bring along a trainer.

It was springtime in Paris. The cherry trees near the Eiffel Tower wore fluffy pink blossoms, and in the Jardin du Luxembourg children rode their favorite animal on the city's oldest carousel. Halliburton hurried over to the zoo and met with the keepers. He then spent two days trying to convince the police to let him take Dally for a walk on the Paris streets. They remembered his adventures last fall and refused.[71]

Halliburton didn't give up and they finally gave in. It was a good thing they had made no promises, because Dally was still averse to cars. Halliburton stood there thinking of how to fix the situation when a truck rumbled past. The elephant perked up—following trucks was her new favorite game.

Now that he had his elephant, he needed to plot his route. Halliburton spent much of July shuttling between Paris, Rome, and Lausanne. He had finalized insurance for the elephant with Lloyd's of London and received permissions from Italian and Swiss officials to enter the country with her. He also scouted the planned route. He drove up the St. Bernard Pass in a used truck, for which he paid $100. At the top, he had tea with St. Bernard Hospice priests and patted their big, lumbering dogs. Halliburton checked to see whether the monks had enough space for Dally to sleep and keep warm.

Back in Paris once more, Halliburton got ready to become the Carthaginian military commander, only instead of leading an army of hundreds, he would be an army of one. Under cover of darkness, Halliburton, one of the trainers, and Dally made their way through the streets of Paris to a waiting train. After loading the elephant onto a freight car, he boarded a passenger train to Lausanne. He met Dally in Martigny, Switzerland. As they wound their way up the St. Bernard Pass, he stopped at a children's hospital. Dally blew a few notes on a harmonica to the children's amusement. Three days later, on July 21, he and Dally arrived at the alpine monastery.

Aside from the monastery's fifteen monks, about two thousand men, women, and children gathered to welcome Dally and Halliburton. A clutch of photographers and newsmen mixed with the crowd. Dally spent the night in a garage on a carpet of soft, sweet hay. Halliburton spent a restful night inside the monastery under a downy quilt.

The first pie-shaped rays of light filtered through his window. After a quick breakfast, it was time for Halliburton to part. On their way down the mountain, they passed a company of mountain soldiers who fired a cannon volley in honor of the adventurer and his elephant. The barrage sent Dally stampeding. "The animal also began to balk because of the altitude after he had ascended beyond the 8,000-foot level." They marched on. And on. After tramping down gravel-strewn switchbacks, sores covered the elephant's feet. On the other side of the pass, in Aosta, Italy, a brass band turned out, courtesy of the Fiat Motor Company. The mini-adventure over, Halliburton loaded Dally onto another freight car and shipped her back to Paris.[72]

Back home, Halliburton's fans joyfully watched newsreels of his jubilant reenactment. His detractors found much to mock. Halliburton bristled from the criticism. A letter from Chambers gave him some perspective. "On considering the elephant stunt, I would not let the wise cracks of the New York columnists upset me too much. After all what they have said has never made very much difference with the sales of your book. I do not see myself, any harm in the exploit provided that in writing it out, you kid yourself. And your books have always been the better for their variety and style and treatment. The singling of grave and gay," wrote Chambers.[73]

Halliburton touched American soil on August 9. His parents greeted him at the dock in New York City. Four days later he flew to Memphis; his parents followed in their car.

He stayed in Tennessee until September to finish his book, and after some reworking, *Seven League Boots* was released in 1935. An elephant marched across the cover, a nod both to Dally and to his treasured childhood book *Stories of Adventure*. The new release shared shelf space with Edna Ferber's *Cimarron* and Margaret Mitchell's *Gone with the Wind*. It found company in stores with self-help books such as Dale Carnegie's *How to Win Friends and Influence People* and Dorothea Brande's *Wake Up and Live!*, and of course John Steinbeck's *The Grapes of Wrath*, Pearl Buck's *The Good Earth*, and Kenneth Roberts's *Northwest Passage*. Like these other books, *Seven League Boots* played to the strength and tenacity of the human character, a favorite inspirational theme during these troubled times.[74]

This fifth book was more serious than his previous works. For the first time, critics stepped back and considered Halliburton as something more than fluff. In *Seven League Boots*, he effectively combined history and politics with his travel writing.

9

Hangover House

THE TRAIN WHISTLED A forlorn cry as it chugged along, carrying Richard Halliburton to another lecture in another city where he would sip cocktails and make conversation. He traveled from Texas to Massachusetts. He spoke to two thousand college students at the Museum of Fine Arts in Detroit and signed books at the Jordan Marsh department store in Boston. At each stop he jumped from one engagement to another with barely time to finish one talk before starting another. During one day in Chicago, he spoke at a woman's club in the morning, attended a small gathering at a tea party, auditioned at a radio station, and then rushed over to Marshall Field's department store for an evening book signing. He spoke until his voice grew hoarse and shook hands until his fingers were numb.[1] He felt frayed around the edges and, before quashing the thought, he briefly wondered how long he could sustain this pace. His family and friends were concerned. They saw a man who needed to, but wouldn't, slow down.

So when his father suggested he fly to Memphis, he boarded the first plane available. Wesley was hosting a dinner party for fifty of his friends and he wanted his son there. Halliburton only knew a few of the guests as he had spent so little time in Memphis in the past several years. Still, he had a fine time, though the postprandial drinks were barely poured before he left for Miami. He hoped four days in the sun would cure all. It didn't.

And so, with grandmotherly affection, Ammudder tucked five dollars into a letter and nudged Richard to buy himself vitamins A, B, and D. He laughed, writing back that all he needed now was a daily dose of cod-liver oil and his mother's yeast tablets. If he stuck to that regimen, not only would his health be restored but also he'd never have to eat again. Clearly he was teasing, since yeast tablets were marketed to women in the 1930s as a way to gain weight, attract men, and "get bikini ready."[2]

Halliburton felt he had no alternative but to make light of his health. He often fretted that the moment he stopped meeting the demands of celebrity would be the moment he would lose relevancy. That explained part of his drive. He also believed he owed his fans his personal presence. They read his books; they followed him in the news. The least he could do was show up, treat them to a first-person account of his latest exploit, shake hands, and sign books. "As a box office attraction, he has few rivals in the field," reported one newspaper.[3]

Nonetheless, his cinematic personality didn't translate into record sales for *Seven League Boots*. Chambers rang Halliburton with an update while he was on the road. So far his fifth book had sold 22,500 copies instead of the hoped-for 25,000. While it was but a small dip in sales, it was nonetheless concerning for an author who was accustomed to six-figure sales for a book's first run. Moreover, most of the sales were to stores that had plenty of stock, signaling sales had plateaued almost as soon as the book had been released. Halliburton expected to earn his $11,000 in *Boots* royalties, but he constantly worried that the remainder pile was but a shelf away.[4]

Though *Seven League Boots* didn't achieve the same commercial success as *The Flying Carpet*, it was nevertheless warmly received. One reviewer described it as "an adventure that makes *Arabian Nights* dull by comparison."[5] Another reviewer wrote, "Every youth dreams of doing the things Richard Halliburton has done. . . . Of course everyone can't be a Richard Halliburton, but his successful career, his exciting adventures are a challenge to all red-blooded young Americans."[6]

Readers too adored the new book, which he'd dedicated to Mary Hutchison, his Ammudder, "who with patience and understanding first taught a small boy to love ages that have passed and places that are far away." In turn, Halliburton sought to inspire readers to embrace the exotic. Virginia Reese, seventy, whose great-aunt Mora "Ermie" Garrison was related to Wesley, has read all of Halliburton's books, in part because her great-aunt "had such a devotion to Richard. She and Wesley were of course pretty close. But my mother and Ermie talked about Richard as if he was a first cousin," Reese said. "Well, *Royal Road to Romance* was my favorite because it was the first one I read. It just really fired my imagination, but all of them were so exciting. I loved the adventure where he goes around the world in an airplane and the one where he rides an elephant down the mountain."[7]

To Reese, and scores of other readers, Halliburton lived impulsively, going wherever he fancied, whenever he fancied. Once upon a time that was true. He had run away from Princeton University and sailed to Europe on the *Octorara* without a plan in his pocket. Even when he and Mike Hockaday left Princeton on their postgraduation trip, they didn't follow a rigid itinerary. But that was years ago. Now everything he did was carefully crafted, designed to meet deadlines and fulfill readers' expectations. In his quest for fame he had become captive to a hamster wheel of publicity and market demands. More than a decade into a prolific career, he had simply perfected the art of writing about the things he did "as if they were just impromptu, they just happened, but he would set them up really so that they would happen that way. . . . Then they actually happened, but he'd write about it as if, well, it just occurred all by itself," Moye Stephens said in an interview many years later, adding that he hated how Halliburton was regarded with "disdain by contemporary writers. They were always picking at his work."[8]

That same year John Richard Finch, editor of the *Five Star Weekly*, interviewed Halliburton. After their wide-ranging discussion, Finch invited Halliburton to contribute "from his own pen, on any subject he might choose."[9] For the first and only time in his career, Halliburton inveighed his critics. He chose to strike after receiving a letter from

Milton McNeil, a nineteen-year-old freshman in "an eastern university" who wrote that although he considered Halliburton's books his bibles, his friends and critics dubbed the adventurer a modern-day Baron Munchausen. Never had a fan letter spoke to him the way McNeil's letter did.

"This letter brings up many of the petty, unsubstantiated, and frequently ridiculous charges that have been made against the authenticity of my books for over a period of 11 years—charges which have afforded me not a little amusement," Halliburton wrote. He addressed each time he was questioned or doubted—including the Taj Mahal swim, climbing Mount Fujiyama, and spending time on Devil's Island. He took issue with being dubbed a ladies' club darling and a fake.

His lengthy article concluded with a message to Milton, and the rest of the world: "His books are their own defense. Truth, like murder, will out, and the eleven years since 'The Royal Road to Romance' appeared, have been time enough to give Fate the chance to dispose of it, and its successors, justly. Obviously, had these books been false they would soon have died."[10]

Halliburton sculpted his image in person as well as in print. When he strode on stage he was the celebrity journalist his audience expected—the one with spit-shined shoes and a glint in his blue eyes—not the gritty man emerging from a week in the jungle with a shaggy beard and unwashed body. Of course, thirteen-year-old John Maize didn't really care how Halliburton dressed. He was just eager to hear the author speak at Memphis's Goodwyn Institute.

Founded in 1906 by the philanthropist and cotton businessman William A. Goodwyn, the Goodwyn Institute boasted a large auditorium and a sizable library. Its mission was to give the young people of Memphis a chance to learn from many different professionals.[11] Maize's father had a real estate office on the second floor of the stately redbrick building, and the teenager often visited him at work. One afternoon, Maize noticed a sign advertising an upcoming lecture. He couldn't believe *the* Richard Halliburton was coming to speak. He had read every single one of his books and clipped most every story about the writer.

Maize remembered how every time a story ran in the *Commercial Appeal*, people talked about it for days. "There was no television, no Internet, it was not like today," Maize said.[12]

When the appointed afternoon came, Maize couldn't stop fidgeting in his seat. Then, when he felt he could take it no more, Halliburton walked on stage. The crowd clapped loudly; their native son was home.[13]

"I was enthralled by Richard Halliburton. I'd search for his stories and his writings every week. I followed one adventure to another in the paper and it got better with each succeeding one," the now ninety-two-year-old said. "To me he was my hero. I enjoyed his adventures. Someone once said he was an explorer. No, he was an adventurer."[14]

Late spring found him on a whistle stop tour of the west. In Omaha he visited with his *Glorious Adventure* companion Roderic Crane and his bride. In Kansas City he met up with his friend Mike Hockaday, now a partner in a brokerage firm. While sitting at dinner his mind wandered. Spooning dessert into his mouth, Halliburton toyed with the idea of packing a bag and running off to Tahiti or Hawaii to bask in the sunshine. Instead he flew to Colorado, where three thousand people filled a lecture hall to hear him speak, and then skipped over to Utah, where two thousand came to hear him in the Mormon Tabernacle.

By the time Halliburton reached California in late May, he felt aimless, unsure of his next step. However, David Laurance Chambers and the entire Bobbs-Merrill team knew what their star should do. They wanted another book and pitched what they thought would be an irresistible idea: a two-part young adult series titled *Richard Halliburton's Book of Marvels: The Occident* and *The Orient*. They imagined the series would celebrate America's latest civil engineering feats and bring "the wonders of the world to schoolchildren."[15] Chock-full of photographs, the books would combine adventure, geography, and history. Halliburton embraced the idea, foremost because the project required little travel.

He envisioned each volume as a guidebook for young readers. In the first book, *The Occident*, he would take them floating down Yosemite National Park's Merced River, to the edge of the Grand Canyon, over Niagara Falls, and through the bustling streets of New York City. In the second book, *The Orient*, he would transport readers to the foot of the statue of Zeus in Olympia, up the steps of the temple of Diana at Ephesus, and inside the tomb of King Mausolus. Readers would stand awestruck before the Colossus of Rhodes, the lighthouse at Alexandria, and the Great Pyramid of Giza, upon which Halliburton had slept in 1922. The project lent some much-needed structure to his summer. He welcomed this renewed sense of purpose.

In June he moved out of the Roosevelt Hotel in Hollywood and into a new apartment situated like a crow's nest high over San Francisco's harbor. Halliburton enjoyed watching the ships and waves in San Francisco Bay. "I feel I can write here," he said of the beautifully furnished flat. He toyed with the idea of buying a reconditioned Ford and enjoyed taking time to ride horses in the park. Swimming and sunbathing became as part of his daily routine as brushing his teeth—he couldn't do without either.[16]

Halliburton threw himself into his project, spending long hours in the library doing research. He also wanted to do as much onsite research as possible. Planning to feature California's great bridges in his book, he toured the eight-mile-long Oakland Bridge. Wearing a hard hat, work trousers, pinstripe blazer, and sturdy shoes, Halliburton walked along its unpaved surface and climbed the unfinished bridge. He paused, hand on rail, and squinted up at the cables. "It *is* marvelous—not nearly completed, so my guide and I had to walk on cat walks, and sometimes on hands and knees atop girders. Scary but not really dangerous," he said. He was eager to scramble over the cables of the Golden Gate Bridge, too, thinking it the more spectacular of the two bridges.[17]

The sight of all this new construction, of a city moving forward, cheered Halliburton. He had been distressed over the death of his uncle John, his father's brother. He knew his uncle's strength was fading, but even so the news came as a shock.

"I was also won to him by the astounding resemblance he had in face and manner to Dad. I wonder if Wesley Jr. and I would have grown to look more alike as we matured."[18] His uncle's death pushed to the surface the feelings of loss over his younger brother's death twenty years before. It was impossible to think that his towheaded kid brother would now be a thirty-three-year-old man. Richard never stopped feeling like an older brother, just as his parents never stopped feeling like they had two children—even though one was living and one was dead. John Halliburton's death stirred their grief, and for a time Halliburton's parents became a mite more overprotective concerning his health.

They prodded their son to see a doctor when he complained about "the old exhaustion" of his youth.[19] An examination diagnosed low blood pressure. Word got back to Chambers, who urged his favorite writer to put his health first, and then "with all eagerness and enthusiasm I am hoping that you will be able to do the *Marvels* for publication this season. It will mean a lot to have it. There is no tonic like sunshine, and if you can take it easy and follow the line of least resistance you may find that some work each day gives you pleasure and relief, and does not prove a serious burden."[20]

Halliburton did his best to balance work and rest. He kept to a daily schedule of sunbathing for two hours every morning and then a full afternoon of writing and researching.[21] Toward the end of July, Halliburton went to Bohemian Grove, "a glorified camp where prominent San Franciscans go for two weeks each summer in the big trees."[22] He returned home and continued his sunbathing routine until August, when Mooney yanked Halliburton away from his desk. The two piled into Halliburton's secondhand Dodge coupe (he never did buy that Ford) and drove the 175 miles to Yosemite National Park. Under skies worthy of a Frederic Edwin Church painting, Halliburton took in the narrow valley flanked by El Capitán on one side and Half Dome on the other. He photographed the wilderness with his accordion-style fold-up Kodamatic and rode horseback for at least an hour every day. One afternoon, wearing worn shoes and crumpled shorts, but no shirt, he climbed Half Dome, rising forty-eight hundred feet above the valley floor.[23] He returned to San Francisco refreshed.[24]

The summer fog rolled out to sea as September arrived in San Francisco. Halliburton decamped for Laguna Beach. Though he enjoyed seeing friends, the endless interruptions made it difficult to get any serious writing done on the two *Marvels* books. Halliburton had first visited the sleepy town in the early 1930s when he rode horseback along its coast and hiked through its steep coastal canyons covered in sage scrub. This time Halliburton rented a quiet seaside shack and few people, except of course Mooney, Pancho Barnes, and his parents, knew he was there. He put himself on a rigorous schedule, aiming to turn out a new chapter every two days. The solitude and light ocean breezes invigorated him as he set to work.

Mooney had helped Halliburton with *Seven League Boots* and before that *The Flying Carpet*. Now, he helped shape the *Book of Marvels*. Mooney's skills impressed Halliburton, and he shared his opinion with his editors and with his parents. His father was dismayed. In fact, Mooney's presence in his son's life so upset Wesley that he insisted all correspondence between the two lovers be burned. Richard swore he'd see it done.[25]

Moye Stephens shared Wesley's feelings regarding Mooney. Halliburton's attraction to Mooney baffled the pilot. He found the man reckless, aloof, and temperamental.[26] "There wasn't anything special about Paul Mooney. That's one of the reasons you can't get any dope on him probably," Stephens later recounted. "He wasn't an impressive person in any way. Well, Dick was a dominant sort of person, and Mooney was anything but. So maybe that was what brought them together. Of course, Mooney was undoubtedly intelligent. I mean I'm sure he helped Dick considerably in his writing."[27]

On the other hand, Ione Lee Mooney, Paul Mooney's mother, seemed more accepting of her son's relationship with Halliburton. In a letter to William Alexander, she wrote of spending "a pleasant evening with Dick. At the lecture, during his dissertation on the Imperial fade-out, a lady in the audience, whom I recognized as one of Lyn's Russian friends, screamed out in agony. Ho-hum . . . Dick is certainly sweet. I like him a lot, and was glad to see him."[28]

Whether it was Mooney's presence or the somewhat more leisurely pace of life in Laguna Beach, Halliburton started imagining living in the balmy sunshine year-round. He had lived out of a suitcase or a knapsack for the better part of a decade, moving from his parents' spare bedroom in Memphis to a rented house in Siasconset to a residential hotel in Brooklyn. Now he wanted more than a room to call his own.

He had fallen in love with a plot of land about two-thirds of the way up Aliso Peak, part of a ridge that hugged Laguna Beach. Halliburton first saw the land one afternoon in 1930 while horseback riding on the beach. He remembered looking up and being struck by the way a particular ridge rose eight hundred feet from the shore. Halliburton rode up to the summit to take in the view. The vista stopped him in his tracks. The Pacific Ocean lay to the south, the Palos Verdes Peninsula lay to the west, and the San Gabriel Mountains were to the north. He could see the valley below, nestled between two mountain walls that seemed to close together in the distance.[29] He paid $1,100 for the land. Eventually Halliburton planned to swap his parcel with Mooney, who owned the adjacent plot.

Some weeks earlier Halliburton had stopped writing his parents about Mooney and his California plans. His mother had met the idea of her son building a house so far from Memphis with hostility.[30] He couldn't put off telling her anymore. He explained it was "exactly what I want to do" and there was no reason, from his perspective, why it should bring any unhappiness to them. Especially if "my happiness is yours and you want me to be happy more than you want anything else in the world."[31]

He also told his parents, in no uncertain terms, of his intention to live with Mooney once the house was finished. He softened the news, adding that Mooney would eventually build his own house on the adjoining lot. Ever mindful of appearances, Richard knew separate houses would maintain the facade of friendship to the outside world.[32] Still, the letter was a declaration of independence. Since he was nineteen, Richard had been living life on his own terms professionally. Now thirty-six, he needed to live his life on his own terms personally, far from the public's prying eyes. He gained a measure of peace knowing he would have a place of solitude.

Halliburton hired Mooney's former lover William Alexander, a relative newcomer to the architectural scene. Alexander boasted he had studied under Frank Lloyd Wright.[33] Well into the 1980s, people remembered seeing Alexander drive his old Toyota station wagon through the Hollywood Hills he called home. In later life he became a philanthropist, donating hundreds of thousands of dollars to the arts. But when the New York University graduate designed Halliburton's Laguna Beach home he was just twenty-six years old.[34]

"You'll love the design—severely simple, but compact and efficient," Halliburton wrote home.[35] The design reflected the Modern Movement style of celebrity architects such as Walter Gropius, Rudolph Schindler, and Richard Neutra. The innovative design included a garbage disposal, central heating, and a dumbwaiter connecting all three floors.[36] Alexander planned to incorporate industrial materials like concrete, steel, and glass. The house would be elegant in its minimalism.[37]

The title cleared in November and construction began.[38] The contractors estimated the house would cost at least $8,000. Halliburton needed $5,500 to cover the first payments to the architect and contractors. He figured his royalties from *Boots* and his earnings from the upcoming lecture season would more than cover the bill. He didn't want to touch what remained of his stocks and bonds and he didn't want to invest one cent of his *Boots* earnings into the jittery stock market. Instead he made another kind of investment: a house and land.[39] Undertaking such a project when his own income had stagnated might not have been prudent, but prudence wasn't Halliburton's strong suit. Buying the land and building the house was keeping with his *carpe diem* philosophy. If he wanted a house, he was going to have one.

Once the house got underway, Halliburton turned his attention to his father. For several weeks he'd carried Wesley's "serious" letter in his pocket. His father worried about his son seeming unsociable and growing solitary nature, and again urged his son to marry and have children. Halliburton agonized over his response. He loved his father dearly and didn't want to hurt him, but the writer needed his father to more fully understand the difference between his public persona and his private self.

"I've always been wearied by the company and minds and hearts of most human beings—ever since early childhood. But this in no way comes from sourness or misanthropy. I'm not in the least antagonistic— just not interested. One who allows himself to speak to 2,000 people every night, shake hands with several hundred, isn't a hermit. It's only individually I'm not interested in dining, or talking at length, to anyone in the 2,000."[40] Before an audience of hundreds the Princeton graduate was animated, friendly, ready with a quick smile and firm handshake. Alone, away from the crowds, Halliburton wanted to shrink into himself, he told his father.

He told him, too, that his Lawrenceville and Princeton friends were his anchors. That's why he visited with Hockaday, Sweet, Leh, and Seiberling whenever he could, even if only for a quick dinner on his way to or from a book talk. Apart from striking up the occasional new friendship, he'd rather not collect friends and companions for the sake of having friends and companions. He found small talk boring; he'd rather spend his time reading and writing. He found it difficult to relate to people on a day-to-day basis.[41] Privacy meant harmony.

"Likewise the women situation is no cause for alarm. They play a very small part in my life, chiefly because their minds and natures bore me worse than men's. There are exceptions—these as free of local prejudices as myself—those wise, tolerant, and understanding. But they are extremely rare—and never younger than myself. Please don't be distressed because I'm the way I am. Just be grateful that I'm so much happier than most people and growing in a continually up-climbing curve, rather than marking time with the masses who have all come from the same regulation mold."[42] Although he never said the words directly, the letter was a plea for his father to accept him as he was: homosexual, wanderer, writer, and son.

The construction of the aptly named Hangover House—a modern house of concrete and glass perched on a cliff—quickly exceeded the budget. It tested Halliburton and Mooney's relationship in ways their frequent separations did not. It pushed Mooney's friendship with Alexander. Halliburton was absent during much of the construction; hence, he supervised the work through letters. These letters, mostly written in 1937, contain a surfeit of candy-coated zingers. Money was the source of much of the hostility and tension in the letters. Egos were bruised and tempers flared. Ultimately, the project pushed Halliburton to the edge of a nervous breakdown.

Halliburton wanted his house to be monumental, but having never before undertaken such a project he didn't appreciate the job's complexity. This led to friction between client and contractor. For instance, before Alexander could break ground, workers needed to blast a road to the rather inaccessible site. Next, Alexander needed to carve a workspace out of the hillside. He had workers build a seventeen-foot retaining wall "as strong as Gibraltar . . . and strong as Gibraltar it is!"[43]

That it looked like Gibraltar was precisely the problem, Halliburton wrote Alexander after looking at a photograph of the retaining wall. "It looks like one of the foundations for the Golden Gate Bridge. It's beautiful, and god knows enduring. It looks big enough and strong enough to hold up a mountain. But the trouble is it cost (Paul admits this much) $1000. When we needed every available penny for window, bath tubs, light, heat, etc. was it wise to spend $1000 for a retaining wall?"[44]

The quarrel over the wall exemplified the wide gap between Halliburton and Alexander regarding how to build a house. Halliburton wanted something unique, and something that required a feat of engineering, but he didn't, or wouldn't, grasp how what he wanted translated into cost. Alexander saw an incredible professional opportunity and didn't appreciate what he viewed as Halliburton's incessant harping over finances.

During the entire enterprise, Alexander rarely confronted Halliburton, or Mooney, directly. Instead he poured out his frustrations about his clients to his friends. "Paul drinks nightly, procrastinates with the chapters Dick has sent for revision. The next book, about world wonders, for children will be full of pictures. Acquaintances in town stop in, admire Paul's 'joie de vivre' and keep him company in the evening. . . . Beauty IS difficult; and with Paul's idea of exchange, expensive and with his chameleonic personality, innerving. Dick insists upon signing over the title of the property to himself exchanging another lot uphill with Paul; Dick howls about costs in his letters, advises the purchase of more land to secure the privacy of the proposed house, howls again about the radio purchase he himself offered, becomes subdued by a letter from Paul regarding his inconsistencies. I am often left in a quandary as to whether or not all the plans will be carried out. . . . At times, Paul is malicious, at other times the most wonderfully subtly tempered person alive."[45]

Halliburton complained to his parents, to Mooney, and to Alexander. He held nothing back when writing to tell the architect that he felt "the house has run wild, and off the track."[46] He tried in vain to impress upon Mooney and Alexander that if they didn't control the spending they would end up living in an empty house with unfurnished rooms. The house, which was to be his refuge, had fast become his albatross.

Certainly trying to oversee such a mammoth project from the road was nearly impossible, but the more incensed he became, the more he welcomed his time away. However, with so much at stake he could no longer stay away; he needed to see the site in person. He returned home to Laguna in April, just in time to see the workers pour concrete. For twelve hours the men worked like demons. Then a rainstorm struck. The violent wind tore down temporary electric lines, cutting off light and the concrete mixers. For four hours, the men, together with Alexander and Mooney, toiled in sodden clothes to stop the flood of water from washing away the newly poured concrete walls.[47] The deluge abated, the sun scrubbed the sky, and the work resumed.

The moonstone-colored dwelling rose above the canyon. In the early morning, when the fog rolled in, the lines of the house softened. On the other mornings, the bright white sunlight streaked over the canyon, illuminating the house. Then it was all angles and corners. "The house rushes along," Halliburton wrote home. "It is *the* most wonderful house in the world. But our rotten luck with the elements continues to follow us. Freezing weather and floods have delayed things for weeks this winter, but a good spell of weather has allowed us to hurry along this past month."[48]

The house became a local sensation. Workmen contended with a parade of the curious who blinked in astonishment and surprise once they reached the top of the winding drive, with its two hairpin turns.[49] Built-in teak desks stood in each bedroom and a dining nook with a brightly upholstered bench wrapped around three sides. Light spilled across the floors and through glass bricks in the interior walls. A full-color, seventeenth-century world map printed on canvas decorated one wall. If Halliburton and Mooney stood in the living room, they could look through the plate glass windows into the canyon on one side and, on the other side, admire how a twenty-foot-by-eleven-foot window framed the ocean.[50]

A circular staircase led to the rooftop terrace where Halliburton looked forward to sitting under the night sky with Mooney. Another flight of concrete stairs rose from the garage to the bronze front door. Initially there was no handrail; and although Halliburton thought it looked smart, he was anxious that "without a hand rail some drunk is going, literally, to break his neck. There may be lawsuits, and certainly plenty grief."[51] Alexander added the rail and illuminated the steps.

In the midst of the construction chaos, the *Book of Marvels: The Occident* was published. It was a bright spot for Halliburton, who had meticulously planned the inside photograph. He had wanted a photograph of himself reading from the book to a group of children sitting on the floor, looking up at him as he read. In his mind, the ideal picture would show them sitting before the fireplace inlaid with the blue-and-white delft tiles he had sent home from Holland so many years ago. A miniature herd of the twenty carved ebony elephants he'd sent home from India marched on the mantel above, their ivory eyes and tusks gleaming.[52]

Always eager for the latest Halliburton book, Marshall Field and Company in Chicago launched the first volume, *The Occident*, to great

Richard Halliburton built Hangover House in Laguna Beach, California. He planned to live there with his longtime partner Paul Mooney. *Author's collection*

fanfare. Children packed the stairwell leading from the reception room when it became too crowded. Jordan Marsh in Boston likewise fêted the book's release. Today an octogenarian, Marilyn Fais remembers shaking Halliburton's hand and waiting patiently while he autographed her book, her hair neatly parted on the side.[53]

"I must have been in junior high then and the program was held in my high school library. I had been a fan of his for some time and, of course, took his book with me to the program hoping to get it autographed. Of course his book was being sold there but when I passed my book to him for an autograph, it was plain to see it had been owned and read by me before his personal appearance at my school," Fais said. "I laughed to see when he passed my book back to me he had misspelled my first name as 'Marinlyn' instead of Marilyn . . . of course that made the autograph more special!"[54]

Marilyn Fais waits patiently while Richard Halliburton autographs her copy of *Book of Marvels. Courtesy of Marilyn Fais*

Inscription to Marilyn Fais. Note her name is misspelled, a mistake Fais said made the book more special. *Courtesy of Marilyn Fais*

Fan mail poured in. Anne Precht, a junior at Wautoma High School, wrote to Richard Halliburton in May 1937. She had to make a booklet on her favorite author and their works. She had admired his writings but couldn't find anything other than a small biography about him in *Who's Who in America*. Would it be possible, she asked Halliburton, for him to send her a letter telling about his life before he wrote *The Royal Road to Romance* as well as what he's been up to as of late? "I wished from the time I started reading it until I finished that I could have traveled along with you. I wish you would have stayed a little longer in Germany," wrote Precht, who was born in Germany.[55]

Other fans begged Halliburton for life advice. The celebrity journalist graciously declined. "But as for offering you my philosophy of life under forty in one page I'm no good," Halliburton wrote to Frances Singer of New York City. "I could have done this easily and glibly when I was 21—but now at 37, I am of the opinion that no profit can come to anyone from reading lessons in living out of a book. Please don't let my non-cooperative spirit discourage you. It's just that I personally realize how far I am from being a wise-man, and would turn hot from embarrassment if I felt anyone were using me as an ideal or example. But for those who feel they have a 'message' all good wishes. Cordially, Richard Halliburton."[56]

With so many people interested in the house, Halliburton decided it opportune to arrange for some formal publicity. He wanted to control the content and thought the best way to do that would be to invite a photographer of his choosing. Roger Sturtevant, a well-known architectural photographer, offered to shoot the house for a magazine for $125. Halliburton balked at the fee. He wrote to Alexander from the Chancellor Hotel in San Francisco. He didn't mince words: "The present financial circumstances [make] this out of the question." The house remained unfurnished and unpainted and he didn't see that changing in the foreseeable future. He had to mortgage the house to pay living expenses over the summer. His financial circumstances were grinding him down. "It takes a lot of will power to keep me from hating the place with all my heart. If ever I can escape, I intend to live in a tent or a boxcar."[57]

Halliburton got another chance to publicize the house. George Haight, another California-based architectural photographer, asked for permission to capture Hangover House in black and white. Halliburton hadn't intended to sell the house when he first conceived of it, but as time wore on he started thinking he needed to keep that option open. As such, he insisted the photo essay emphasize the house was under construction, because "if the house is presented—barren, harsh, cold—a half-finished engineering project—as R. Halliburton's happy home—my last hope will be destroyed for a sale."[58]

Mooney planted flowers in the window boxes and around the pool. He also wrote the press release for Alexander to use: "Something on the order of what I've written will be better, and if it connects your name with Dick (*he's* the story, you're still the wagon) and with a photo of a house, that ought to be enough."[59]

After a weekend getaway with Halliburton, Mooney wrote to "Billushkin," his sometimes nickname for William Alexander, telling him about their visit with Tom and Wilson, artist friends who lived on the outskirts of Laguna Beach. None of their new paintings spoke to either Mooney or Halliburton, except for one of Laguna Canyon with a dead white tree in the center. "There is movement afoot to have Dick buy it for me for Christmas or birthday or something."[60]

Fifteen months after the first bulldozer cleared a path, construction on the Hangover House was finished. Looking down over the sand and sea, the three-bedroom residence on 31172 Ceanothus Drive was indeed an architectural wonder of its day.[61] It was also, at $40,000, one of the most expensive.

Regrettably for Halliburton, he was saddled with unpaid bills for the house. Tired of being stonewalled, Alexander confronted the author. "How do *you* think I felt, after living months of such an endeavor, to be offered my fare back to Brooklyn? As your books, once written, have to be vastly re-written, so this house (once planned) had to be replanned [*sic*]—chiefly through Paul's intercession. Neither your abhorrence of my race, nor your resentment of the sums of 'house money' which Paul says you know he drank down, nor your seemingly total inability to appreciate the house I've built for you, seems to release you from your contractual obligation towards me."[62]

Halliburton lashed back. He was incensed that Alexander never understood the stress the house caused him physically and mentally. He told Alexander that the grind of trying to meet his financial obligations caused him to lose his voice and send his blood pressure plummeting to 80. "You claim that you have been the goat in this house project. But I must insist the honor is all mine," he concluded.[63]

In spite of the arguing and the bitter feelings, the house did bring joy. It echoed with raucous parties where writers, film stars, and aviators came together.[64] Ayn Rand, a friend of Alexander, was a guest of Halliburton's in 1937. She reportedly based *The Fountainhead*'s Heller House on Hangover House.[65]

And yet, though his house—his anchor—was completed, the familiar dread of staying put tapped at his soul. Halliburton never spent much time in the house. He felt the siren whisper of the sea. Halliburton was at the peak of his celebrity when he decided to embark on an over-the-top seafaring adventure, one that would make the *Arabian Nights* dull by comparison.

10

A New Inspiration

A S VICE PRESIDENT AND manager of the San Francisco Convention and Visitors Bureau, it fell to Walter Gaines Swanson to schedule tours of the unfinished Oakland Bay Bridge. So it was that he found himself walking along its unpaved road with Richard Halliburton one sparkling afternoon. Standing 525 feet above the cold, greenish waters of the San Francisco Bay, Swanson turned to Halliburton, a question in his eyes. Did the writer really want to sail a replica Chinese junk nine thousand miles across the Pacific Ocean from Hong Kong to San Francisco?

If Halliburton said yes, it would satisfy a nagging problem for Gaines: how to open the 1939 San Francisco Golden Gate International Exposition, a celebration of East and West, with a show-stopping splash. For Halliburton, the idea of sailing underneath the Golden Gate Bridge's majestic Art Deco towers sent his heart racing. He imagined flag-waving fans clustered on the pier, eager to welcome him home. The idea of such an international and illustrious figure joining in the ceremonies galvanized Swanson. The two men agreed to meet at the fair offices as soon as possible to work through the details.

On the appointed day, the adventurer arrived in a dark gray suit tailored just so, the starched cuffs of his shirt extending exactly two inches from the sleeves. A silk handkerchief was tucked into one cuff.[1] Clyde M. Vandeburg, the curly-haired director of publicity and promotion for the fair, sat wearing an expectant look on his face. Next to him, Art Linkletter, the up-and-coming radio and television personality, considered Halliburton.

"Opening day ceremonies were always a problem, and in the search for offbeat attractions more than one fair expert has reached the nervous breakdown stage," Linkletter later wrote in his autobiography *Confessions of a Happy Man.*[2] The committee concurred: Halliburton's triumphant entry on opening day would add that extra pop of glamour and color to an already outsized event. As a symbol of daring adventure, he would attract thousands of people and help sell thousands of tickets.[3]

Even knowing Halliburton's thirst for adventure, they didn't take his participation for granted. They told him how he would join a roster of an already outstanding group of entertainers slated to perform. Benny Goodman was scheduled to play the clarinet and Bing Crosby was ready to serenade audiences in the evening. Jack Benny would tickle people's funny bones and Robert Ripley's *Ripley's Believe it or Not!* would shock them just enough. The burlesque dancer Sally Rand planned to perform her famously risqué ostrich feather fan dance and bubble dance. Linkletter would write and narrate the pageant scripts.[4]

The fair committee expected upward of two hundred thousand people to converge on Treasure Island, a flat artificial island attached to Yerba Buena Island in San Francisco Bay starting in February 1939. The Army Corps of Engineers built the artificial island between 1936 and 1937 specifically for the fair. Great exhibition halls would showcase the world today and the world to come. The General Electric Kitchen of the Future promised modern appliances. Visitors walking through the Hall of Air Transportation would see the Pan Am Clipper, capable of flying passengers across the Pacific, as well as a translucent Pontiac automobile. In another pavilion, miniature models of gold mining equipment would "mine" a million dollar "mineral mountain" of ore to celebrate the history of the California Gold Rush.[5]

Once Halliburton arrived in San Francisco aboard his Chinese junk, he would dock in the "Lake of All Nations" and he and his boat would become another fair attraction. The committee traded ideas on how to boost publicity. To add yet another dash of flare to the event, Linkletter proposed meeting Halliburton offshore with a film crew to get an exclusive report on his trip for a network show. The lean, impeccably groomed Tennessean listened.

Halliburton saw endless commercial possibilities regarding the trip. For instance, he could earn much-needed cash taking passengers for a tour around the Golden Gate Bridge and the San Francisco–Oakland Bay Bridge aboard the boat for one dollar a ride. He suggested selling Chinese junk–themed souvenirs, stamps, and pins. Because it would be difficult to broadcast the crossing live, Halliburton came up with the "*Sea Dragon* letters." For five dollars, he would offer his fans a chance to subscribe to exclusive letters that he would mail from Hong Kong and other stopping points throughout the voyage. The idea floored the committee; nothing like it had ever been done before.

A grin camped on Halliburton's face and the faint creases in the corners of his eyes crinkled upward. In the space of one afternoon, Halliburton rekindled his passion for adventure. He hadn't felt this kind of thrill regarding a trip since flying around the world in his scarlet-and-gold airplane with Moye Stephens. He stood and shook hands with Linkletter, Vandeburg, and Swanson. Each man wished Halliburton good sailing. The thirty-seven-year-old walked out the door, resplendent in his confidence.[6]

"I've a new inspiration. They cheered over my Chinese junk plans, and wanted me to stop everything else and develop this idea," Halliburton wrote his parents.[7]

The adventure would sate his boyhood fantasy. Once upon a time he had dreamed of owning a white-sailed schooner and sailing it across the vast Pacific Ocean. Yet as one adventure and one book gave way to another, he put aside the fantasy. Years before he became the best-known adventurer of his time, Halliburton happened to visit the harbor of Foochow in China. It was 1922. There he saw hundreds of boats, and was immediately drawn to the Chinese junks with their horseshoe-shaped sterns and painted hulls.

Excited to share his plan with Paul Mooney, Halliburton took off for Laguna Beach. It was an easy drive along the coast from San Francisco; on one side lay the ocean, on the other creased ridges reached skyward. Sleek and solid, Hangover House rose above the canyon like a fortress. He was eager to sit outside in the garden and listen to the waves breaking on the sand below, surrounded by goldenrod and sagebrush. The small copse of eucalyptus trees he had previously planted stood that much taller. The house never ceased to cast a spell on the writer. "If I can't get nearer the Eternals in that house, then it's not in me. I never saw a house so far away from man and so close to God. The peace and serenity of that canyon at my feet is enough in itself to make me relax and dream," he wrote.[8]

And dream he did.

As an American literary fixture, his was a household name. His seven books were now available in fifteen languages. The first of his two-volume young adult books, the *Book of Marvels: The Occident*, received glowing reviews upon publication, exceeding his and his publishers' expectations. Book reviewers admired the way Halliburton ignited his readers' imaginations and whet their appetites for more knowledge of the world.[9] Even those born a generation after the book's publication raved about the wonders within. "Even years later Richard Halliburton's *Complete Book of Marvels* offered a vivid illustration of what I could never be: utterly at home in the world. Halliburton moved in space and time in a way I knew I never would . . . plus he painted a portrait of a wonderful, colorful world that was innocent and open and undiscovered and full of people who didn't hate Americans," said the late essayist David Rakoff.[10]

R. W. Apple, the late *New York Times* reporter, recalled his most treasured possession while growing up in Ohio in the 1940s was "a book with a dark blue cover and impressive pictures of far-off places inside . . . it helped give me a case of incurable wanderlust."[11]

The Orient, with its navy cover and gold lettering, was scheduled for a September 1938 release, but it would be delayed several times because of production glitches; the hot New York summer kept the ink from drying.

Yet, even with this approval, Halliburton suspected, or maybe feared, that interest in his brand was fading. He sometimes woke in the middle of the night with a creeping sense that he had lost his ability to entertain. He worried he wasn't as clever, as brilliant, as he once was. True, the largest magazines, such as *Ladies' Home Journal* and *Cosmopolitan*, still featured his work, and newspapers still covered him hungrily and ran his byline. But tastes were changing. People favored the movie theater over the lecture hall. They watched Katharine Hepburn and Cary Grant in *Bringing Up Baby* and Bette Davis in *Jezebel*. T. H. White's *The Sword in the Stone*, Ayn Rand's *Anthem*, and *Rebecca* by Daphne du Maurier were among the most popular books. Outside of entertainment, the world's attention was shifting to the dual menace that was Germany and Japan.

But if done right, this next adventure could be just the thing to revive his readers' excitement. It would echo his earlier expeditions where he traced literary and historical figures such as Ulysses or Cortés. Like his leap into the Well of Death, setting forth in a Chinese junk called forth something ancient. And like his Panama Canal swim, it would highlight his perseverance and ability to break records. The trip was vintage Halliburton.

Once committed to the idea, Halliburton wasted no time pursuing financial backing. He didn't have the funds to finance the trip, and while the fair organizers would certainly promote him, just as they promoted the other exhibitors and entertainers, they were not going to directly invest in his project. He had financed the *Flying Carpet* journey with the sale of magazine rights, lectures, and previous book sales. That wouldn't be enough this time. He needed to find sponsors to secure the necessary $35,000.

Halliburton boasted a vast network of contacts and he mined his list until he found San Francisco–based agent Wilfred Crowell, a "high pressure promoter who knows moneyed people" in San Francisco.[12] Crowell would handle the finances and, for a fee, Richard Townsend, a San Francisco attorney and Dartmouth graduate, would supervise the overall management. Through such a corporation they planned on selling stock to raise the $30,000 needed to purchase a boat, pay the crew, and stock the ship's stores. The plan called for the original stockholders to receive 40 percent of all profits over $30,000—their initial investment. Halliburton would receive 40 percent of the profits and Crowell would receive the remaining 20 percent.

Since Halliburton was the San Francisco exposition's star attraction, it made sense to approach the city's local Chinese entrepreneurs. After considering a list of names, he and Crowell tapped four men as possible investors. Halliburton and Crowell told the merchants they could count on recouping their investment through ticket sales, souvenirs, radio programs, stamps, junk-themed merchandise, and the subscription letters.[13] It was a first-class example of cross promotion.

Halliburton's keen eyes carefully scanned the documents for the Richard Halliburton Chinese Junk Expedition a final time before filing with the secretary of state in Sacramento. Two months after the corporation was formed, Halliburton hit a snag. While in Indianapolis to deliver a lecture about *Seven League Boots*, he learned his Chinese backers had withdrawn from the deal, "not because of percentage, but because they fear the Japs will prevent our sailing," Halliburton wrote home. Fear not, he told his parents: "This doesn't discourage me. All my other projects have stood still several times before they succeeded."[14]

After Indianapolis he flew to El Paso and then took a train to Baton Rouge. There he lectured and attended a party at the home of the assassinated governor Huey Long, where he met Long's "very pretty and attractive daughter and a nineteen-year-old son who had his father's brains." One evening of hobnobbing later, he boarded a train to Deming, New Mexico, and a bus to Silver City; he then took a car and drove to Laguna, where "the house was shining. The rains all spring have made everything intensely green. There are only a few sand spots in the canyon. In fact grass has about taken the yard and slopes, but I've got to imitate Dad and do a lot of weed-pulling."[15]

Halliburton only spent a couple of days in his retreat. He needed to return to San Francisco and continue his quest for financing. He was not at all hopeful. "A letter from my agent says the junk prospects look black," he wrote home.[16]

Acting on Crowell's advice, Halliburton reached out to the corporate world beyond California and arranged for a meeting with Buick Motors in Detroit. His experience there became one more example of the highs and lows he encountered. Some decades later John Nicholls Booth, his fan turned friend, recalled the story.

Booth and Halliburton both happened to be visiting Detroit for different speaking engagements. Halliburton was to give a lecture at the Museum of Fine Arts. Eager to catch up with his friend, Halliburton told Booth to phone him at the museum shortly before he was to speak, but well after he concluded a meeting with Buick. That way they could pick a time and place to meet for a late dinner. Booth called promptly at 8:00 PM. A stagehand grabbed the ringing phone. Booth asked him to please tell Mr. Halliburton that "John Booth is calling." "Well, I'm Napoleon," the stagehand snickered before slamming down the phone.[17] Momentarily taken aback, Booth dialed again. No one answered. Booth didn't see Halliburton until the next afternoon. The author broke into peals of laughter as soon as he spotted Booth walk through the restaurant's doors.

Just as in show business, timing was everything. Booth's call came precisely as Halliburton was entertaining his audience with stories about Dr. Samuel Mudd's imprisonment at Fort Jefferson, his price for setting John Wilkes Booth's broken leg. "Imagine the stagehand's reaction when you called saying you were John Booth," Halliburton said.[18] Laughing felt so good after the disappointing meeting with the executives at Buick Motors, he said.

Halliburton updated Booth on his plans. He explained how he hoped to air several Sunday night broadcasts during his Pacific crossing, radio signals permitting. He wanted the car company to sponsor the shows. The businessmen seemed most taken with the idea. Then, just as the meeting ended, and the men in suits pushed back their chairs to stand, Halliburton cast his eyes about the room. A skeptical look flashed across the face of one executive. He thought it a terrible idea for the brand Buick to appear in any kind of advertising campaign that used the word *junk*. In an instant the promise of sponsorship was lost.[19] Unfortunately, Buick's rejection became just one more stumbling block in the way to getting the necessary $35,000. Booth felt for his friend and tried to assure him he would get the funding he needed.

On another occasion, Swanson arranged for a meeting between Halliburton and San Francisco's Chinese Six Companies, also known as the Chinese Consolidated Benevolent Association. Founded in 1882, the Six Companies represented Chinatown's political, economic, and social elite. Swanson believed they could easily convince the association to back Halliburton's upcoming adventure, as they were already heavily invested in the exposition.

Halliburton detailed his plan to the board members. The men peppered Halliburton with questions—how long would the voyage take, how many crew would he hire, what would he do to promote the book—and took copious notes. After Halliburton finished his presentation, the group politely asked him to leave the room. They motioned for Swanson to remain. Halliburton paced nervously in the corridor. The minutes crawled. After what felt like an interminable amount of time, Swanson came out of the conference room, gently closing the door behind him. His furrowed brow told Halliburton everything: the businessmen had unanimously turned down the request. They didn't see the financial benefit of sponsoring Halliburton's trip. They were simply not convinced that they would get a good return on their investment. Instead, they decided backing a floating casino tethered to Treasure Island would be more lucrative. Halliburton tried to ignore the dejection that now threatened to slink up on him. No money, no boat.

Halliburton went home and brainstormed. He realized part of the answer to his financial conundrum was perched above the caramel sand of Laguna Beach. He mortgaged Hangover House for $4,000 and began looking for someone to rent the three-bedroom house. Next, he decided it was time to call upon his cousin Erle P. Halliburton. After all, the oil magnate had on one occasion offered him a free plane for his around the world *Flying Carpet* trip. Surely, Halliburton thought, he would be interested in this new venture.

Halliburton rehearsed his pitch on the way to the ranch. He would propose taking Erle Jr. along as an assistant to his radio operator in exchange for the capital. "I've already talked to Jr.," Halliburton wrote his parents. "He says he'd 'give anything' to go. His eagerness will be a powerful persuader to Sr."[20]

The businessman and the writer retreated into the living room. Halliburton knew better than to launch right into the business at hand. He needed to finesse Erle and his wife Vida to part with their dollars. Still, he was certain he could convince them of the great opportunity he offered. His confidence was a tad premature. In fact, his meeting stalled before it started. Halliburton spent the night, but once Erle learned what his younger cousin wanted, he wouldn't give him a chance to talk about it.[21]

Halliburton refused to let that be the final word. He vowed to try again. This time he planned to ask only for $7,500—not up to $30,000—in exchange for bringing their son along on the adventure, but that their son should bring someone. During his recent trip to the ranch, Vida mentioned her son's friend might be interested in the trip. Since he had wealthy parents, money wasn't an issue. Halliburton said he would take the pair for $15,000 if he could raise the remaining $15,000 from other investors.

Vida ruminated on it for a few days before phoning Halliburton. She was sold on the idea and asked him to count her in. Halliburton drove back to the ranch to thank his cousin's wife. When he got there he learned Erle Jr. was in the hospital about to undergo eye surgery. Vida didn't think her son would recover in time to go on the trip, but she still wanted to invest.[22]

As Halliburton worked to fit the pieces of his financial jigsaw puzzle into place, he began assembling his crew. He tried to go about it quietly, but the press got wind of the plan. Mixed in with the upbeat coverage were articles like the one in the *New Yorker*, which devoted several inches of copy to needle the writer. "He wants to sail across the Pacific Ocean in a Chinese junk. Why do some people want to do things the hard way? It's easier than swimming, isn't it?"[23]

Once the word got out, the letters started pouring in. Sitting in his room at the Chancellor Hotel in San Francisco, the author opened envelope after envelope. Halliburton received nearly one thousand letters from women and men begging for the chance to sail with the famous daredevil. The letters sounded the same; not one stood out. Then his phone rang. A John Wenlock Welch was on the line. His booming voice reverberated through the speaker.

Halliburton agreed to interview him for the captain's spot. The Australian-born Welch had served in the British Navy during World War I and had sailed his fair share of difficult voyages. After his discharge, he moved to the United States and became an American citizen. As a master mariner, Welch once helmed grain clippers around the Horn of Africa and sailed United Fruiters to Central America. He had also worked as a movie consultant for Universal and Fox Studios.[24] His experience was more than enough to convince Halliburton; he signed the forty-two-year-old for $250 a month.

Next, Halliburton hired Henry von Fehren to be his engineer. Originally from Germany, the naturalized American now lived in San Francisco. He boasted six years' experience working with diesel engines in motor sailboats and seemed to possess "complete control of all the black magic of machinery."[25] His radio operator had spent time in the Coast Guard and participated in the Mid-Pacific effort to help locate Amelia Earhart when her Lockheed Electra went missing.

After Halliburton filled these key posts, he spent the rest of the summer rounding out his crew. He wanted bright, dynamic people filled with energy. Although he received inquiries from women and men, there is nothing to suggest Halliburton considered bringing women along on a trip that was expected to last weeks. And though he received stacks of applications, he ended up relying on word of mouth and personal recommendations to fill the positions.

Vida and Erle Halliburton's daughter Zola Catherine shared several promising leads with her beloved cousin. A Wellesley University student, she told Halliburton about her friend John "Brue" Potter, the son of wealthy parents. A member of Dartmouth University's Class of 1936, he grew up in Maine. He started sailing in elementary school and now owned a "New York 40," a sixty-five-foot ketch, which he loved sailing through the restless waters off the North Atlantic coast.

Through his niece and Potter, Halliburton met Gordon Torrey and Robert Chase, both Dartmouth alumni. Torrey graduated from the university in 1935 and was staying in Boston while awaiting the probate results of his father's will. Late one Friday afternoon, he received a call summoning him back to Maine, but "having to kill some time before I could catch a train for Maine, I went into the Copley Plaza Merry-Go-Round bar to do some thinking about my problems, with the help of a drink," Torrey said.[26] Across the carousel-themed bar, which opened when Prohibition ended, Torrey spotted Potter, a fellow class-mate, and Robert Chase, a rising senior at Dartmouth. He pulled up a red upholstered chair, ordered a drink, and then introduced himself to the fetching woman seated next to Chase. It was Zola Halliburton.[27]

The conversation turned to everyone's summer plans. Potter, named class "Hot Dog" at Dartmouth, planned to spend his time sailing in Maine and, if his mother permitted, take his boat to the West Coast and perhaps on to Hawaii. The young men seated around the white linen–covered table thought it a grand idea. The only hitch, Potter said, was that he needed a crew. He invited Torrey to join him. Torrey knew Potter from school and from Mount Desert Island in Maine, off the coast of Bangor.[28] Potter was a summer resident of Southwest Harbor, a fishing community on the island near where Torrey lived year-round. The two spent a lot of time in Northeast Harbor, on the other side of Mount Desert, sailing in regattas.

"Then the young lady (Zola) said something to the effect that he sounded about as crazy as her cousin who planned to have a Chinese junk built in Hong Kong and sail it to San Francisco to be exhibited at the forth-coming World's Fair," Torrey said.[29]

It all sounded incredibly outlandish to Torrey, who was soon to return to Maine and care for his younger brothers until school resumed in the fall. But he also couldn't deny it: the idea sounded incredibly appealing. Adventure trumped pragmatism. He would go to Maine, see to his brothers, and then maybe he could make time to do something slightly impulsive and decidedly bold. He had enough available cash to pay his way to Hong Kong and about six months' available time before needing to seriously go about finding a job. As an added bonus, Torrey would meet *the* Richard Halliburton, whose books he'd devoured in his youth.[30]

Potter also agreed to invest $7,000 in the project on the condition that he could come along on the seafaring adventure. "I want to purge myself of the wanderlust," said Potter. He wanted to get "the roaming fever" out of himself before settling down to a career in the diplomatic service.[31]

Zola Halliburton also told her cousin about George Barstow III, who was studying piano at the Juilliard School in New York City. His mother, Bertha Barstow, was eager for her son to be associated personally with Halliburton, thinking the chance offered a better education than one year in college.[32] As such, Bertha invested $4,000 in the Richard Halliburton Corporation. She insisted she didn't want to receive one cent, note, or stock in return. She wanted Halliburton to receive any and all benefits derived from her investment. Halliburton ignored her wishes and sent George Barstow his stock.[33]

Halliburton signed on all the Dartmouth men; they ended up investing more than half of the money Halliburton raised.

Ever creative, Halliburton moved ahead with his idea to sell subscription letters to school-aged children. Eventually children in all forty-eight states and several countries subscribed to the *Sea Dragon* letters. He aimed to sell ten thousand letters at five dollars each; Halliburton would receive two-thirds of the profits and the corporation would receive one-third.

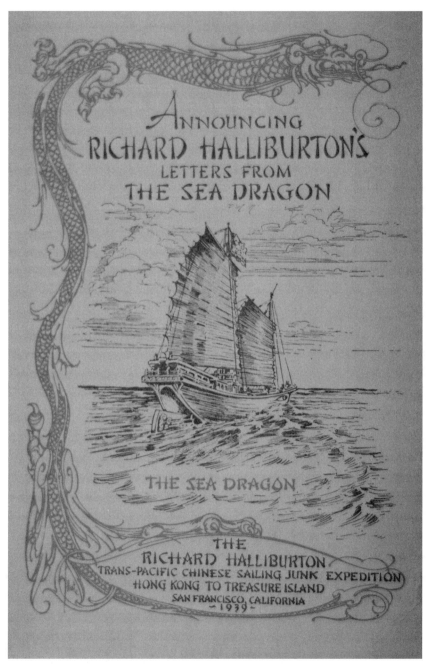

For five dollars, children could subscribe to exclusive letters about Richard Halliburton's voyage from Hong Kong to San Francisco. *Courtesy of Marilyn Fais*

Figuring out how to divide the profits was easy; figuring out the logistics of printing that many letters was harder. Each of the letters had to be stamped, addressed, and autographed. Halliburton needed to bring along a mimeograph machine on the trip and an assistant to run off copies, stuff envelopes, and affix postage. He hired Mooney as his assistant. "He'll be splendid with some intense adventurous job—and he will be paid well for his services—the same as I would have to pay anybody else. He's in a rut in Laguna—drinking and smoking too much—this violent change will stir him up and give him a new interest in life and work. He's overjoyed over the prospects of going along—and so am I as I'll have that much *more* protection."[34]

Though Halliburton sometimes complained that he and Mooney "clashed on almost everything," he told his parents that "it is this very warfare that makes his friendship provocative and stimulating. His companionship provides a daily shock to my own complacency and a spur to my intellect."[35] The two were bound to each other.

Nearly two decades after Halliburton started crisscrossing the globe, his parents had grown more or less accustomed to their son's departures for the untamed reaches of the world. But now, as the world disintegrated a bit more every day—between the Spanish Civil War and the Ethiopian War, between Nazi Germany's rearmament and Japan's designs on Asia—Wesley opposed the trip. Richard tried to reassure his father. He wasn't ignorant of the hostilities brewing in Japan, but rather he felt impervious to any danger.

"Dad if I could talk to you about the junk trip I'm sure you would lose all your hesitation about it," he wrote shortly before he left. "Never was any expedition so carefully worked out for safety measures. I've a wonderful captain and engine and engineer. I'll have two months to choose my junk with the best possible help."[36]

All across San Francisco, excitement about the fair was reaching a fever pitch. Chicago had hosted the Century of Progress Fair between 1933 and 1934. New York City would hold the World of Tomorrow Fair between 1939 and 1940. But now it was San Francisco's turn to present an idealistic view of the future, a hopeful note amid the intensifying tension between the United States and Japan. As President Franklin D. Roosevelt told the nation on opening day, "Unity of the Pacific nations is America's concern and responsibility; their onward progress deserves now a recognition that will be a stimulus as well. . . . May this, America's World's Fair on the Pacific in 1939, truly serve all nations in symbolizing their destinies, one with every other, through the ages to come."[37]

On the eve of its opening in 1939, invisible rays from the India Sunbeam tower illuminated the Golden Gate Exposition. Men and women, old and young, gathered awestruck to watch from the hills or from inside windows of taller office buildings in the bay as Treasure Island glowed in the light. At least a hundred thousand people passed through the entrance gate before noon the next day. They spread out blankets, unfolded lawn chairs, and settled in to watch the highly anticipated Pageant of the Pacific. Treasure Island, so named after the sand that was hauled from Sierra Nevada Mother Lode during the Gold Rush, was awash in merriment, from "a baby that had seen less than a year of life to an octogenarian whose hope was of 'seeing another California fair.'"[38]

The revelry lasted well into the night and long after dawn. Not one bar closed that night as celebrators strolled through the city from Washington Street to the lake and back.

"Life, color, and action were swirled together in a spontaneous explosion of hilarity that turned the city topsy-turvy for a parade that lasted 3 hours and 15 miles," reported the *Oakland Tribune*.[39]

The date approached for Halliburton to once again take leave of the United States. He put his affairs in order. He mailed his mother a confidential letter, instructing her to hide it in her lock-box once she finished reading it. It detailed how Hangover House, now worth around $20,000, should be disposed of in case he predeceased either his mother or his father. If he died before his parents, the house would become their joint property. It stipulated that the Halliburtons could sell the house only if they were in dire need of capital for living requirements. After the three of them died, he wanted the proceeds from the sale to establish a library at Princeton University: Halliburton Library.[40] (The library never came to fruition, and the gift was at some point associated with the university's map collections, but only temporarily.)[41]

His estate in order, Halliburton visited with friends and family. There was something about this trip that made him want to take stock. Perhaps it was being on the edge of forty.

Halliburton drove to Greensboro, North Carolina, to spend time with his younger cousin Juliet Halliburton. She had last seen him about a year ago. He told his newly wed cousin all about his plans for the Pacific crossing. She was fearful about the hazards of such a trip, but he shrugged off her disquiet, telling her he considered it less dangerous than flying over the Sahara with Moye Stephens in the scarlet-and-gold *Flying Carpet*. But before he left, he confided to her that this was surely going to be his last trip. The world was changing and he needed to change with it.

Halliburton also drove to Kansas City, Missouri, to visit Mike Hockaday. The two old friends sat in the kitchen. Hockaday's wife puttered around, listening with amusement while the two boyhood friends reminisced about dorm life and their European adventure. Bouncing his little son, and Richard's godson, four-year-old Irvine Jr., on his knee, Hockaday sat engrossed, listening to the details of Halliburton's latest plan. Halliburton was only half-joking when he proposed his friend join him on the Pacific Ocean adventure. Tempted as he was, Hockaday turned him down.[42]

Then it was back to the West Coast to pack. Halliburton booked passage on the *President Adams*, which was set to sail from San Francisco for Hong Kong in August. Several days before leaving, he motored over to Treasure Island to inspect his anchorage. He proclaimed his ship would be the most exciting concession at the fair.[43] At this point Halliburton had raised $21,000 for his trip. And then, as was par for Halliburton's course, the trip was delayed. He used the time to tie up some loose ends regarding Hangover House. He rebooked passage on the SS *President Coolidge.*

He thought about how the next time he sailed across the indigo sea, it would be standing at the helm of his own vessel. The end rush of preparations left him "bewildered and dizzy" and so he was thankful for the time spent with his mother. He arranged to meet her at the Biltmore Hotel near Los Angeles's Pershing Square and drove back down the coast to Laguna, where he threw himself a party "to say goodbye to my friends."[44] During their short week together, his mother shed the last ounce of her resentment and anger over Richard's move west. She saw contentment in her son, a peace.

"Mother and I did the best we could with the fleeting moments we had together. They were very sweet and very happy—and she was patient not to get too restless . . . seeing what a mature, experienced captain and engineer I have, she can feel at ease. Both these men think no more of this new sailing job than they think of every one of the dozens behind them. It never occurs to them that there is any 'peril.' Discomfort, yes—but they plan to be back in San Francisco on schedule and nothing will prevent them," he wrote home, trying again to reassure his father.[45]

The Tennessean had great expectations for the trip, and he wrote his father that he looked forward to "living on salt beef and hard tack cooked by a Chinaman."[46] His magazine articles would provide for a lively, dramatic opening for a new book, a sort of *Royal Road to Romance* in the United States. About one hundred books on American history now lined the shelves of the library in Hangover House. He planned to use his voyage from China as the opening act for a pre-Columbian "discovery" of America story. He wanted to spotlight historical sites such as Williamsburg and Yorktown. He would feature the Grand Coulee Dam and the Empire State Building. Perhaps he could even reenact John Wilkes Booth's escape from Ford's Theatre.[47]

On September 23, at 3:00 PM, the *Coolidge* blasted her horn and announced its departure. It was to arrive in Yokohama, Japan, on October 7. Nineteen years earlier, Halliburton had run away from Princeton University and worked his way across the Atlantic Ocean aboard the *Octorara*. Now, as he watched San Francisco recede from view, Halliburton felt just as elated as when he first went to sea in 1919.[48]

11

The *Sea Dragon*

THE *COOLIDGE* DROPPED ANCHOR in Yokohama after fifteen days of hot sun and calm seas.[1] The only break in the nearly eight-thousand-mile journey was a ten-hour stop in Honolulu. Halliburton and Mooney refreshed themselves with a quick swim at Waikiki beach and fit in a short visit with some friends they knew on the island.

Halliburton welcomed Mooney's company. Initially, he had reservations about the scope of the adventure, but as the plan formed, Mooney decided—for better or worse—the escapade was not to be missed. The night before Mooney left, he and William Alexander spent a great deal of time burning Mooney's personal correspondence in the fireplace.[2]

During the crossing, Halliburton and the *Sea Dragon* captain, John Welch, spent long hours in the bridge with Captain Dale E. Collins, chief officer of the *Coolidge*. Heads bent over charts, the three men discussed possible routes, weather, and currents. Collins offered advice; he knew the route well, having sailed between Hong Kong and San Francisco many times. Halliburton wanted to follow the most direct route that would also keep them far from Japanese reach. He had already secured permission from the US Navy to use the Pan American islands dotting the Pacific as way stations to resupply and, if need be, to rest. This meant the *Sea Dragon* would never have more than "a 1,200-mile hop between places."[3] Collins recommended the men set forth from Hong Kong by January, but certainly no later than mid-February. After that the furious seas and hammering rains of monsoon season would pose more danger than any Japanese gunboat.

During mealtimes and walks about the deck, the ever-garrulous Welch entertained passengers and crew alike. "The lusty talks were always well seasoned with a seaman's phraseology and yet, to the ladies he would be as courtly and gallant as any knight in King Arthur's Court," Collins said.[4]

Nothing is known of Mooney's interactions aboard the liner. Halliburton kept his lover out of his letters home.

Halliburton impressed Collins as a quiet, unassuming man—even a bit shy. "But when he spoke, our attention was immediately and irresistibly captured by his slow, soft spoken tones, his flawless manipulation of the 'King's English' and his inexhaustible vocabulary."[5] Collins recalled an amusing incident during the early part of the crossing when a crewmember on the *Coolidge* mistook Halliburton for a stowaway. It was three nights after they'd left San Francisco. Just before midnight, the night watchman bounded up the metal stairs to the bridge and pushed open the door. He rushed up to Collins, babbling something about there being a stowaway. The fugitive was none other than Richard Halliburton.[6]

Now Halliburton stood on the deck of the *Coolidge*. He watched the sailors secure the ship's lines to the anvil-shaped moorings and felt a shiver of anticipation as the crew lowered the gangway. He crossed the narrow metal ramp and, for a moment, was suspended between sea and land. It was a moment of promise—his entire adventure lay before him.

Ahead, Mount Fuji appeared like a Hokusai woodblock print. The murky skies hid the solitary snow-fringed peak, its base swaddled in the mist below. On a clear day one could see all the way to the gumdrop-shaped mountain. Halliburton waxed nostalgic upon seeing the mountain again. He remembered making the icy climb to the summit more than a decade ago.[7]

Once in Yokohama, Halliburton phoned Ambassador Joseph Grew. He had met the diplomat in Constantinople during his flight around the world with pilot Moye Stephens. Having exchanged the Turkey posting for Japan, the ambassador now helped Halliburton arrange for appointments with key Japanese Navy officials in Tokyo. The author needed to make sure the Japanese didn't object to his endeavor.

Halliburton last visited Tokyo in 1932. Seven years later, he hardly recognized the capital. It now resembled a modern American city; subways zipped underground and above grew a forest of skyscrapers. He remembered that only a small slice of the populace wore European-style suits and dresses. Now western dress was the norm.[8] Walking the streets he saw few signs that "Japan is engaged in a great war for the subjugation and annexation of the most populous country on the globe. Wartime Tokyo never seemed so prosperous."[9] The city's hotels overflowed with guests, spectators packed theaters for nightly performances, and glitzy department stores stayed open late.

But the buzz of the city masked the country's ferocious authoritarianism—a state of affairs Halliburton found most oppressive. He discussed it in length in his letters home. "It regulates what they think and spend, and they seem to obey without complaint or criticism. The Government has decreed that the people must cheer more loudly for Japan's alliance with Italy and Hitler. So the theatres are told to feature German and Italian music, uniforms, flags. The theatrical hit during my visit was called 'Hello Berlin.' . . . In America we may take this Japan-Germany-Italy alliance very lightly, and wishfully think that it has no real foundation other than the momentary politics of those three countries. But in Japan you soon learn otherwise."[10]

Two months earlier a group of uniformed Hitler youths arrived in Yokohama on the battleship *Gneisenau*. Upon their arrival, they marched onto the quay. Standing in a ruler-straight line, they thrust their arms upward in a "Heil Hitler" salute. Their cry, "*Dai Nippon banzai!*" ("Long live Japan!"), rang through the waterfront.

After declaring war against China in June, the Japanese Navy blockaded Chinese port cities and had sunk thousands of Chinese junks along the coast. In spite of this overt military force and aggression, officials working in Tokyo assured Halliburton he had nothing to fear. Nonetheless, Halliburton decided an abundance of caution was in order. "I have the safe-passage documents in my pocket and will carry them with me—even to the bottom of the China Sea," he wrote.[11] He also planned to display three oversized American flags on his boat. He would fly one from the mast and have one painted on each side of the hull. "This is the general custom in the war zone out here nowadays," he wrote home.[12]

His business in Japan concluded, Halliburton, Mooney, and Welch took a British steamer to Hong Kong. They sailed southwest down the coast, planning stops at several ports to find a suitable junk. Halliburton finished his first dispatch and posted the article from Japanese-occupied Shanghai. Well aware of the legion of Japanese intelligence officers devoted to suppressing the press, Halliburton refused to self-censor. He filled his article with his impressions and thoughts about his forthcoming voyage and about wartime Japan.

He had no luck in Shanghai. Most boats—junks, sampans, or fishing—had fled the Japanese military shortly after the invasion. In Wenchow, Halliburton admired the faded beauty of several white-and-scarlet junks but distrusted their seaworthiness. He pressed on. Ningpo. Amoy. Foochow. Not one port had what he wanted or needed; moreover, every boat owner and shipyard knew about the wealthy white American interested in buying a junk. They had no qualms about jacking up prices. His last hope for a fair deal lay in the British colony of Hong Kong.

The steamer approached the trade city. Tung-stained junks with painted eyes staring from their bows bobbed in the congested harbor alongside sampans and ferryboats. Ships from all nations anchored in the waters. Oil, fuel, rotting fish, vegetables, and fruits made for a piquant fragrance. The golden morning light skipped off the waves. Cheery fishermen shouted greetings as the boat wound its way past various fishing fleets and Japanese naval vessels anchored in the harbor's mouth.

Eager to find a proper junk, Halliburton examined at least fifty. Some looked like they'd been cobbled together with plywood and push pins. Some looked as if they had seen their last best days during the Ming Dynasty. Others were so battered they had more holes in them than solid wood. One was too big; one was too small. None looked capable of withstanding the weight and vibration of the heavy auxiliary motor they would need. Then there was the *Gin Drinker's Bay*, a ninety-foot-long junk with polished teak deck, scarlet sails, and red lacquered cabins. It cost three times what he could afford.[13] He found another junk almost as handsome as *Gin Drinker's Bay*. It had five iron cannons to defend its crew from pirates. Just before Halliburton closed the deal, he discovered the hull planking was a mere inch thick.[14]

"And so it went, ship after ship. Inevitably, in the face of all these disappointments, we soon reached the only possible conclusion—we must build a new junk suitable to our needs, regardless of the time it took," Halliburton wrote.[15]

In principle, building one from the keel up meant a safer boat, if done right. It would also allow Halliburton to design a ship to his exact specifications. Halliburton estimated the project would cost $4,000, about what he originally planned to spend on a remodeling a used junk.

Locals steered Halliburton to Fat Kau's Shipyard in the Kowloon section of the peninsula. Fat Kau enjoyed a reputation as "Hong Kong's best junk-builder."[16] Halliburton told the round shipwright he wanted a Ningpo-style junk, or a three-masted trading vessel. Fat Kau told Halliburton he required neither blueprints nor drawings. An explanation and simple drawing would suffice. Halliburton explained he wanted a seventy-five-foot-long ship, with a twenty-foot beam. He wanted it "extra sturdy" and "adorned with every possible flourish."[17]

Halliburton's interest in Chinese junks reached back through the years to his childhood. When he turned twelve, his parents gave him a foot-long model of a junk, complete with the traditional eyes painted on the bow. With its small mat sails properly hoisted, he raced his new treasure across a neighborhood pond. It was "faster than any other sailboat I ever owned. And it *never* turned over," he wrote.[18] In the game, one side of the described pond was Canton, the other San Francisco. The aim was to have the toy junk "sail" across the Pacific Ocean until it reached American shores. There it would unload its cargo of tea and silk. "This same game I plan to play again. . . . The cargo will be one thousand model junks—exact miniatures of the ship that's carrying them," he wrote.[19]

Halliburton found a picturesque but vulnerable city in Hong Kong. Its steep slopes cupped the harbor, as if offering protection from the coming violence. Already more than five hundred thousand Chinese had found refuge there after escaping the Japanese Imperial Army. As many people had succumbed to cholera and malnutrition as they had to Japanese bullets and bayonets. The rest, the barely living, streamed onto the island pushing and pulling wooden carts and rickshaws, piled high with mattresses, rice sacks, and stoves. Some refugees wore cotton-padded clothes, typical of those from the North and further inland; others came swaddled in rags.

The most destitute scratched out a living not far from Fat Kau's Shipyard. The majority of the housing had no inside plumbing. Women trudged to public water spigots several times each day. They filled pails with water for cooking, drinking, and bathing. Even so, the refugees endured frequent water shortages; the Japanese controlled Hong Kong's water supply from the mainland.[20]

Until 1939, between 60 percent and 70 percent of war materials reaching the Nationalists in Hong Kong arrived in Kowloon via Canton on trains and on junks. Thus, the Japanese military viewed ships like Halliburton's with suspicion, as they could have been used to supply enemies of the Empire. That he was an American writer provided zero immunity. The government knew foreign writers and journalists wrote anti-Japanese propaganda. Consequently, they faced the possibility of arrest and deportation.[21]

War was on Halliburton's mind. He read the English-language press and knew how Orson Welles had panicked countless Americans with his "War of the Worlds" broadcast and that in Nazi Germany, Jews suffered from increasing violence. In Asia, by the end of the year, President Franklin Roosevelt would approve lending Chiang Kai-shek $25 million, further provoking Japan's ire against America and thereby endangering Americans in Japan. Still, in his letters home, Halliburton downplayed the danger, insisting, "the war is hardly noticed here" and that "life seems normal in every way."[22] He sought to calm his parents, particularly his father, who also thought a lot about Amelia Earhart.

She had vanished over the Pacific some ten months earlier. His father was also anxious about the impending war. In truth, Richard harbored no such illusions about the Japanese menace. He wrote about "torpedo season" and the brutality of the Japanese Army, but he banished such thoughts from his mind. He had no time for fear.

Halliburton worked out a precise timetable that would ensure he leave for San Francisco on New Year's Day 1939. That was in less than three months' time. The writer allotted no more than sixty days total for the work: forty-five for the workers to lay the keel and finish the hull, fifteen more to rig the three sails and train the crew. Of course, Halliburton should have known better. First, he was at the mercy of Fat Kau, the builder's four wives who worked in the shipyard, and all the carpenters in Fat Kau's employ. Second, Halliburton had to supervise his own crew. Welch and von Fehren knew what to do, but the other men would need direction when they arrived. Last, he could guarantee neither the cooperation of the weather nor the on-time shipment of building supplies.

Halliburton started awake every morning feeling the ticktock of his deadline. Upon leaving Walter Gaines Swanson's office that late summer afternoon, he had given his word that he would arrive in time for the Golden Gate Exposition's opening, less than a month from now. The tight time frame forced Halliburton to devise ways to make construction progress as efficiently as possible. For example, he persuaded the builders to stop hand-sawing every plank and piece of timber and instead carry the lumber to a nearby sawmill.[23] Sometimes he thought he would be stuck at the shipyard for ten more months rather than arriving at Treasure Island when he was due.[24]

And so Fat Kau's was a hive of activity, day in, and day out. Halliburton snapped instructions to his translator in English, punctuated with short bursts of Mandarin. His wishes sometimes got lost in translation, but by and large the work continued smoothly . . . until the morning Halliburton approached the shipyard only to see a black cloud billowing through the air. The acrid smoke burned his eyes and nose. Flames shot into the sky. Despairing that all was lost, he blamed the carpenters. "Why did the Chinese have to be such infuriating fools!" he wrote in one of his letters.[25] Had Halliburton known anything about shipbuilding, he would have known the carpenters were bonding the planking to make it conform to the curve of the hull. To do this, the carpenters first balanced each thirty-foot plank across two sawhorses six feet apart. Then they weighted down the ends with stones and built a bonfire under the middle. Whenever the plank caught fire someone doused it with water.

The *Sea Dragon*'s hull took shape. Though Halliburton said he wanted the boat built in what he described as "the ancient manner," he made certain concessions to modernity, such as using iron bolts instead of wooden pegs.[26] His addition of several unconventional touches, including a large saloon and skylights, also departed from tradition.

After the carpenters finished the keel, Halliburton threw them a raucous party, though not because he was a gracious host. The workers had walked off the lot, leaving Halliburton rather flummoxed. For the life of him, he couldn't understand what had instigated the walkout. He asked Fat Kau. The chubby shipwright laughed at Halliburton's unfamiliarity with local customs. "Ship-owners always give a party when the keel is laid—the men expect it," he told Halliburton.[27] If Halliburton wanted work to resume, he'd better treat the carpenters to a little merriment, advised the shipwright. For nine dollars Halliburton bought barrels and baskets of Chinese food, and enough rice wine to float the *Sea Dragon*. The fifty men working on the job got drunk, very drunk. "And then—the climax of the evening—they all helped themselves to opium. Without the opium, so I was told, no party was worth being invited to."[28] Satisfied, the carpenters returned to work the next day and redoubled their efforts; "the pounding, sawing and nailing could be heard from afar."[29]

Every once in a while, Halliburton stopped and considered his surroundings—the way the birds dipped and soared above the harbor, the constant jostle of people on the wharf. He watched and wrote about the shipyard for his newspaper articles. "It sprawled along the waterfront in a wild confusion of timbers, bamboo poles, babies, old cannon, cooking fires, carpenters, and wives. Hens roosted on the big two-man saws.

Tailless cats prowled, slant-eyed, among the logs of teak and camphor work. Cached in every cranny were the workmen's bed-rolls—for all the workmen sleep at the job at night."[30]

Thanksgiving approached. Smells of sawdust, not pie crust, filled the air. Halliburton agonized. Fat Kau was overscheduled and the project was running over budget. Lately Halliburton noticed Welch lacked not only boatbuilding expertise but also management skills.

What had begun with such promise was now mired in frustration; it brought to mind the problems he had had with Hangover House. He wrote home of his growing irritation with the Chinese shipbuilders. His letter painted the workers in broad-brush strokes of generalization and stereotypes. "The Chinese do everything backwards and everything slow. Even so, local people say our progress is astonishing. The entire skeleton of the junk is almost finished," he wrote.[31]

Meanwhile, Mooney threw himself into the subscription letter project with gusto. "He works harder than anybody and pulls more than his own weight," Halliburton wrote his parents.[32] A quick study, Mooney mastered the mimeograph machine. He couldn't control the movement of the junk on the sea, so Halliburton asked his readers to forgive him if the print was a touch blurry.[33]

At last the rest of his crew arrived. Some had had a rougher journey than others. Gordon Torrey's trip from Bar Harbor, Maine, to Hong Kong was an adventure in and of itself. On the morning of September 21, he caught the train from Bangor to New York. "The 1938 New England hurricane hit that morning. What a trip! When I finally got to New York I had a fairly good idea what to expect from a typhoon, if we were ever to encounter one," Torrey said.[34] Torrey met up with George Barstow and the pair then went west, arriving in Hong Kong on December 1. Potter and Chase arrived two weeks later.

Halliburton introduced the four Americans to the rest of the crew, including Jim Sligh, a cook whom Halliburton had hired in Hong Kong. Sligh had cooked on the ships of at least a dozen nations. George Petrich, a radio operator who had previously worked on the Matson Line, joined them as well.

The crewmembers rented rooms in a boarding house near the ship-yard. At first they all got along, relatively speaking. A real gentleman, von Fehren put everyone at ease, able to joke and talk with each member of the crew. Welch, on the other hand, was starting to show himself to be ornery and temperamental. A dictatorial streak ran through the sailor, which immediately grated on the four college students. Halliburton forgave his captain this quirk, deciding it wasn't necessarily a poor trait for a sea captain. There would come a time when his word was the only word that would matter.[35]

Tension soon radiated from the shipyard. The stress affected the crew; they wondered if it might affect the trip's success.[36] They became increasingly querulous. Small factions formed. The college students banded together in one group, the Chinese crew in another. Welch hated Mooney and Mooney hated Welch. The captain's animosity stemmed from his open disapproval of Halliburton and Mooney's relationship, "but he [Welch] wanted the money and so did it [the job]."[37] The boisterous, but amiable, sea dog who had traveled with Halliburton aboard the *President Coolidge* had vanished. There was also some grow-ing friction between Halliburton and Mooney, according to Torrey, who noticed that the author was spending a fair amount of time with a Chinese man; Torrey assumed the man was Halliburton's lover.[38]

Eager to avoid clashes, Potter and Torrey decamped from the board-inghouse and moved to another in Kowloon to escape Welch's outbursts. Von Fehren remained content so long as he kept his interactions with Welch to a minimum. "The captain and engineer still hate each other and it takes all my diplomacy to keep them working together," Hal-liburton wrote home.[39] Likening Captain Welch to Captain William Bligh of the HMS *Bounty*, he complained to his parents that it was wearying to play the detached mediator.

Just as Halliburton's manuscripts required rewriting, the *Sea Dragon* required several remodels. The carpenters tore up the ship's interior at least four times. The final time was to install the engine where the main cabin had been. It was the only way to balance the junk and carve out a little more living room. They needed quarters for twelve people and storage space for ten weeks' worth of food and water. Every bit of available space would be packed with equipment, supplies, and crew. The diesel engine took up a lot of room, leaving little space for the spare fuel tanks. Halliburton planned to use only the engine, which could power the boat through the water at 5.5 knots, for entering and leaving ports and in the event of an emergency.[40]

Halliburton would not share a cabin with Mooney. Instead he chose to share it with "the finest and jolliest and fattest statue of Tai Toa Fat that could be found anywhere in Hong Kong."[41] Two additional cabins were located over the stairs on the poop deck. Welch got one and the other served as the chart room. The four college students shared one four-bunk cabin. The engineer, radioman, and Mooney shared another. The cook and cabin boy were assigned in a space toward the bow. Their mascots, two white Chinese kittens, would have the run of the vessel.

Of the college graduates who joined Halliburton, Potter and Torrey kept the most detailed account of their time in Hong Kong. Their letters home and recollections in their hometown newspapers reveal complicated feelings toward the famous author. Idolization gave way to mounting irritation, bordering on contempt. For Torrey, meeting the man behind the legend was like pulling the curtain back on the Wizard of Oz. "Having read his books when younger, I was disappointed with the real article and lost interest in the potential association, with him and the junk trip, when it finally materialized in the form it did," Torrey said.[42]

Additionally, the writer's tendency to occasionally disappear from the construction site irritated both Torrey and Potter. They couldn't imagine whom Halliburton was meeting or what he was doing; Halliburton shared none of his private life with his crew, save for Mooney. And so for the Dartmouth men, Halliburton "was not particularly fun to be with or too sociable with us."[43] What the two didn't know was that

Halliburton visited an orphanage run by a woman from Long Island, New York. He also favored the cocktails at the Hong Kong Hotel bar.

And sometimes he just needed to steal the occasional moment to meander alone through Hong Kong's winding streets and alleyways. Shop signs hung from posts like flags. An inveterate collector of souvenirs, he hunted for trinkets to send home to Memphis. He wanted his parents and Ammudder to receive their Christmas gifts on time. He wished he could see his mother beam when she unwrapped the mah-jongg set, which was nestled inside a red lacquer box with a tray, and he knew his father would appreciate the cigarette box. He also sent china horses, ivory Buddha statues, and the ebony stands on which to display them. Inside another package, he sent one or two of the few thousand *Sea Dragon* models he planned to sell at the fair. It can only be seen in photographs, as no existing models remain.[44] One black-and-white print shows a Mary Lou Davis and her two children, Dorothy and Tommy. They stand before the front door of Hangover House, where they would live for nearly a year. In the snapshot the three pose with one of the junk models.[45]

As the weeks passed, Torrey, with his many years of experience sailing Maine's restless waters, watched the *Sea Dragon*'s construction with more than a soupçon of unease. He couldn't believe how the junk was "left wide open below from stem to stern" to accommodate the diesel engine and elaborate living and office space below decks. He didn't think three watertight bulkheads were enough to contain flooding should there be a breach in the hull. Torrey was apprehensive the boat would sink under typhoon conditions, which were not unusual in the western Pacific.[46]

Then, there was the design. Torrey considered it garish and impractical. "To have it pictorially Chinese, as an exhibit item, it was given a Soochow river-type junk spoon bow and a great, towering poop section aft, to accommodate the painted dragon. Both features being unsuitable for off-shore work, particularly the type of conditions a trans-Pacific crossing involves."[47] Lastly, there was a long trunk-type raised section to accommodate glass skylights so the junk could have "nice working light during days in the below deck area."

But Halliburton had very definite ideas about the boat's decoration, supervising the work like a set designer. He enjoyed choosing the paint colors and the ornamentation. He loved watching how the bamboo scaffolding rose like an exoskeleton around the boat and how workers scrambled over the upper decks like acrobats. Painters hoisted buckets of red, black, yellow, and white paint up a pulley attached to the upper scaffolding. He looked at the junk like a giant canvas and imagined it graced with fantastical pictures, so bright they'd be visible in the night.

Two enormous, fire-spitting dragons, painted on each side of the soaring poop, writhed upward as though trying to climb the mizzen mast. On the stern, the three-foot gilded Chinese characters—*Sea Dragon, Hong Kong*—gleamed in the moonlight. One flag flew from each of the three masts, an orange fore sail, a white mainsail, and a scarlet mizzen. He had already crated the typical mat sails and sent them ahead on a San Francisco-bound steamer. He would change sails once on Treasure Island.[48]

Every junk bore a pair of "eyes" on its bow. According to custom, the eyes helped boats see through any weather, day or night. Halliburton ordered a set measuring thirty inches in diameter. He wanted the *Sea Dragon* to wear the "finest and biggest eyes possible." A carver spent two days shaping the ovals from camphor-tree logs, and it took four men to lift the wooden eyes into place and nail them to the hull. Fat Kau explained only a trial run could reveal whether the eyes were properly positioned. If the junk ran into storms, or if things went poorly, it meant the eyes "have seen badly, and taken the wrong course."[49] They would need to be moved.

With all the strain, Halliburton unsurprisingly felt a bit of schadenfreude upon learning another junk had washed ashore off Formosa (now Taiwan) in its bid to reach San Francisco. The buzz around the shipyard was its captain had left Shanghai for San Francisco on October 15 but was waylaid by a storm. Apparently its captain was forced to anchor in Hong Kong for a refitting before starting anew. His unfortunate "misadventures may cost him a month and give me ample time (with my engine) to get there first. For him to have arrived just before me would have been disastrous."[50]

Halliburton's livelihood depended on the *Sea Dragon* arriving first to the Golden Gate International Exposition. If he didn't, the fair sponsors would give away his berth. He would lose any chance at profiting from the sale of his models, tours of the bridges, and commercial concessions, and even turning the trip into a bestseller would be in jeopardy.

Halliburton was pleased to run into Charles Jokstad. The captain of the *President Pierce* happened to be in Hong Kong. The two had met more than a decade before when an emboldened young Halliburton tried to stowaway on Jokstad's ship. Rather than boot him from the ship, Jokstad let the youth earn his keep with bucket and mop. They laughed at the memory and went out for lunch to catch up on the years since. Jokstad had liked the "personable, adventurous young author" and had read his books.[51]

Halliburton respected Jokstad. Born in Norway, Jokstad immigrated to the United States at age fourteen and then became the youngest captain in the US Merchant Marine. He went on to captain passenger cruise liners and author several books, including *The Captain and the Sea*. Jokstad accepted Halliburton's invitation to examine the junk.

The captain walked around the *Sea Dragon*, surveying its exterior. "Carved, gilded, and painted in dazzling colors, it was the gaudiest thing on the waterfront," Jokstad thought.[52] Just as they were about to board the junk, an eight-inch rat scampered off the gangplank onto the wharf and straight into a heaping pile of trash. Jokstad asked Halliburton if he too saw the obese rodent. He had. It was, Jokstad added, bad luck. "It is a superstition among the white race that when rats walk off a vessel it ordinarily means the vessel will go down with all hands," he said.[53]

Jokstad continued inspecting. He didn't speak the entire time, only nodded to himself now and again. He looked everywhere. In the cabins and in the chart room. In the supply room and in the galley. He examined the bolts and the portholes. He noted the rigging and the engine. Welch followed closely, angry at what he considered a rude intrusion.

Jokstad's review exposed numerous design flaws and he enumerated each and every one of them to Halliburton. To start, there wasn't enough ballast in the keel. If the winds were high enough, the junk would tip or heel. It might capsize. The heavy diesel engine wasn't securely mounted to the ribs. The rudder stuck out too far; a strong wind could snap it in half with no more effort than it took a breeze to snap a twig. The rigging was not only poorly secured to the ship, it was secured to the vessel with leg screws when it should have been bolted straight through the planking. Jokstad faulted the glass ports; a gale would smash them to smithereens.

No, Jokstad thought, this ship was most definitely not seaworthy. Welch listened with barely concealed rage. Other members of the crew, including Torrey, Potter, and Chase, had also followed the captain. Their faces turned chalk white when they heard Jokstad pronounce the vessel unfit to reach California.

Jokstad made numerous recommendations. Neither sailor nor shipwright, Halliburton promised to get to work on the repairs, though he told Jokstad he had spent all his money. At least he would nail some boards across the portholes. But Halliburton had been bitten by the bug of overconfidence, and Jokstad doubted any of the changes would be made. Jokstad's gut twisted. He had a feeling he'd never again see the author.[54]

Later, the *Coolidge*'s Captain Collins assessed the *Sea Dragon* in an article for the US Naval Institute's magazine *Proceedings*. The junk's hull was constructed of sound wood. Galvanized iron bolts held the hardwood frames in place. But Halliburton's decision to raise the height of the poop deck eight feet made the *Sea Dragon* extremely difficult to handle in heavy weather. Its masts were too high and its sails too large.[55]

Jokstad and Collins weren't the only ones harboring reservations about the junk's construction. British naval officers drinking in the Hong Kong Hotel mercilessly teased Halliburton. They told the writer if the boat didn't sink within minutes of leaving the harbor, the Japanese would blow it sky-high.

In all his letters, to his parents as well as the *Sea Dragon* letters he sent to children, Halliburton showed not one whit of concern.

"People have asked if my shipmates and I are not reckless—trying to sail a clumsy junk across the Pacific, and in winter. If they know (as I have learned) how seaworthy junks can be, they would not consider our expedition so perilous. The season and the small-ness of our ship multiply the hazards, it is true; but the *type* of our ship reduces them," he wrote in a *Sea Dragon* letter from Shanghai.[56] He reminded readers that for the four thousand years junks had navigated Chinese waters there had been scarcely any changes made to their design. He wrote that they were among the most seaworthy of vessels, capable of sailing between sixty and seventy miles a day.

He confided in his readers that it wasn't just the construction that was difficult, so was managing the different personalities. At this point, the crew certainly had had its share of screaming matches, Halliburton said. More than once someone had vowed to leave the expedition and board the next available boat for America. But as the departure date approached, those vows to leave the expedition were forgotten. Harmony was restored. "Once we're at sea, fighting the Pacific in our cockleshell, the common struggle will probably draw us even closer together," Halliburton wrote home.[57]

None of the fighting shows in photographs taken during this time; they convey joviality and determination. Halliburton planned to bring on a professional cameraman when the ship reached Honolulu. Until then, he and his crew shot both stills and film. Chase, who took the most footage, mailed the reels to his brother in Milton, Massachusetts. He in turn colorized the black-and-white film.

A snippet of the film now plays on an endless loop in the library at Rhodes College in Memphis, Tennessee. The stuttering footage depicts several scenes. The Dartmouth graduates in dress pants and collared shirts, sometimes with sleeves rolled up. The crew with arms around each other's shoulders, proud and tall. Halliburton standing protectively behind the group, his arms crossed. His close-mouthed smile tired and worn.

Shortly before the *Sea Dragon*'s trial run, Halliburton stopped in a small temple located near the shipyard. Halliburton might not have been a religious man, but he respected tradition. It was time for the opening of the eyes ceremony. Halliburton invited the priest to perform the ritual. He wore white-and-yellow robes and a large black square hat. He carried a tom-tom in one hand, incense in the other. Walking about the deck, the priest beat his drum loudly. One by one he fixed paper prayers to the mast. He bathed the eyes in *samchu*, Chinese rice wine. Next, the priest threaded a three-foot-long string of firecrackers. Dressed in a white turtleneck, scarf, and double-breasted peacoat, Halliburton ignited the explosives. Incense burned. One hand lightly holding a rope, Halliburton peered into the bright sunshine. Stress etched his face. The great eyes dripped wine, the firecrackers popped, and the junk slipped into the bay.

Nearly a year before Halliburton set sail on the *Sea Dragon*, he received a letter from Dick Halliburton Wells, a little boy who lived in Hinesville, Georgia. He was not related to Halliburton, just named for him. "Dear Mr. Halliburton, School has closed at last, and am I glad! Aren't you glad you do not have to go to school? We hope to read your last books soon. I'd like to travel and write like you do. It must be fun. Don't let your boat sink coming across the Pacific."[58]

12

So Good-bye Again

RATHER THAN ENJOY A late New Year's Day breakfast, Richard Halliburton and his crew, most of whom were "the greenest of green crews," boarded the *Sea Dragon*.[1] It was time to put the *Sea Dragon* through its paces on the open sea. The crew also needed experience handling the junk in real time.[2]

Halliburton believed Captain Jack Welch could sail the *Sea Dragon* in his sleep.[3] He had only confidence in Henry von Fehren, a veteran engineer. John "Brue" Potter had enough sailing experience in his twenty-five years to serve responsibly as first mate. And he felt certain Gordon Torrey and Robert Chase too possessed the necessary skills. "But the rest of us! A piano student, a journalist, and myself—scarcely know port from starboard," Halliburton said, referring to George Barstow and Paul Mooney.[4] Another American, Richard L. Davis, was newly signed on.

The diesel engine rumbled to life. As it was a test run, few people stood on the pier and watched the junk slowly move through the fishing boats. Halliburton stood on the deck next to Welch. Joining him were Barstow, Potter, Chase, and Torrey. Once the *Sea Dragon* cleared the harbor, Welch ordered von Fehren to kill the engine. He called for the raising of the orange foresail. Next he ordered the crew to hoist the enormous snow-white mainsail. Last, the small scarlet mizzen fluttered into place. The three sails caught a brisk wind and the *Sea Dragon* tasted the sea.

228

The whitecaps galloped like Lipizzaner stallions. Beautiful to look at, but more than most could handle. Soon the cabin boy, Mooney, and even Halliburton lay on the polished teak deck. "I—the world's worst sailor—lay prone on the deck, praying for a wreck, a pirate attack, or for Doomsday, for anything, in fact that would end this oscillation."[5] Barstow was one of the few still standing. He filmed the ship as it rode the swells, sneaking in a few shots of the crew as they heaved over the rail. "We could gladly have killed him, only we didn't have the strength," Halliburton wrote in the first of his *Sea Dragon* subscription letters.[6]

Welch paid the ailing crew no mind. His only concern was handling the junk. The ship slanted and heaved. The timbers groaned and the rigging creaked. There was nothing unusual about that, but he did not like how the heavy diesel engine weighed down the junk, causing it to run deep in the water. He also would have preferred the ship to respond more quickly to the rudder. Finally, several leaks sprang in the hull.

A few hours later, once they were back in port, Welch, von Fehren, and Halliburton sat together. It didn't take a detective to decipher what was wrong with the *Sea Dragon*. They made a list of every weak point in the junk, but overall they felt the junk was nearly ready. "We've lost the last vestige of uneasiness we may have had about her seaworthiness," Halliburton wrote home.[7]

Halliburton could speak for himself, thought Fat Kau. Upon reaching the harbor and feeling solid ground beneath his feet once again, the shipwright declared he would never again sail in a junk.[8] He accompanied Halliburton on the sea trial, along with his third wife, who spent most of the trip moaning and groaning. A shawl wrapped around her head, her seasickness paled next to his.

Fat Kau promised to get started on the repairs straight away. Halliburton estimated it would take at least seven days to caulk some of the seams and refit the equipment. He just wanted to make sure none of the repairs would detract from the *Sea Dragon*'s aesthetics. "If we can just hold on to the gay colors till we get to San Francisco, we'll be a real sensation. . . . I've lost none of my enthusiasm," he wrote home.[9]

Halliburton might not have lost his enthusiasm, but after the trial run some of the young crew were decidedly less keen about the endeavor. Torrey worried the *Sea Dragon* was a floating catastrophe. He knew hundreds of junks had crossed the Pacific, some larger than the *Sea Dragon*, some smaller. But those boats were designed for that single purpose: to cross swiftly and safely. They didn't have skylights and they didn't have diesel engines that were too heavy. They didn't have a poop deck built so high the ship's balance was threatened. As far as the Dartmouth graduate was concerned, Halliburton put too much importance on realizing his artistic and creature comfort fantasies and not enough attention on sound design and construction.[10]

Torrey feared the *Sea Dragon* would be in a grim situation were it to face the kind of rough seas he'd experienced on his way to Hong Kong while crossing the Formosa Strait aboard a passenger ship. He predicted that even in moderate seas a wave could wash right over the junk's low bow, potentially shattering the skylights and swamping the lower deck. The added weight of the diesel engine would send the boat plummeting to the ocean floor. "In Admiralty law parlance, I feel it could be alleged that both the vessel and the crew were 'unseaworthy,'" Torrey later wrote.[11]

Torrey took Potter, Chase, and Barstow aside. He tried convincing his peers to back out of the trip. They were uninterested in what he had to say. For one, Potter's sizable financial investment in the project made it difficult for him to leave. "Naturally this led to unpleasantness and I became disassociated from the others," Torrey recalled almost fifty years later. He was left alone to wrestle with his dread.[12]

Meanwhile, Halliburton, Welch, and von Fehren continued tackling the long list of repairs. The work strained the already tense crew; they clashed more than usual. Halliburton held his tongue and acted as the rudder, carefully steering between the captain and crew. He trusted the group would settle down once they got underway. No matter what people said about the junk, he would never call it quits. He had a reputation to maintain and anyway, the drama added the right burst of color to his articles and would help sell his planned book on the adventure. Halliburton would let readers "follow him around the earth and back again . . . on wings, on foot, on camels, elephants, carts, and autos . . . flying, riding, swimming, fighting, laughing his way through man's immortal treasure-house of romance and adventure."[13]

But before his readers could follow him, he needed to take a break from all things *Sea Dragon*. As he sailed halfway across the earth with notebook in his coat pocket, Halliburton headed north to Canton. He wanted to bear witness to the continuing carnage.[14] Like a dagger, the Japanese Army pierced the heart of the river port city eight days after landing on the coast. Prior to the October invasion, the Japanese Air Force had bombed the city without respite for weeks, the bombs turning the city, and thousands of its civilians, into rubble and ash. Hundreds of thousands of more Cantonese fled, hoping to melt into the countryside. For three days and three nights survivors trudged along the pockmarked roads to Hong Kong, swaddled in so many layers they no longer looked human. These were the refugees Halliburton had seen upon reaching Hong Kong last November.

Finding transportation took a dash of ingenuity and more than a dollop of enterprise. The Japanese stopped permitting foreign commercial ships near the city several weeks before Halliburton decided to make the trip. For more than twelve years, the *Mindanao*, an American river gunboat, had cruised between Hong Kong and Canton, protecting American ships from piracy. After Japan seized Canton, the gunboat was charged with guarding American neutrality. Taking on civilians was outside its mission. However, always persuasive, Halliburton convinced the captain to ferry him the ten hours up the coast. He didn't quite absorb what he was seeing.

"Canton was proud of its wide avenues, and of the dense care-free throngs that once filled them. But walking along them now, between charred and blackened ruins, one sees scarcely a single hint of life. Some of the streets are lined with trees. Even these, the fire has scorched to death. The trees stand, but they are lifeless and black," Halliburton wrote of the city he had last visited in 1922.[15]

Like he had done during his time in the Soviet Union, Halliburton showed a reporter's instinct to capture emotion without being emotional. His writing was spare, devoid of the flowery prose so prevalent in most of his books. He was eager to send it stateside, but knew he had to wait until he at least reached Macao, a Portuguese port about thirty miles from Hong Kong. The Japanese rigorously censored the mail, and sending it from Canton would surely attract unwanted attention.

Meanwhile, back in Hong Kong, Barstow, Chase, Potter, and Torrey roamed the city's warren-like streets. They rode the funicular tramway up the thirteen-hundred-foot-high Victoria Peak and enjoyed the broad vistas; below, the ships in the harbor looked like models. They shot rolls of films and took in street theater.[16]

Mooney spent much of this time alone. He hadn't accompanied Halliburton to Canton and he didn't particularly like the college graduates. After watching them in action he wrote, "One boy a Connecticut Yankee of the worst [sort]; another longing for his habitual background of zebra stripes at El Morocco; still another fresh (how!) from Dartmouth and full of anti-Roosevelt jokes."[17] But having Mooney in Hong Kong was vital to Halliburton; he was a calming presence "and I love him for that," he wrote home.[18]

Once back in Hong Kong, Halliburton checked in with Welch and von Fehren. All the repairs seemed to be on track; however, a new development vexed the two men. Each day scores of curious people descended on the pier, eager for a glimpse of Hong Kong's most famous junk. "The ship has tremendous box-office appeal. So be happy, and proud of the expedition, and don't worry one minute about any danger."[19] There were so many people climbing on and around the junk it resembled "a floating crazy-house."[20] Halliburton hired guards to stop gawkers from getting in the way.

Among those in the crowd vying for a glimpse of the Sea Dragon was twenty-eight-year-old Robert Pullen of California. A former member of the merchant marine, the bushy-bearded amateur photographer stood before the ship in wonderment. Halliburton's bestselling books were among his favorites. Spying the author on deck, Pullen called up and asked for permission to come aboard. Halliburton waved him on.

As he crossed the gangway, the photographer buttoned his woolen peacoat against the raw, damp air. He eyed the rigging and admired the colorful artwork on the ship's hull. Pullen pointed his Kodak-style folding camera at the *Sea Dragon*. He shot picture after picture on 2½-by-4¼-inch black-and-white film. His close-up photographs show the junk in stunning detail. The *Sea Dragon* and homeport of Hong Kong emblazoned in Chinese characters stand out below a yin-and-yang symbol. The elaborate painted image of a phoenix soars next to several Chinese mythological scenes. Horses prance and the dragon looks ready to claw its way up and over the rails.

Pullen jealously guarded the negative and print for the remainder of his life. His daughter donated the photo to Halliburton's alma mater Princeton University upon her father's death.[21]

On February 5 at 4:00 PM, just before the *Sea Dragon* shook off its lines, Halliburton sounded three blasts on its electric horn. As it inched away from the wharf, he telegrammed his parents: "Junk Sea Dragon Via San Francisco Have Sailed Next Port Keelung Formosa Alls Well High Spirits Love."[22] Halliburton and his crew also sent jubilant radio messages to their respective families. The families radioed back their congratulations. For good measure, Halliburton burned an extra stick of thanksgiving incense before the shrine of the ship's good-luck god.

Halliburton perused the checklist. There was enough oil to fuel their auxiliary engine for ten days. The three-month supply of food for twelve men and two thousand gallons of fresh water were stowed in the galley. In case of pirates, an arsenal of shotguns stood locked in a cabinet; only Halliburton and Welch had the keys. Last, he patted his trousers' pocket and felt for his letter from the Japanese government requesting safe passage.[23]

Slowly, the *Sea Dragon* made for the harbor entrance. Its orange foresail flapped cheerily in the breeze. Halliburton was pleased and relieved. "This was the day I had waited for and worked for, these many months. The discouragements, the quarrels, the despair that had hung over us for the long period of shipbuilding and outfitting vanished. In the battle with bills and Chinese procrastinations, the words romance and adventure had faded from our vocabularies. But now, in one exhilarating moment, these words came back again," he wrote.[24]

This photo of the *Sea Dragon* was taken by Robert Pullen, twenty-eight-year-old amateur photographer. It has never before been published. *Princeton University Library*

Victoria Peak slid from view in the warm twilight. On their way out, Halliburton nodded at several fishermen who stared unbelieving at the *Sea Dragon* with its bat-like sails. "One entire fleet of fishers crept close to stare, to exclaim, to shout at us and find out if we were real," Halliburton wrote.[25]

A brilliant moon floated above. All through the night the crew kept a sharp lookout for the Japanese Navy and pirates. They saw neither. In fact, the crew saw nothing more than fishing junks and passenger ships. This surprised them. Over the radio they learned there were numerous Japanese liners, battleships, and freighters in the vicinity. There were also rumors that Japanese were indiscriminately sinking junks. Not for the last time did Halliburton wonder if his letters from Japanese officials would offer any real protection.

Welch planned to sail up the China coast, following the main steamship line. He would turn east toward Keelung.[26]

The stars fell away. Dawn came. They had covered one hundred miles in fourteen hours. Giddy with optimism, Halliburton started running the numbers in his head. He figured if they covered at least 170 miles a day, or 1,190 miles a week, they could reach San Francisco in less than seven weeks.

His optimism was premature. During the second day at sea they made no progress; a lighthouse they had passed on the China coast the day before was still within view. Welch changed course and headed southeast, thinking it best to sail around the southern tip of Formosa rather than the northern. At midnight, or very nearly close to it, a vicious monsoon raced in from the northeast. Black clouds broke Halliburton's reverie and extinguished the sun. Roiling seas threatened to overtake the vessel. The winds lashed. Everything and anything not fastened down rolled and flew about the ship. The two kittens mewled and the two Chow dogs, new additions, whimpered. In the galley, pots and pans clattered to the floor. The noise was ear splitting. Patrick Kelly, the seventeen-year-old mess boy, lay with his knees curled into his chest. Born in Canton to an American father and a Portuguese mother, Kelly desperately wanted to see America. He possessed a US passport and so Halliburton took him aboard, after warning him of the "terrors ahead."[27]

"We were heading into a storm," Halliburton wrote.[28]

Welch gripped the wheel and held steady. The wind tore the radio aerial from the mizzenmast. The wire struck like a cobra. Meanwhile, Ben Flagg, another new hire, sat in the bosun's chair. A gust nearly sent the recent Bowdoin College graduate airborne. Regaining his balance, Flagg grabbed the mast and held fast, his knuckles white. He tried to nail the thrashing aerial in place. Flagg was a crewmember aboard the *President Pierce* but had missed his ship in Hong Kong. "We practically shanghaied him aboard our junk," Halliburton said.[29] Flagg stopped the aerial from slicing anyone.

Welch shouted. His bark cut through the din—someone needed to turn the auxiliary engine on full power. He yelled for someone to close the engine room hatch. Even so, the fumes from the freshly painted tanks and bulkheads seeped through to the main cabin. The crew started coughing.

Every time the hull leaned too hard, the portholes rolled under water. Once again the hull sprouted leaks.[30]

Then first mate Potter fell sick with what they thought might be acute appendicitis. Actually he sustained a smashed rib and a few sprained muscles when the boom of the staysail struck him while the ship yawed.[31] Halliburton told him to rest. One by one the crew went down. Torrey injured himself on the boom. Mooney fell down the hatch and broke his ankle.

All the while the weather continued its assault. The elephant-gray clouds were now jet black, the sheet of rain was unremitting. Halliburton took turns standing watch with Flagg, Barstow, and Chase. Four hours on. Four hours off. Day and night. In pairs. Two men were needed to hold the course in this weather. After a time their oilskins no longer shielded them from the force of spray and rain. They were wet and miserable in this rain-soaked world. All the while Potter languished on his bunk, his condition worsening.

But "nothing seemed able, really, to discourage us. We knew what we were in for, when we set out to cross the Pacific in a junk. We also knew that just as our first idyllic day had run its course and passed—so would this cursed storm. Then the sea and wind would calm down, and we'd soon forget how miserable we'd been."[32]

The junk was now about fifty miles from the southern tip of Formosa. Welch counted on passing through the worst of the storm in a few more hours. He hoped everyone could hang on for just a little longer.

It was not to be. Potter had not been able to keep down water or food. Alarmed at how ill the Mainer looked, Halliburton and Welch conferred. Keelung, on the northern tip of Formosa, was the next possible port, three hundred miles away. While they considered taking Potter there, they knew the Japanese might turn down their request to anchor.

And refuse him they did. Halliburton's request came shortly after the *President Hoover*, an American Dollar Line ship, had run ashore in the vicinity. The Japanese suspected the *Hoover*'s accident was a ruse to put American spies ashore in the heavily fortified area. "They distrusted Halliburton and were under the impression that his desire to put me ashore was simply another hoax to land an agent," Potter later said.[33]

Deciding to forge ahead and hope for Japanese mercy was out of the question. If they tried for Keelung anyway and were still refused entry they wouldn't be able to stop until Midway Island, nearly four thousand miles away. By then it might be too late.

"One more look at Potter's flushed face and fevered eyes, and we voted to turn around. A life—and a very fine life—might be at stake. So we sung the tiller with a mighty swing, spun the ship about, and set our course back to China," Halliburton wrote.[34]

The *Sea Dragon* limped into the harbor under cover of darkness. Welch steered it around reefs until it reached the all too familiar wharf. "We were glad it was midnight, and that no one was on hand to see our ignominious return. . . . Before going ashore I glanced at our good-luck god, still sitting and smiling in his little temple. I decided it was a fake and a hoax," he wrote.[35]

Halliburton called for help when they reached the shore. He helped load Potter onto a gurney and watched the ambulance speed to a local hospital. A short while later, Halliburton arrived at the hospital with Mooney. He stayed at Mooney's side while doctors wrapped his partner's ankle in a cast. Mooney insisted on going back to the *Sea Dragon* even though he would have to hobble on crutches for at least three weeks.

From his hospital bed, Potter announced he would forgo his spot on the ship. It wasn't because he needed to recover. In truth, those few days on the *Sea Dragon* convinced the nephew and grandson of *Titanic* survivors that the junk would never reach California. He figured Halliburton's trip was a fool's errand. Potter returned to the States in the spring of 1939, whereupon he joined the US Navy. For the remainder of World War II, Potter served as an attaché to British naval intelligence in Bombay, India.[36]

Potter's leaving precipitated a domino effect among the young crew and all Halliburton could do was watch the exodus. The next to go was Torrey. That inner voice of doubt shouted for him to stay put; the passage was too risky. He spent the rest of 1939 in China working as an interpreter for a French journalist.[37] Next, Patrick Kelly resigned from the crew, telling Halliburton five days of seasickness was too much to bear. He would travel to America some other way, some other time. He couldn't envision one week aboard the *Sea Dragon*, let alone ten or more. Only Robert Chase and George Barstow stayed. Had they known what was to come, they too would have walked away.

A chastened Halliburton scrambled to find replacements. This time he wanted professional crewmembers so when he started again "we'll have two or three real seamen who know what to do."[38] Early one morning, when the author stopped at the dock to check on the progress and scout for potential new hires, he saw the *President Coolidge* tied next to the *Sea Dragon*. He asked Captain Dale Collins to spare some crew. The chief officer said no. Having seen the problems surrounding the *Sea Dragon* and the lack of experienced crew, he couldn't in good conscience recommend one of his men to Halliburton.

"The fact still remains that it certainly takes more than six days, or six weeks, to train landsmen into competent deep water sailormen," Collins later wrote. "Any sailor who has experienced the interminable

40-knot winds that blow off the Penghu Islands, off the northwest coast of Taiwan, from October to March, will know this is probably the last place in Asia to test an inexperienced crew in a new vessel."[39]

Again the *Sea Dragon* sat in dry dock. Halliburton decided to change the keel to a fin keel in order to move the ballast weight as low as possible in the water. He hoped the change would stop the ship from rolling too much. He knew the diesel engine was too heavy, but he did not have the luxury of time to sail across the great blue.

He also made sure Fat Kau's construction workers got busy spreading tar inside the hull to plug the leaks. "The delay has been exasperating, but I'm sure will add to our security, and to our ultimate success. I'm tired and impatient, of course, but in no way downhearted. Don't you be," a haggard Halliburton wrote to his parents, making sure to send them "hugs."[40]

The delay stretched on. One week turned into two. News of the German battleship *Bismarck*'s Valentine's Day launch reached the men. They heard that in San Francisco the Golden Gate Exposition opened with much pomp. Several more days passed. Then came Chinese New Year, and for four days Hong Kong ground to a standstill. Nothing sailed in or out of the harbor. Halliburton returned to his cheap but clean little backstreet hotel in Kowloon. Gordon Sinclair, the *Toronto Star* reporter who first met Halliburton at the Raffles Hotel in Singapore, happened to be in Hong Kong.

Sinclair trotted up the steps of the hotel and walked into the lobby. He looked around for a moment, his eyes passing over Halliburton. The change in Halliburton caught him off guard. Gone was the vibrant man of just a few years ago. Then Halliburton had been full of vim and vigor, ready to go snake hunting or meet a group of headhunters in the jungles of Borneo. Now he was a bundle of frayed nerves, sipping cans of tomato juice and popping vitamin pills.[41]

Sinclair knew all about Halliburton's woes. There were no secrets at the wharf. He knew Halliburton was having a hard time finding a replacement crew. He heard the *Sea Dragon* wasn't seaworthy. He knew about the personality conflicts and the interminable delays. "If anyone wishes to be driven rapidly and violently insane, and doesn't know how to go about it, let me make a suggestion: try building a Chinese junk in a Chinese shipyard during a war with Japan. From personal experience I know this to be a most effective method. In fact I don't see how it can fail—I'm a mental wreck," Halliburton wrote.[42]

The chatter on the waterfront filled Sinclair's ears. He heard how the junk's engine, extra water and fuel tanks, navigation equipment, and wireless made it too heavy for even a calm crossing of the mighty Pacific. He heard Halliburton's crew had virtually fled from the scene. He heard tell of raging fights between the captain and the remaining crew and of cowering mess boys. What was gossip and what was true, he didn't know. Regardless, something was clearly wrong.

"I imagine for every alleged expert who told me these grim predictions there were a dozen who told the same, or worse, to Halliburton," Sinclair said.[43]

Sinclair's account offers a different perspective from the one Halliburton presented to his reading public. His letters home and mimeographed copies of *Sea Dragon* letters maintained a facade of good cheer. In truth, the pressure threatened to consume the adventurer.

There was, however, a touch of good news. Around the time Halliburton reconnected with Sinclair, he hired three Chinese sailors: Sun Fook, Kiao Chu, and Wang Ching-huo. He also hired Liu Ah-shu as a mess boy. And in Velman Fitch of Minneapolis he hired one more. He believed this new, and professional, crew could feasibly slash between two and three weeks off his sailing time. For the first time in weeks a faint smile crooked his face.

Additionally, it was a relief knowing the weather would soon turn. Though they would have to sail through the stormy month of March, most of the passage would be during the calmer weeks of spring. Right now he banked on arriving in San Francisco sometime in mid-May. His last letter from his manager Wilfred Crowell reminded him of the big barge anchored in the small ships' basin at Treasure Island. A large sign reading RESERVED ANCHORAGE FOR HALLIBURTON'S *SEA DRAGON* hung for all to see.[44]

The *Sea Dragon*'s destination was the Golden Gate International Exposition in San Francisco. Halliburton was to dock the ship off Treasure Island, pictured here on this commemorative postcard. *Author's collection*

As a longtime Pan Am Clipper pilot, Horace Brock frequented the Asia route. So it was that on March 4, 1939, he found himself in Hong Kong on a layover. With time to spend, he strolled down to the waterfront to see Richard Halliburton and the *Sea Dragon*; he had followed the story in the papers and was thrilled to see the real thing. "The junk was a beautiful boat, maybe 50 to 60 feet long, all teak rubbed with Tung oil, no bottom paint, fully painted on the bow so it could see. Joss sticks were burning in the huge and elaborately decorated main saloon and all Chinese rituals to ensure a safe passage were rigorously complied with," Brock said.[45]

Halliburton and crew waved to the people ashore. Sinclair, who was soon leaving for Canada, stepped aboard the *Sea Dragon*. The men chatted for a few moments. Sinclair raised his camera and snapped a dozen or so pictures while a small group of Chinese looked at it with what he later described as "a peculiar lack of interest."[46] "On that last day I had a feeling that Richard Halliburton was pretty close to a nervous breakdown. His face was gaunt and lined and I couldn't coax one single smile for the last picture that was ever taken of him," he said.[47]

Then the time came for one last letter home. "We sail, again, in a few hours—far more seaworthy than before. The delay now has been heart breaking, but worth it. My spirits have sprung back again, now that we're getting away from Hong Kong and its troubles. I'm going to enjoy the trip and be happy I've gone to such an effort to make it. I'm in perfect health—if somewhat weary," Halliburton wrote. "So goodbye again—I'll radio you every few days, so you can enjoy and follow the voyage with me. Think of it as wonderful sport, and not as something hazardous and foolish. I embrace you all—and will give my sweet Mother an extra hug on her birthday. You know how much I love you.—R."[48]

The Hong Kong Observatory forecast easterly winds and overcast skies with drizzle and light rains.

The *Sea Dragon* shook off its moorings. The sun was a hazy smear in the sky above. Wearing a white sweater under a topcoat, Halliburton stood on the high stern and waved again.[49] Fine lines creased his eyes as he looked over the crowd. Airplanes flew overhead. A smattering of firecrackers popped in salute from the shore as the boat sailed out of Hong Kong harbor and headed northeast toward Formosa. Halliburton exhaled, knowing he would arrive on time in San Francisco—just.

Two days later, the March 6 edition of *South China Morning Post* ran a small news item about its departure. Twelve days later, the *Sea Dragon* sent a radiogram, presumably from Guam, requesting Clipper plane service forward any and all mail to Midway Island.[50] The *Sea Dragon* was due to reach the halfway point on or about April 5.

At the same moment, the *President Coolidge* was en route to Hong Kong from Hawaii. On March 19, Collins, the chief officer on the *Coolidge*, received a message from Halliburton and Welch. The *Sea Dragon* reported its location at 29.50 latitude and 144.20 longitude east, or about two thousand miles from Hong Kong. "All well left fourth (March) appreciate letter please keep contact outward."[51] The junk was still on course.

Collins and his captain, Karl A. Ahlin, examined the chart. They calculated that the *Coolidge* would pass fairly close to the *Sea Dragon* in about four days' time. On March 21, Ahlin wired Welch and Halliburton. If the weather cooperated, the *Coolidge* would stop, lower a boat, and supply the *Sea Dragon* with fresh provisions and water.

The *Sea Dragon* radioed its answer on March 23. Heavy northwest swells hinted at the weather to come. Welch cut the junk's speed to four knots. They looked forward to linking up with the *Coolidge*: "Happy to cooperate with you. Welch and Halliburton."[52]

In the space of a few hours, the weather intensified. Southerly gales and pounding waves thumped the *Sea Dragon*. The steady rain became a full-fledged storm. Miles away, the *Coolidge* plowed through gigantic seas. Collins cut the liner's speed from twenty knots to six knots, and then from six to a dead slow. As they were "experiencing very high seas," he ordered the passengers to remain confined in their bunks for their safety.[53]

The *Sea Dragon* kept going. It sailed straight into the onyx clouds and angry seas. The wind picked up, catching and tearing at the sails. It howled like a banshee. Welch fought against the heavy swells, some the height of a four-story building. Walls of water between forty and forty-five feet high crashed over the foredeck. Torrents of water gushed belowdecks. The crew slipped and skidded on the top deck. There was nowhere safe.

The *Coolidge* received the *Sea Dragon*'s final radio transmission reporting its position as twenty-four hundred miles west of Midway Island. "March 24 Radio: Captain John Welch of the Sea Dragon To Liner President Coolidge Southerly Gales Rain Squalls Lee Rail Under Water We Bunks Hardtack Bully Beef Having Wonderful Time Wish You were here instead of me."[54]

All through the night the radio operators on the *President Coolidge* tried to raise the junk. Silence. They put out a general call to all ships and stations, giving the *Sea Dragon*'s last known position, course, speed,

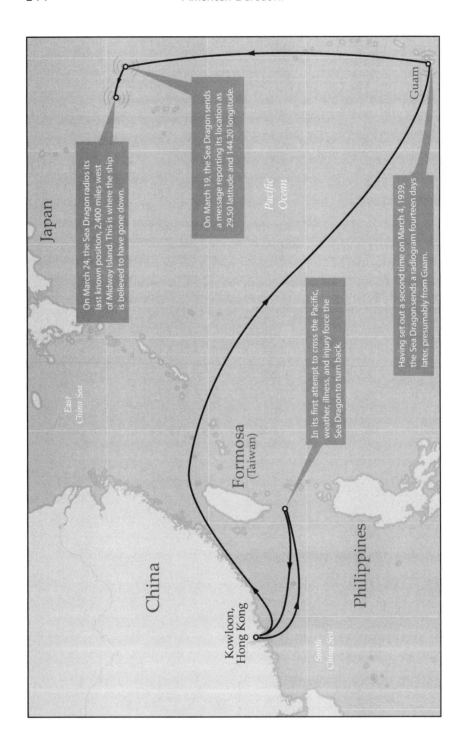

On March 24, the Sea Dragon radios its last known position, 2,400 miles west of Midway Island. This is where the ship is believed to have gone down.

On March 19, the Sea Dragon sends a message reporting its location as 29.50 latitude and 144.20 longitude.

In its first attempt to cross the Pacific, weather, illness, and injury force the Sea Dragon to turn back.

Having set out a second time on March 4, 1939, the Sea Dragon sends a radiogram fourteen days later, presumably from Guam.

Japan

China

Formosa
(Taiwan)

Philippines

Guam

Kowloon,
Hong Kong

Pacific
Ocean

East
China Sea

South
China Sea

and weather. All ships in the vicinity were advised to keep a sharp lookout for the junk and, if sighted, alert the *President Coolidge*, which would have been about three hundred miles from it.

The next morning the *Coolidge* was still diving into seas of "awe-inspiring heights, the waves curling and breaking at crests due to their excessive speed and height."[55] By noon the weather calmed just enough that Captain Ahlin was able to increase their speed to about fifteen knots. He sailed toward the last known position of the *Sea Dragon*. Double lookouts stood on each wing of the bridge and in the crow's nest.

An object was spotted: a large glass ball, the kind used by Japanese fishermen, bobbed innocently on the surface of the water.

13

No Trace

D AVID LAURANCE CHAMBERS DIALED the familiar Memphis phone
number. Each unanswered ring meant one more moment in Wesley and Nelle Halliburton's world where their oldest son still lived.

Nelle went inside from where she was sitting with her husband and picked up the phone. She wilted upon hearing the news. In the minutes and hours following, the grief slashed its way through every fiber of their being. It was as though their life had been sliced into three. In part one, there were four Halliburtons: Wesley Sr., Nelle, Richard, and Wesley Jr. In part two, Wesley Jr. died and Richard traveled the world, writing his way into fame. Now came part three, where though their two sons were gone, they remained parents all the same.

Editors and reporters across America stared in disbelief as the first reports of the author's disappearance came across the wire. AUTHOR LOST; RICHARD HALLIBURTON MISSING 5 DAYS, read the headline across the front page of the *Nevada State Journal*. In the *New York Times*: "No Trace of Halliburton: Writer and Crew of Ten on Chinese Junk Still Unreported."[1] The news triggered coast-to-coast media coverage in papers large and small.

Halliburton's fans gasped. One librarian became so overcome when she heard the news that she went home for the rest of the day. A devoted fan, she was proud of her autographed collection of his books.[2] Others hoped their boyishly handsome hero might turn up alive. Perhaps he had staged another Hellespont-style publicity stunt and was at this moment waiting outside to make a triumphant arrival at Treasure Island. Author and playwright Tennessee Williams, a fellow Laguna Beach resident, thought it possible: "Incidentally he has apparently met a tragic end in crossing the Pacific. . . . People around here say that Paul Mooney, mentioned as his collaborator, actually did most of his writing for him. They both went down in the junk—unless it all turns out to be a big publicity stunt."[3]

Perhaps the nine words of the *New York Journal*'s headline best captured America's mood: BUT RICHARD HALLIBURTON LOST? IT'S AN INCREDIBLE IDEA.[4] An incredible idea indeed. Eighteen years ago Halliburton sailed forth from New Orleans determined to wring as much from life as possible. It was incomprehensible to his admirers, to the reporters who covered his every move, to his friends and family, that the man who swam the Panama Canal, flew around the world in an open cockpit airplane, and interviewed an assassin had simply vanished. Marilyn Fais, who had met the author in Mentor, Ohio, just two years before, had been one of the many children who had signed up to receive the *Sea Dragon* letters, "but sadly he disappeared and no more letters were sent. I was devastated."[5]

The news also stunned his colleagues. The Golden Gate Exposition fair organizers, including Walter Gaines Swanson, could not believe there would be no grand arrival in San Francisco, no queuing up for tickets to hear the author speak about his adventures on the high seas.

Putting aside their grief, his editors at the Bobbs-Merrill Company worked to keep ahead of the story. The publishing house sent a press release to newspaper and radio editors from Boston to San Diego and all points in between. They implored editors to resist speculating over their beloved author's fate. The release offered the barest outline of what Bobbs-Merrill knew to be true.[6] In time, dispatches from various ships operating in the vicinity, transcripts of last radio contacts, and telegrams between Halliburton and his parents would provide some semblance of a timeline of the events leading up to the tragedy.

The *Sea Dragon* last made contact with the SS *President Coolidge* on March 23 when it reported its location to be about 2,480 miles from Midway Island, so named because it lies about halfway between Asia and America.[7]

This headshot of Richard Halliburton accompanied many of the articles announcing the author's disappearance at sea. *Author's collection*

S. W. Fenton, the marine superintendent of the Mackay Radio Company, reported the station last made contact with the junk at 5:00 AM on March 24.[8] Halliburton's voice was unmistakable. Fenton recognized it from having previously spoken with the author. When the station failed to hear from the *Sea Dragon* at the next appointed time, Fenton started broadcasting two messages every half hour on the dot. One message tried to raise the junk; the other message requested all ships at sea to remain vigilant. "Lookouts on ships cruising west of Honolulu and radio operators on ships and at shore stations in the Hawaiian Islands and on the mainland searched unavailingly Thursday for Richard Halliburton and his junk the *Sea Dragon*," the Mackay radio station's Fenton reported.[9]

Back in San Francisco, Wilfred Crowell, the manager of the Richard Halliburton Expedition, immediately notified the US Navy, the US Coast Guard, and Pan American Airways. Thus began the search.

The SS *President Pierce* reported observing wreckage of some kind floating on the water. However, it could not confirm what the debris was or whether it came from the seventy-five-foot-long *Sea Dragon*. At twelve hundred miles west of Midway Island, both the *President Taft* and *President Adams* had been near Halliburton's last known location. The two ships reported no signs of the ship. Neither did the *Roger Taney*, a 327-foot Coast Guard cutter sailing near Jarvis Island, an uninhabited coral island in the South Pacific.

For six days and nights, ships combed more than 160,000 square miles of ocean, an area slightly smaller than the whole of France. It was like looking for a white cat in a snowstorm. The ocean yielded no signs of Halliburton or his crew.

"'No trace' was the word flashed again today from ships at sea and Pan-American Clipper planes in the unofficial search for Richard Halliburton's Chinese junk *Sea Dragon*."[10] On April 4, not two weeks after the *Sea Dragon*'s disappearance, the US Navy called off the search. It could no longer justify the dedication of resources to so vast an area; the likelihood of finding anything was remote.[11] The ever-shifting winds and currents of the Pacific Ocean act like a giant conveyor belt, carrying away debris like suitcases on a baggage carousel.

The decision to end the search distressed Halliburton's parents; not knowing their son's fate was the worst kind of suffering. They pleaded with the navy to keep looking.[12]

"We just don't know what to do or think," Wesley Halliburton told a local paper. "Since the last message of March 24 we have heard nothing. Richard has been through dangers before where we had about given him up for lost, and all we can do now is to wait and hope. But it is a terrible suspense just waiting and not knowing what the next word may be."[13] Friends of the family joined the Halliburtons' entreaty.

Feeling the pressure, Admiral William D. Leahy, Chief of Naval Operations, assured the Halliburtons the search would be reopened. It was now mid-May and in reality it was no longer a search but rather a recovery operation.

Captain Richmond Kelly Turner, the commander of the USS *Astoria*, a ten-thousand-ton cruiser, was in Guam on May 21, having taken part in a successful operation to refloat the *US Grant*, a US Army transport ship. When the orders came through to hunt for Halliburton, Turner headed north toward the author's last known position. The *Astoria* combed the area until May 29.

"The result of my search was negative," Turner said.[14]

Two months later, in May 1939, Gay Beaman, who represented Halliburton for the A. G. Beaman Agency Ltd., wrote to Hangover House architect William Alexander. A telegram had announced the incident weeks before; only it had taken time for Beaman to gather the energy to write. He refused to accept that neither his client nor Mooney ("whose last letter was quite cheery!") were going to anchor at Treasure Island. After all, he wrote, maybe the *Sea Dragon* had reversed course and headed back to Hong Kong when the weather turned deadly. Or perhaps Halliburton and his crew were stranded on a deserted island. Beaman didn't accept the US decision to stop looking and hoped to persuade the Japanese government to conduct its own independent search. Or, at the least, assist the Americans in their search.[15]

What Beaman couldn't know was that Secretary of State Cordell Hull was already personally involved. The chief diplomat had reached out to the Japanese Foreign Office and asked them for assistance. Japan agreed to limited help. Japanese shipping companies requested their vessels to be on heightened alert for possible radio signals from the *Sea Dragon*. Several weeks later, the Japanese Foreign Office reported back to Hull: they had no information as to the fate of the missing vessel.[16]

With no firm answers, speculation flourished. Perhaps the typhoon blew the *Sea Dragon* just enough off course that it missed Midway Island, suggested Fenton, the Mackay Radio official. If that were true, the *Sea Dragon* might still be sailing toward San Francisco. Halliburton's expedition manager Crowell likewise told the public he believed the *Sea Dragon* was afloat and drifting off course somewhere in the mid-Pacific. Privately, however, he grew ever more alarmed.[17]

Albert Richard Wetjen, a friend of the *Sea Dragon*'s Captain Welch, weighed in with his own theory. As the author of several shipwreck novels, the cigar-smoking Wetjen surmised the intense winds and current had forced Welch to continue straight toward San Francisco. The junk likely no longer had an operational radio or enough fuel for its auxiliary diesel engine. Soon, he said, the *Sea Dragon* would sail triumphantly under the Golden Gate Bridge, its colorful sails waving in the breeze.[18]

But after nearly two months of fruitless searches, the public understood their beloved author was gone. Newspapers started running obituaries and letters from readers. Grace K. Ebright of Altoona, Pennsylvania, found a letter Halliburton had once sent. She read it over several times before sitting down to write an obituary. Ebright reflected on what motivates people, even when the odds are stacked against them—as they so often had been for Halliburton. "Our great geographic discoveries were made by such gallant soldiers of fortune as this. Columbus set out in the face of every known obstacle—but he had a dream and he stuck to it . . . that was the kind of thing he loved to do. He was made of the kind of stuff that welcomes danger, defies hardship, invites the unusual experience."[19]

⸻◦◦◦◦⸻

Many fans wrote to Bobbs-Merrill postulating all kinds of scenarios. Some insisted the Japanese had taken Halliburton prisoner, because they discovered the writer was a spy and had been on a secret mission for President Roosevelt. Others surmised the writer, fed up with publicity, was living on an atoll somewhere in the Pacific with only his crew for company. Seeking to quiet the conjecture, Captain Dale E. Collins, the *President Coolidge*'s chief officer, summed up what he knew in an article for the US Naval Institute's magazine *Proceedings*. His connection with Halliburton coupled with his experience lent authority to the piece. There was nothing mysterious about Halliburton's disappearance the night of March 24–25, Collins wrote less than a year after the tragedy.[20] The exact date remains unknown, as the junk was crossing the International Date Line at the time.

Collins outlined three possible scenarios in his article. One, the *Sea Dragon* tried to outrun the typhoon instead of dropping a sea anchor and trying to ride out the storm. Two, the winds snapped the *Sea Dragon*'s mast and it toppled with the force of a giant sequoia, punching through the top-deck. The torrents of water washing over the rails would have drowned anyone below, and anyone standing near the mast when it fell would have been swept into the sea. Three, the force of the waves simply capsized the junk.[21]

Naturally, Collins couldn't verify any of the three scenarios proffered, or even say which of the three was the most plausible; he simply wanted to present the facts, as he knew them. But having been privy to Halliburton's trials and tribulations, Collins wasn't trading in sensationalism when he called the expedition ill fated from its inception.

As *Time* magazine described it, his disappearance was "the only unpremeditated adventure of Adventurer Halliburton's career."[22]

In the weeks to come, Halliburton's family and friends reluctantly accepted the truth: a brutal typhoon had swallowed the *Sea Dragon*.[23] Halliburton was dead. The sea also claimed the lives of John W. Welch, captain; Henry von Fehren, engineer; George Petrich, radio man; Richard Davis, assistant engineer; George Barstow III, crew; Robert Chase, crew; Paul Mooney, crew; Ralph Granrud, seaman; Ben Flagg, seaman; Velman Fitch, seaman; and Sun Fook, Kiao Chu, Wang Ching-huo, and Liu Ah-shu.

Perhaps the editors at Bobbs-Merrill said it best when they issued this statement to the public: "What the end was must remain forever one of the unsolved mysteries of the sea, but anyone who has seen the usually tranquil Pacific in one of its rare moods of tempest will know that there was high adventure indeed in those last final hours, and that for Richard Halliburton it must have been an end set to the tempo of a gallant life."[24]

One month after the *Sea Dragon* disappeared, Alicia Mooney, one of Paul Mooney's younger sisters, wrote to William Alexander. "No report—just general guessing that a typhoon sank the junk. . . . My favorite brother never was destined to die in bed; he got one more thrill when he looked upon a typhoon making toward him; and if fast thinking yet could save him, he's still around," she wrote.[25]

One year later, on St. Patrick's Day 1940, Mooney's mother, Ione, celebrated her sixty-second birthday. Grief had long settled into the eaves of her house. She thought about her son's last message. She knew she needed to be more present, but Mooney's death crippled her and her relationship with her four surviving children: "They know they cannot take his place. But who am I to expect to miss the 'slings and arrows of outrageous fortune'? It's just life."[26]

Gordon Torrey learned about the *Sea Dragon*'s disappearance while still in Hong Kong. He had last seen Halliburton from a hospital bed.[27] Torrey remained in China after his recovery and went to work for the Texaco Oil Company (China) Ltd., first in Shanghai and then in Haiphong, Indo-China, which by then had become the major trans-shipping point for all of the strategic war materials destined for interior

China, particularly petroleum products.[28] Eventually, the waters around Mount Desert beckoned. Torrey spent summers on the island, but after Hong Kong, he and Potter never saw each other or spoke again.

Torrey forever believed the tragedy of the *Sea Dragon* was avoidable. Instead of sailing a replica junk halfway across the world, Halliburton ought to have shipped it aboard a freight bound for San Francisco. Once near the California coast, he could have had the junk unloaded and then sailed to his mooring at Treasure Island. This would have saved lives and still allowed for commercial success at the Golden Gate Exposition. "Having moderately enjoyed forty-eight plus years of living beyond the others, I have always felt that a decision to sail as the *Sea Dragon* did should not be left to the whims and commercial aspirations of one person, as in this case," Torrey wrote many years later.[29]

Seventy-five years after her father nearly perished at sea, Sarah Betts Alley, Torrey's daughter, admonished the *Sea Dragon* adventure. "Adventure to fulfill monetary and commercial needs, while ignoring obvious risk to others' lives is not an event to celebrate."[30]

Seven months later, on October 5, 1939, a Memphis chancery court declared Halliburton, Mooney, and the rest of the crew officially dead. The ruling allowed the First National Bank of Memphis to probate Halliburton's last will and testament regarding his estate, believed to be worth about $100,000. The decision also meant Prudential Insurance Company of America would pay a total of $20,099.60, the sum of two policies, to Wesley Sr. and Nelle Nance Halliburton.[31]

After the court rendered its verdict, Dr. Ernest L. Fitch, the father of Velman Fitch, spoke with the Associated Press. The younger Fitch had cabled his father on March 5 with his exciting news that he was sailing for San Francisco with *the* Halliburton. Fitch held out no hope that his son still lived, "but members of his family feel that if a tiny Chinese junk sighted off northern Vancouver Island, could stay afloat 106 days, there is still hope for Halliburton and Fitch."[32] The grief-stricken father was referring to the *Taiping*. Captain John Anderson of

New York, a retired Yangtze River pilot, and his twenty-five-year-old wife had left Shanghai three weeks after Halliburton sailed from Hong Kong. According to Anderson, the *Taiping* trailed the *Sea Dragon* "until we were separated by a typhoon." Before the Andersons had been sighted off the cost of northern Vancouver Island, they had been "battered and tossed for weeks in 30 foot boat . . . almost hysterical, waving white rags on bamboo poles."[33]

Like frost heave, the court decision pushed tensions between Halliburton, Mooney, and Alexander to the surface. The elder Halliburton, who had no use for his son's friends or the family of his son's lover, found attending to his son's estate a comforting distraction.

Bitter about his friend's, and former lover's, death, Alexander directed his attorney to write to Halliburton's father. He stopped short of accusing him of rushing the official declaration of death so he could get his hands on his son's money. "I am sure that weighing dollars is the principle of a man in the Farm Investment business and not in the profession of Architecture . . . I am informed that it was you who hastened the proceedings to declare your son dead, while Alex Levy has not lost hope of his safe return."[34]

As for Mooney's mother, she was angry with Halliburton's father for not having yet paid the remainder of Hangover House's outstanding debt. She was angry that Lloyd's of London had so far denied her insurance payments. And she was angry that Halliburton's death overshadowed her son's death. "I have no heart for anything anymore. . . . Paul and I were too close, I fear."[35]

She then took to bed for two weeks with a nasty bout of influenza. Thoughts of Mooney crowded her every waking hour. At night she dreamed of finding his diary. She asked Alexander to ship her some paintings and other things of her son's that were in storage, including a brass bowl. "Bringing Paul's things here has probably cost me more than they are worth intrinsically, but naturally I wanted them—especially his books."[36]

There reportedly was a Halliburton diary that Lee Hutchings, a mutual friend of Alexander, had saved, "but after he died his physical therapist went into the apartment and threw it out, with everything else. The diary was falling apart," Michael Blankenship, a friend of Alexander's, said.[37]

Soon after the *Sea Dragon* disappeared, condolence letters from readers inundated the Halliburtons' Memphis mailbox and the Bobbs-Merrill Company offices. The carefully affixed foreign and domestic stamps were poignant reminders of the nearly one thousand letters Richard sent his parents over his lifetime and the countless places he had visited. Fifteen years after Richard and his crew vanished, the letters kept coming. "A lot of Halliburton's fans just won't take the publisher's word for it that the great adventurer is dead. One woman, finally convinced, insists on keeping up a correspondence just the same," reported David Dempsey in the *New York Times*.[38]

The Halliburtons tried to answer as many letters as possible, just as their son had once answered his fan mail. One response to the Reverend George Lapp, who had met Richard in both Calcutta and Hong Kong, showed the stoic heartbreak that now sheathed the Halliburtons. Wesley wrote how he recently started rereading his son's letters, starting from his first days at Princeton University all the way until he went missing. "We are grateful for your sympathy, and it is just such letters as these that help us pass through the valley without too great a strain upon our emotions. We naturally expected Richard to meet a dramatic end, but, of course, we hoped that he would be with us until we had passed to our reward. At this late date in our lives it leaves our future here rather drab, but it can't be helped, so we will make the best of it," Wesley wrote.[39]

But of all the letters they received, it was the one from twelve-year-old Roma Borst Hoff of Wisconsin that captured Wesley's heart. Penned two years after their son's disappearance, her words moved the grieving father. In her he saw the grandchild he would never have.

"It would be inhuman if we did not appreciate most deeply the delicacy of your feeling towards our sorrow and your desire to soften our disappointment because we can have no grand-child, the fear of which was the cause of lamentations in a letter to Richard," Wesley Halliburton wrote in answer to her letter. "It is a sad defeat, my wife and I must acknowledge, that though she bore us two fine sons, they are both gone, and there can now be not any to carry on. We must try to think in the long last, it was for the best. We do not know or perhaps believe it to be true, but accept it we must."[40]

The two grew close, and from 1930 until his death in 1965, Wesley's grief found an outlet in ink. Through their letters he continued the conversation he had begun with his son so many decades before. When he told Hoff how proud he was of her, he was also saying how proud he was of his son. When he wrote to her of harnessing each day, he was speaking to his son of courage and opportunity. In Hoff he saw the enthusiasm and imagination his elder son once possessed.[41]

In 1950 Hoff's grandfather died. It was eleven years after Richard went missing and thirty-two years after Wesley Jr. succumbed to rheumatic fever. Wesley Sr. offered his sympathy in a two-page letter that was affecting not for its words of comfort but for the way it spoke of his own infinite anguish. "Your grandfather's passing was normally timed. I am disturbed when youth, unfinished untimely, passes. My Wesley was fifteen. What might he not have added to this world that was worthwhile? Richard passed in full flower with much yet to do that we know was good. And here I am, and their mother, old and useless, linger on for no good."[42]

If the sympathy letters offered a degree of succor, the number of purported *Sea Dragon* sightings did not. Two of the most credible incidents dashed hopes as quickly as they were raised.

The first came in the spring of 1940 when Captain Charles Jokstad of the *President Pierce* wired his supervisors. While steaming across the Pacific from Yokohama to Honolulu, the officer on watch sighted a fair amount of wreckage in the distance. Jokstad grabbed his binoculars and trained them on the horizon. He scrutinized every piece of debris. "To my amazement we sighted the very rudder of the *Sea Dragon* which I had condemned! This same rudder, as well as the other timbers, had about a year's growth of barnacles," Jokstad later wrote. The state of the debris corresponded with the timeline of the junk's sinking. But choppy seas coupled with a touch of engine trouble prevented him from salvaging anything. He went to his grave sure with "little doubt that I had witnessed the last chapter of Halliburton's adventures."[43]

Another jolt of hope came in 1945 when wreckage from a small craft washed ashore on San Diego's Pacific Beach. According to newspaper reports, it appeared to be the waterlogged hull of a small wooden vessel similar to the *Sea Dragon*. The piece was a flat-bottomed section of heavy timbers, held together with huge brass bolts.[44]

The article speculated the timbers were the exact type, size, and kind used in the *Sea Dragon*'s construction. It said the carvings and workmanship were unmistakably Chinese. "It is indeed possible that these timbers were part of the once proud Sea Dragon but it is only conjecture and circumstantial evidence, and perhaps a little dramatic wishful thinking," Collins said. "Anyway it makes a fitting end to the story of Richard Halliburton that sections of his latest adventure would come finally to reset near his former home at Laguna Beach."[45]

Maritime experts agreed the debris was Chinese or Japanese in origin, but they doubted it came from the *Sea Dragon*. So too did the ever-practical Nelle Halliburton. She told the newspapers her son never mentioned anything concerning brass fittings in all his letters about the *Sea Dragon*. "Having never seen the *Sea Dragon* we would not be able to identify it even though this *Sea Dragon* wreckage was that of the small boat, and from what we have learned through news releases from that point we are positive that the *Sea Dragon* is not the vessel involved."[46]

Memphian John Maize was almost sixteen years old when the *Sea Dragon* vanished in 1939. He held close the memory of hearing Halliburton speak at the Goodwyn Institute, although because of the impending war, "I wasn't thinking about his disappearance or Richard Halliburton anymore at the time."[47] Two years after the *Sea Dragon* sank, the Japanese bombed Pearl Harbor. Maize was now a freshman at Southwestern, as Rhodes College was called, and school seemed frivolous. He enlisted in the Army Air Corps and became a B-25 pilot. He spent the better part of his war stationed in the Philippines.

Toward the end of the war, Maize experienced what he called his own personal sequel to Halliburton's Hong Kong sojourn. On June 22, 1945, Maize and his squadron were assigned to reconnoiter the Chinese coast and verify that the Japanese had withdrawn from their position in Hong Kong. They flew upriver and checked every boat to see if there were military personnel or supplies on board. Observing nothing, they flew back to the Philippines. Concentrated as he was, Maize didn't realize he had flown over Hong Kong in the course of his mission.

"That has bothered me ever since. Then when I looked at the exhibit at Rhodes and I watched the film very carefully I realized that was Hong Kong. That's where Richard Halliburton built his junk and where I was just a few years later," Maize said. "I didn't see anything like what he saw. The harbor was—all empty. There was not a rowboat anywhere, but I know I was exactly where Richard Halliburton was."

Many decades later, whenever Maize traveled, whether it was to roam through the antique cities of Europe or to explore the lush islands of Hawaii, he said, "I always had my traveler with me, and my traveler is Richard Halliburton."[48]

In late 1939 Halliburton's parents marked the passing of their elder son in a quiet ceremony at the Forest Hill Cemetery in Memphis.

Halliburton's empty grave lies next to his brother's. His parents considered burying all of their son's letters in an empty casket. But Juliet Halliburton Davis, Richard's younger cousin, convinced them otherwise. Davis asked her uncle to think about editing the correspondence and publishing them as a book. She accompanied Wesley to his office in the First National Bank Building, where he kept all the letters locked in a safe. After rereading just a few, Halliburton decided burying them would be like burying his son; instead he wanted to give the world a look at the private Halliburton, albeit a heavily edited look.[49]

With sharpened pencil in hand, he removed any passage he felt would reflect negatively upon his son. He deleted anything alluding to his long-term relationship with Mooney, and he scratched out anything that spoke of Mooney's literary contributions to his son's books. When in 1937 Halliburton wrote home about his work on the *Book of Marvels* to say, "I've been so busy with Book I've had no time to work on house. Now that I'm here Paul would rather I take charge," his father deleted the second sentence entirely.[50] Nevertheless, the end result was a book that took readers from Halliburton's innocent boyhood days through his last adventure.

In 1940 Bobbs-Merrill signed a contract with the Halliburtons to publish a book of their son's letters. According to the contract, his parents would receive ten free copies of the book.[51] Bobbs-Merrill released *Richard Halliburton's Life of Adventure: His Letters to His Father and Mother* in June that same year. On its cover, the *Sea Dragon* leans into the wind, making its way over the sapphire sea. An American flag snaps in the wind high above the orange, white, and scarlet sails.

Hundreds of thousands of copies sold in the United States. A dozen countries abroad printed the book, which contained but a fraction of the thousands of letters Halliburton wrote. Halliburton represented the young men and women whose best years lay between two world wars—restless, questioning, dissatisfied, curious, bored by inaction. The *New York Times* called it "engaging and revealing" and said, "If, as has been rather strongly intimated, he was a show-off, these personal writings prove that he was conscientiously and consistently such. He was, moreover, a showman, not only in connection with his deeds but with his thoughts; his letters to his parents prove this."[52]

Aside from the book, of which the Halliburtons were proud, they wanted to further memorialize their elder son. They chose to have a redbrick bell tower erected on the campus of Rhodes College so the city might forever remember their "Memphis Boy." Neither parent lived to see the tower dedicated, but today when the massive bronze bell, cast in France, rings, it can be heard across campus.

Throughout the years, Halliburton's life continued to touch even those whom he never met, from generation to generation. Mary Chapman remembered how her grandfather J. Penfield Seiberling frequently regaled them at family dinners with stories from his youth. Many of these stories centered on Halliburton, his old college friend. One story in particular haunts her these decades since.

"Grandpa told us that Dick Halliburton was a born adventurer, and they all knew he would never settle down nor marry, but would be a traveler and an adventurer soul all his days . . . and so he was! Halliburton told the roommates, and Grandpa told us, that if he (or they) ever heard a phrase repeated publicly concerning the whereabouts of Dick Halliburton, that they would KNOW by that phrase being made public, that he had already passed away. Grandpa knew that Halliburton had been on a trip to India and the Orient, and was set to return across the Pacific via a Northerly passage. According to Grandpa, Halliburton was on a 'Chinese Junk' ship, off Alaska, and was caught in a violent storm. One of the last cables, perhaps the last cable was from Richard Halliburton, saying simply 'Everything's all right, WISH YOU WERE HERE.' When Grandpa heard the 'Wish you were here' phrase read, he said he told Grandma that Richard Halliburton was dead."[53]

Chapman believes the story was her grandfather's means of coming to terms with his friend's death. A friend whom "one would need the 'tongue of angels' to accurately portray."[54]

The Halliburton family tree spread from its roots in Scotland; it has branches across the United States. Richard Halliburton, seventy, of California, never knew his namesake, but seems to possess the need to crisscross the globe. Each year the former professor publishes a family newsletter, *The Glorious Mis-Adventure.*[55]

For nearly two decades, the Memphian's zest for adventure spurred people to inhale life. Never believing he held a monopoly on adventure, Halliburton encouraged others to experience. The writer spoke to budding writers; to Walter Cronkite, the bestselling adventurer-journalist was a daredevil with movie star looks.[56]

Susan Sontag first read *Richard Halliburton's Complete Book of Marvels* when she was seven years old. He sparked her desire for adventure. "Halliburton's books informed me that the world contained many wonderful things. Not just the Great Wall of China," Sontag wrote in her essay "Homage to Halliburton." For her Halliburton was *carpe diem* personified. "You have something in mind. You imagine it. You prepare for it. You voyage toward it. Then you see it and there is no disappointment, indeed it may be even more captivating than you imagined." And every time she did something big and adventurous like he did, she thought "I've done it. They were on his list."[57]

And though the travel writer Paul Theroux never met Halliburton, he recalled that "reading his books at a certain age filled me with a desire to travel. . . . I believe he was a complex man."[58]

John Nicholls Booth, who first met Halliburton backstage in Toronto in 1933, lived this lesson. "If anyone possessed the world it was Richard Halliburton. He would do something in connection with it—he would sleep on top of Mount Olympus. He became a part of what he was seeing; he made you feel the history. The spirit of Halliburton will remain alive in the world. I think what he did was bring people together better than any formal political efforts," said Booth.[59]

His spirit revealed itself in the late newsman Charles Kuralt, who hosted the CBS show *On the Road*. He remembered curling on his grandparents' porch swing as his grandmother read from Halliburton's travel books.

Indeed, Halliburton's knack for connecting with people revealed itself in the way he persuaded King Abdulaziz to meet him inside a royal tent in Jedda, swayed a Dayak chief to go flying, and convinced the Japanese government to grant him safe passage in wartime. "He was an appealing, confused individual, a US phenomenon, a US symbol. The nice son of a nice US environment, he never entirely either outgrew or betrayed it. He was essentially, if mildly, an artist and a rebel, he achieved neither art nor rebellion. He was an innocent sort of Byron—of his time," *Time* said.[60]

In 1944 the United States Maritime Commission recognized this gift when it named a Liberty ship in honor of Halliburton. As was custom, Liberty ships were named for deceased individuals who made notable contributions to American history and culture. As one member of the naming committee told Wesley Halliburton Sr., he proposed Halliburton because "the spirit of adventure which characterized his career eminently suited him to the honor of having a ship named for him."[61] The *Richard Halliburton* was a 10,000-ton and 430-foot-long cargo ship. A life ring from the boat now hangs in Rhodes College.

"If Richard Halliburton had not actually lived, no novelist or satirist would dare have invented him. Any fictional character who had the time, ability, or inclination to do all the exciting, grueling, and often ridiculous things he did simply would not be believable."[62] So wrote Joe David Brown in a piece for *Sports Illustrated* twenty-four years after Richard Halliburton disappeared at sea.

Esquire magazine's George Weller celebrated the writer in his essay "The Passing of the Last Playboy." Acknowledging Halliburton's polarizing nature, Weller applauded his ability to rise above his fiercest critics. "Probably no adventurer with such meager personal pretensions to authorship ever excited so much dispute in American letters as this man," Weller wrote. Once his critics concluded that Halliburton did what he said, they chose other reasons to lambast him, primarily for his writing style. Weller believed Halliburton had died ten years too late. When the 1920s closed, Halliburton had done, seen, and sampled everything possible. Made of too mercurial, too romantic stuff for the Depression, Halliburton "was an Ariel, left over from the summer of the Jazz Age."[63]

Today, four columns, one for each family member, stand in Memphis's Forest Hill Cemetery. Set in the ground are four rectangular stones engraved with the names of each Halliburton: WESLEY JR., 1903–1918;

Nelle, 1869–1955; Wesley Halliburton, 1870–1965; and Richard, 1900–1939 Lost At Sea.

For thirty-nine years Richard Halliburton sought the kind of immortality enjoyed by the literary heroes of his childhood, but the dream he had chased for so long died with him. The tragedy lay not in his dying young, but rather in his fading glory.

Acknowledgments

THIS BOOK COULD NOT have been completed without the help and support of so many.

Thank you, William Short, Associate Director, Barrett Library, Rhodes College in Memphis, Tennessee, for being a source of all things Halliburton and for photocopying countless pages, opening the archives on a Sunday, and giving me a tour of Memphis. I am grateful to the staff of Princeton University Rare Books and Special Collections, especially AnnaLee Pauls, for guiding me through the extensive collection of journals, letters, and photographs that comprises the Richard Halliburton Papers. This book neither revisits nor includes every single one of Richard Halliburton's adventures. I encourage interested readers to read Halliburton's books for more information, as well as his numerous newspaper and magazine articles.

I am grateful to a number of libraries and historical societies. The Bar Harbor Historical Society, the Mount Desert Island Historical Society, the Northeast Harbor Library, the National Oceanic and Atmospheric Administration, the St. Louis Park Historical Society, and the Rauner Special Collections at Dartmouth University all helped facilitate my research.

To Michael E. Blankenship, for your e-mail correspondence, which was filled with insights and anecdotes. Also thank you to Sarah Alley, Harriet Chapman, Mary Chapman, Maggie Devault, Jennifer Fais,

Marilyn Fais, Richard Halliburton, Irvine O. Hockaday Jr., Roma Borst Hoff, John Maize, and Virginia Reese.

To my agent, Laurie Abkemeier of DeFiore and Company, I am grateful for your wise editing. From the earliest stages of the book proposal to the early drafts of the manuscript and beyond you always understood the essence of what I wanted to convey. I value your counsel and couldn't ask for a better advocate.

Thank you Jerome Pohlen, my editor at Chicago Review Press, for giving me the opportunity to tell Halliburton's story and for your enthusiasm in helping me shape the narrative. To Devon Freeny, for your keen eye as you polished the manuscript. To Sarah Olson for your gorgeous cover design; it truly captures the spirit of Halliburton. Thank you to Chris Erichsen for the maps. Thanks also to Meaghan Miller and Mary Kravenas for your hard work in promoting the book.

Thank you to Jill Swenson for your advice and friendship. To Richard Z. Chesnoff, for your mentorship, I miss you. And to Amy Levine Kennedy, thank you for your humor and friendship.

To my parents, Norma and Marvin Prince, for your never-failing support and encouragement.

To my children, Nathan & Zoë: may you never stop looking at the world with curious eyes. And finally to Pierre, who always believes, you are my lodestar.

Notes

1. Wanderlust

1. Richard Halliburton to parents, July 30, 1921, box 19, folder 1, Richard Halliburton Papers, Manuscripts Division, Department of Rare Books and Special Collections, Princeton University Library, Princeton, NJ.
2. Richard Halliburton, *New Worlds to Conquer* (Indianapolis: Bobbs-Merrill, 1929), 16.
3. Wesley Halliburton Sr. to Roma Borst Hoff, November 14, 1950, courtesy of the Halliburton Archives, Barrett Library, Rhodes College, Memphis, TN.
4. Carolyn Crum, "Richard Halliburton: Adventurer, Writer, Horizon Chaser," *MUS Today*, May 2005.
5. Joe David Brown, "A Rich Blend of Romance and Reality," *Sports Illustrated*, September 9, 1963.
6. J. Penfield Seiberling, as quoted in 1987 bell tower anniversary brochure, courtesy of the Halliburton Archives.
7. Richard Halliburton, "Washington," chapter 8 of *Complete Book of Marvels*, box 1, folder 9, Richard Halliburton Papers.
8. As quoted in Brown, "A Rich Blend."
9. Wesley Halliburton Sr. to Roma Hoff Borst, September 17, 1943, courtesy of the Halliburton Archives.
10. Richard Halliburton to parents, August 15, 1915, as quoted in Richard Halliburton, *Richard Halliburton: His Story of His Life's Adventure: As Told in Letters to His Mother and Father* (New York: Garden City Publishing, 1940), 6–7.
11. Wesley Halliburton Sr. to Roma Hoff Borst, September 14, 1960, courtesy of the Halliburton Archives.
12. Seiberling brochure, courtesy of the Halliburton Archives.
13. Ibid.

14. Obituary of Wesley Halliburton Jr. from Lawrenceville Academy, pasted into Richard Halliburton's scrapbook, box 45, Richard Halliburton Papers.

15. Ibid.

16. Richard Halliburton to parents, November 10, 1918, as quoted in Halliburton, *Richard Halliburton*, 13.

17. Wesley Halliburton Sr. to Roma Hoff Borst, April 24, 1950, courtesy of the Halliburton Archives.

18. Wesley Halliburton Sr. to Roma Hoff Borst, February 1, 1946, courtesy of the Halliburton Archives.

19. Richard Halliburton to parents, January 9, 1918, as quoted in Halliburton, *Richard Halliburton*, 9.

20. Richard Halliburton to parents, October 5, 1918, as quoted in Halliburton, *Richard Halliburton*, 9–10.

21. At one point Halliburton may have tried to pass for eighteen when he was still a year younger; his first passport shows his birth year as 1899 instead of 1900. The original passport is in the collection of the Halliburton Archives.

22. Richard Halliburton to parents, October 5, 1918, as quoted in Halliburton, *Richard Halliburton*, 9–10.

23. Richard Halliburton to Wesley Halliburton Sr., December 5, 1919, as quoted in Halliburton, *Richard Halliburton*, 51.

24. James Axtell, *The Making of Princeton University: From Woodrow Wilson to the Present* (Princeton, NJ: Princeton University Press, 2006), 246; and Richard Halliburton to parents, September 27, 1920, as quoted in Halliburton, *Richard Halliburton*, 61–62.

25. Richard Halliburton to parents, January 9, 1919, as quoted in Halliburton, *Richard Halliburton*, 21–22.

26. Richard Halliburton to parents, October 5, 1918, as quoted in Halliburton, *Richard Halliburton*, 9–10.

27. Hy. S. Watson to Richard Halliburton, February 24, 1921, box 25, folder 20, Richard Halliburton Papers.

28. Richard Halliburton to parents, April 9, 1921, box 19, folder 1, Richard Halliburton Papers.

29. Ibid.

30. Richard Halliburton to parents, April 9, 1921, box 6, folder 10, Richard Halliburton Papers.

31. Richard Halliburton to parents, April 9, 1921, box 19, folder 1, Richard Halliburton Papers.

32. Ibid.

33. Richard Halliburton to parents, April 9, 1921, box 6, folder 10, Richard Halliburton Papers.

34. Wesley Halliburton Sr. to Roma Borst Hoff, December 3, 1950, courtesy of the Halliburton Archives.

35. Richard Halliburton to Nelle Nance Halliburton, May 31, 1921, as quoted in Halliburton, *Richard Halliburton*, 79–80.

36. Richard Halliburton, *The Royal Road to Romance* (Indianapolis: Bobbs-Merrill, 1925), 2.

37. Cathy Pond, e-mail correspondence with author, October 28, 2014.

38. Richard Halliburton to parents, May 7, 1921, box 19, folder 1, Richard Halliburton Papers.

39. Jonathan Root, *Halliburton: The Magnificent Myth* (New York: Coward-McCann, 1965), 45.

40. Richard Halliburton to parents, July 16, 1921, box 19, folder 1, Richard Halliburton Papers.

41. Irvine O. Hockaday Jr., telephone interview with author, October 30, 2014.

42. Richard Halliburton to parents, May 23, 1921, as quoted in Halliburton, *Richard Halliburton*, 79.

43. Harry A. Franck Home Page, accessed March 17, 2015, www.harryafranck.com/index.htm.

44. "Lecture Notes on the *Glorious Adventure* and Other Stories" (copybook), box 6, folder 10, Richard Halliburton Papers.

45. Ibid.

46. Halliburton, *Royal Road*, 5–6.

47. Hockaday, telephone interview with author.

48. J. G. Bennet, Marine Superintendent, United American Lines Inc., to Captain R. W. Tucker, s/s *Ipswich*, July 12, 1921, box 25, folder 22, Richard Halliburton Papers.

49. Ibid.

50. Richard Halliburton and Irvine Hockaday to J. L. Schaefer, July 15, 1921, box 25, folder 19, Richard Halliburton Papers.

51. Richard Halliburton to parents, July 16, 1921, box 19, folder 1, Richard Halliburton Papers.

52. Copybook, box 1, folder 8c, Richard Halliburton Papers.

53. Ibid.

54. Richard Halliburton to parents, July 30, 1921, as quoted in Halliburton, *Richard Halliburton*, 81.

55. Richard Halliburton to parents, December 6, 1920 as quoted in Halliburton, *Richard Halliburton*, 67.

56. As quoted in Charles E. Morris III, "Richard Halliburton's Bearded Tales," *Quarterly Journal of Speech* 95, no. 2 (May 2009).

57. Richard Halliburton to Nelle Nance Halliburton, August 1, 1921, box 19, folder 1, Richard Halliburton Papers.

2. Romancing the Road

1. Irvine O. Hockaday Jr., telephone interview with author, October 30, 2014.

2. Richard Halliburton to parents, August 7, 1921, as quoted in Richard Halliburton, *Richard Halliburton: His Story of His Life's Adventure, as Told in Letters to His Mother and Father* (New York: Garden City Publishing, 1940), 83–84; and Hockaday, telephone interview with author.

3. Richard Halliburton to parents, August 19, 1921, as quoted in Halliburton, *Richard Halliburton*, 88.

4. Sean Dennis Cashman, *America in the Twenties and Thirties: The Olympian Age of Franklin Delano Roosevelt* (New York: New York University Press, 1989), 383.

5. Lucy Moore, *Anything Goes: A Biography of the Roaring Twenties* (New York: Overlook Press, 2010), 315.

6. Stanley Coben, *Rebellion Against Victorianism: The Impetus for Cultural Change in 1920s America* (New York: Oxford University Press, 1991), 46.

7. Richard Halliburton, "Dutch Treatment and London Follies," box 17, folder 2, Richard Halliburton Papers, Manuscripts Division, Department of Rare Books and Special Collections, Princeton University Library, Princeton, NJ.

8. Richard Halliburton to parents, August 19, 1921, as quoted in Halliburton, *Richard Halliburton*, 87.

9. Ibid.

10. Richard Halliburton to parents, April 9, 1921, box 19, folder 1, Richard Halliburton Papers.

11. Richard Halliburton to parents, September 8, 1921, as quoted in Halliburton, *Richard Halliburton*, 93.

12. John Maxwell Hamilton, *Journalism's Roving Eye: A History of American Foreign Reporting* (Baton Rouge: Louisiana State University Press, 2009), 250.

13. Frederic Ballert to Richard Halliburton, January 21, 1927, box 25, folder 22, Richard Halliburton Papers.

14. From one of Richard Halliburton's scrapbooks, courtesy of the Halliburton Archives, Barrett Library, Rhodes College, Memphis, TN.

15. Ibid.

16. Richard Halliburton, *The Royal Road to Romance* (Indianapolis: Bobbs-Merrill, 1925), 8.

17. Halliburton, *Royal Road*, 10.

18. From one of Richard Halliburton's scrapbooks, courtesy of the Halliburton Archives.

19. Halliburton, *Royal Road*, 12.

20. Ibid., 16.

21. From one of Richard Halliburton's scrapbooks, courtesy of the Halliburton Archives.

22. Hockaday, telephone interview with author. Irvine O. Hockaday Jr. scaled the peak in honor of his father and godfather Richard Halliburton after he graduated Princeton University.

23. Halliburton, *Royal Road*, 22.

24. From one of Richard Halliburton's scrapbooks, courtesy of the Halliburton Archives.

25. Richard Halliburton to parents, September 28, 1921, as quoted in Halliburton, *Richard Halliburton*, 94.

26. Richard Halliburton to parents, October 3, 1921, as quoted in Halliburton, *Richard Halliburton*, 97.

27. Hockaday, telephone interview with author.

28. Halliburton, *Royal Road*, 45.

29. Moore, *Anything Goes*, 168.

30. Richard Halliburton to parents, November 20, 1921, as quoted in Halliburton, *Richard Halliburton*, 106.

31. Ibid.

32. Charles E. Morris III, "Richard Halliburton's Bearded Tales," *Quarterly Journal of Speech* 95, no. 2 (May 2009).

33. Richard Halliburton to parents, December 18, 1921, as quoted in Halliburton, *Richard Halliburton*, 114.

34. Richard Halliburton to parents, December 21, 1921, as quoted in Halliburton, *Richard Halliburton*, 115.

35. After Richard Halliburton's death, his father donated his correspondence to Princeton University and Rhodes College. When the time came to edit the collection for the book *Richard Halliburton: His Story of His Life's Adventure, as Told in Letters to His Mother and Father*, Wesley Halliburton deleted references to Halliburton's lovers and any suggestion of homosexuality.

36. Richard Halliburton, *The Glorious Adventure* (Indianapolis: Bobbs-Merrill, 1927), 233.

37. Dorothy Dayton, "Richard Halliburton, 'Prince of Lovers,' Talks about Women and Love," *Illustrated Love Magazine*, March 1930, 38, 39.

38. Halliburton, *Royal Road*, 80–81.

39. Military HQ Gibraltar to Richard Halliburton, February 2, 1922, box 25, folder 22, Richard Halliburton Papers.

40. Richard Halliburton, "Gibraltar," chapter 8 of *Complete Book of Marvels*, box 1, folder 18, Richard Halliburton Papers.

41. Richard Halliburton to parents, April 23, 1922, as quoted in Halliburton, *Richard Halliburton*, 144.

42. Richard Halliburton to parents, May 21, 1922, as quoted in Halliburton, *Richard Halliburton*,152.

43. Richard Halliburton to parents, May 13, 1922, as quoted in Halliburton, *Richard Halliburton*, 148.

44. Notebook entry, n.d., courtesy of the Halliburton Archives.

45. Copybook 1, box 1, folder 32, Richard Halliburton Papers.

46. Halliburton, *Royal Road*, 177.

47. Richard Halliburton to parents, September 17, 1921, as quoted in Halliburton, *Richard Halliburton*, 92–93.

48. Ibid.

49. Notebooks and notes, n.d., courtesy of the Halliburton Archives.

50. From one of Richard Halliburton's scrapbooks, n.d., courtesy of the Halliburton Archives.

51. Ibid.

52. Photo caption, Halliburton, *Richard Halliburton*, no page.

53. Ibid.

54. Richard Halliburton to parents, July 2, 1922, as quoted in Halliburton, *Richard Halliburton*, 162.

55. Richard Halliburton to parents, September 23, 1922, as quoted in Halliburton, *Richard Halliburton*, 175–176.

56. Hockaday, telephone interview with author.

57. Richard Halliburton to parents, November 21, 1922, as quoted in Halliburton, *Richard Halliburton*, 124.

58. Ibid.

59. "Chinese Pirates Seize Vessel, but Lose Fight," *New York Times*, November 1922.

60. Halliburton, *Royal Road*, 295.

61. Richard Halliburton, "Midwinter Dueling with Fujiyama," box 17, folder 15, Richard Halliburton Papers.

62. Ibid.

63. Ibid.

3. Feats and Marvels

1. Richard Halliburton to parents' home, February 13, 1923, as quoted in Richard Halliburton, *Richard Halliburton: His Story of His Life's Adventure, as Told in Letters to His Mother and Father* (New York: Garden City Publishing, 1940), 208.

2. Halliburton, *Richard Halliburton*, 210.

3. Richard Halliburton to parents, May 10, 1923, as quoted in Halliburton, *Richard Halliburton*, 209.

4. Ibid., 209.

5. George Chauncey, *Gay New York: Gender, Urban Culture, and the Making of the Gay Male World, 1890–1940* (New York: Basic Books, 1994), 155.

6. Ibid., 3, 4, 7.

7. Richard Halliburton to parents, May 14, 1923, as quoted in Halliburton, *Richard Halliburton*, 211.

8. Richard Halliburton to parents, May 10, 1923, as quoted in Halliburton, *Richard Halliburton*, 210.

9. Ibid.

10. Richard Halliburton to parents, May 30, 1923, as quoted in Halliburton, *Richard Halliburton*, 213.

11. Wesley Halliburton Sr. to Roma Hoff Borst, April 24, 1950, courtesy of the Halliburton Archives, Barrett Library, Rhodes College, Memphis, TN.

12. Richard Halliburton to parents, May 30, 1923, as quoted in Halliburton, *Richard Halliburton*, 213.

13. Richard Halliburton to parents, June 4, 1923, as quoted in Halliburton, *Richard Halliburton*, 214.

14. Ibid.

15. Ibid.

16. Richard Halliburton to parents, May 14, 1923, as quoted in Halliburton, *Richard Halliburton*, 211.

17. Halliburton, *Richard Halliburton*, 216.

18. Richard Halliburton to parents, September 13, 1923, as quoted in Halliburton, *Richard Halliburton*, 217.

19. Richard Halliburton to parents, February 21, 1924, as quoted in Halliburton, *Richard Halliburton*, 228.

20. Copybook 5, box 1, folder 36, Richard Halliburton Papers, Manuscripts Division, Department of Rare Books and Special Collections, Princeton University Library, Princeton, NJ.

21. Chapters 14 and 15 of "To Hell with Ulysses," box 6, folder 2, Richard Halliburton Papers.

22. Richard Halliburton to parents, September 8, 1924, as quoted in Halliburton, *Richard Halliburton*, 239.

23. Richard Halliburton to Nelle Nance Halliburton, November 10, 1924, as quoted in Halliburton, *Richard Halliburton*, 239–241.

24. Ibid.

25. Irvine O. Hockaday Jr., telephone interview with author, October 30, 2014.

26. Richard Halliburton to parents, June 8, 1925, box 19a, folder 1, Richard Halliburton Papers.

27. Thomas R. Conran to Richard Halliburton, Bobbs-Merrill, April 24, 1925, courtesy of the Halliburton Archives.

28. Richard Halliburton to parents, June 8, 1925, as quoted in Halliburton, *Richard Halliburton*, 241.

29. Lucy Moore, *Anything Goes: A Biography of the Roaring Twenties* (New York: Overlook Press, 2010), 238–239.

30. Stanley Coben, *Rebellion Against Victorianism: The Impetus for Cultural Change in 1920s America* (New York: Oxford University Press, 1991), 52.

31. Ibid., 54.

32. Richard Halliburton to parents, June 8, 1925, box 19a, folder 1, Richard Halliburton Papers.

33. Richard Halliburton to Mr. Hathaway, n.d., box 25, folder 22, Richard Halliburton Papers.

34. Michael Cart, "The Romance of Travel," *Booklist*, September 15, 2009, 50.

35. Richard Halliburton to parents' home, June 8, 1925, box 19a, folder 1, Richard Halliburton Papers.

36. Charles E. Morris III, "Richard Halliburton's Bearded Tales," *Quarterly Journal of Speech* 95, no. 2 (May 2009).

37. Carrie Jacobs-Bond to Richard Halliburton, June 16, 1927, box 25, folder 22, Richard Halliburton Papers.

38. "Innocent Abroad," Books, *Time*, July 8, 1940, http://content.time.com/time/magazine /article/0,9171,795086,00.html.

39. John Maxwell Hamilton, *Journalism's Roving Eye: A History of American Foreign Reporting* (Baton Rouge: Louisiana State University Press, 2009), 111.

40. Nicholas Crosby to Richard Halliburton, June 19, 1927, box 25, folder 22, Richard Halliburton Papers.

41. Richard E. Richardson for Major General Staff to Richard Halliburton, August 25, 1927, box 25, folder 22, Richard Halliburton Papers.

42. Dorothy Dayton, "Richard Halliburton, 'Prince of Lovers,' Talks about Women and Love," *Illustrated Love Magazine*, March 1930, 36–41.

43. Herbert Lincoln Adams to Richard Halliburton, January 29, 1928 (enclosed with June 19, 1936), courtesy of the Halliburton Archives.

44. "Richard Lectured on 'The Royal Road to Romance,'" *Oak Park Oak Parker*, January 22, 1926, 12.

45. Dayton, "Richard Halliburton," 38.

46. Harriet D. Chapman, e-mail correspondence with author, October 28, 2014.

47. Richard Halliburton to parents, July 4, 1925, box 19a, folder 1, Richard Halliburton Papers.

48. Coben, *Rebellion*, 136.

49. Richard Halliburton to parents, June 17, 1925, box 19a, folder 1, Richard Halliburton Papers.

50. Ibid.

51. Richard Halliburton to parents, June 8, 1925, box 19a, folder 1, Richard Halliburton Papers.

4. Following Ulysses

1. Richard Halliburton to Wesley Halliburton Sr., July 4, 1925, box 19a, folder 1, Richard Halliburton Papers, Manuscripts Division, Department of Rare Books and Special Collections, Princeton University Library, Princeton, NJ.

2. Richard Halliburton to Wesley Halliburton Sr., July 24, 1925, box 19a, folder 1, Richard Halliburton Papers.

3. Richard Halliburton to Wesley Halliburton Sr., July 17, 1927, box 19a, folder 1, Richard Halliburton Papers.

4. Richard Halliburton to parents, June 17, 1925, box 19a, folder 1, Richard Halliburton Papers.

5. Richard Halliburton to Wesley Halliburton Sr., July 4, 1925, box 19a, folder 1, Richard Halliburton Papers.

6. Richard Halliburton to Wesley Halliburton Sr., July 17, 1925, as quoted in Richard Halliburton, *Richard Halliburton: His Story of His Life's Adventure, as Told in Letters to His Mother and Father* (New York: Garden City Publishing, 1940), 245.

7. Richard Halliburton to Wesley Halliburton Sr., July 24, 1925, box 19a, folder 1, Richard Halliburton Papers.

8. Roderic Crane to Nelle Nance Halliburton, July 26, 1925, box 19a, folder 1, Richard Halliburton Papers.

9. Richard Halliburton to Wesley Halliburton Sr., August 4, 1925, as quoted in Halliburton, *Richard Halliburton*, 245.

10. Richard Halliburton to Wesley Halliburton Sr., August 4, 1925, box 19a, folder 1, Richard Halliburton Papers.

11. Copybook 2, chapters 26–27, box 3, folder 11, Richard Halliburton Papers.

12. Richard Halliburton to Wesley Halliburton Sr., August 15, 1925, and to Nelle Nance Halliburton, August 15, 1925, box 19a, folder 10, Richard Halliburton Papers.

13. Ibid.

14. Ibid.

15. Ibid.

16. Ibid.

17. "Fear Halliburton Died in Turkish Sea: Letter Tells of Attempt of Princeton Graduate to Swim the Hellespont," *New York Times*, September 6, 1925.

18. Ibid.

19. Iowan Hull, *Sioux County Index*, August 8, 1929, 7.

20. "Finds Halliburton Safe: Father Gets Letter Telling of Author's Swim in Hellespont," *New York Times*, September 7, 1925.

21. Richard Halliburton to David Laurance Chambers, September 10, 1925, courtesy of the Halliburton Archives, Barrett Library, Rhodes College, Memphis, TN.

22. Ibid.

23. Ibid.

24. Irvine O. Hockaday Jr., telephone interview with author, October 30, 2014.

25. Richard Halliburton to David Laurance Chambers, September 10, 1925, courtesy of the Halliburton Archives.

26. Richard Halliburton to parents, September 17, 1925, box 19a, folder 1, Richard Halliburton Papers.

27. Roderic Crane to Nelle Halliburton, July 26, 1925, box 19a, folder 1, Richard Halliburton Papers.

28. "Rupert Brooke's Obituary in *The Times*," Brigham Young University official website, accessed November 20, 2015, http://exhibits.lib.byu.edu/wwi/poets/rbobituary.html.

29. Richard Halliburton to parents, August 15, 1925, box 19, folder 1, Richard Halliburton Papers.

30. Ibid.

31. Ibid.

32. Richard Halliburton, *The Glorious Adventure* (Indianapolis: Bobbs-Merrill, 1927), 40.

33. Richard Halliburton to parents, September 17, 1925, box 19a, folder 1, Richard Halliburton Papers.

34. "Innocent Abroad," Books, *Time*, July 8, 1940, http://content.time.com/time/magazine/article/0,9171,795086,00.html.

35. Richard Halliburton to parents, August 15, 1925, box 19, folder 1, Richard Halliburton Papers.

36. Richard Halliburton to parents, October 27, 1925, box 19a, folder 1, Richard Halliburton Papers.

37. Richard Halliburton, "Where I'll Spend My Honeymoons" (unpublished manuscript), box 17, folder 25, Richard Halliburton Papers.

38. Richard Halliburton to parents, November 17, 1925, box 19a, folder 1, Richard Halliburton Papers.

39. Ibid.

40. Ibid.

41. Richard Halliburton to parents, November 26, 1925, box 19a, folder 1, Richard Halliburton Papers.

42. Ibid.

43. Richard Halliburton to parents, December 6, 1925, as quoted in Halliburton, *Richard Halliburton*, 258.

44. Richard Halliburton to parents, January 21, 1926, box 19a, folder 2, Richard Halliburton Papers.

45. Richard Halliburton to parents, February 8, 1926, box 19a, folder 1, Richard Halliburton Papers.

46. Martha Delaplaine, *Oak Park Oak Leaves*, February 26, 1927.

47. Richard Halliburton to parents, February 26, 1926, box 19a, folder 1, Richard Halliburton Papers.

48. Richard Halliburton to parents, April 6, 1927, box 19a, folder 2, Richard Halliburton Papers.

49. Richard Halliburton to Nelle Nance Halliburton, April 14, 1926, box 19a, folder 2, Richard Halliburton Papers.

50. Richard Halliburton to Nelle Nance Halliburton, June 16, 1926, box 19a, folder 2, Richard Halliburton Papers.

51. Richard Halliburton to David Laurance Chambers, October 25, 1926, courtesy of the Halliburton Archives.

52. Richard Halliburton to parents, February 16, 1928, box 19, folder 1a, Richard Halliburton Papers.

53. Ibid.

54. Richard Halliburton to parents, April 27, 1927, box 19a, folder 3, Richard Halliburton Papers.

55. David Laurance Chambers to Richard Halliburton, February 8, 1927, courtesy of the Halliburton Archives.

56. Ibid.

57. Richard Halliburton to Wesley Halliburton Sr., June 30, 1927, box 19a, folder 3, Richard Halliburton Papers.

58. Copy of F. Scott Fitzgerald letter to Richard Halliburton, June 30, 1927, box 25, folder 22, Richard Halliburton Papers.

59. George Weller, "The Passing of the Last Playboy," *Esquire Magazine*, April 1940, 58.

60. George Chauncey, *Gay New York: Gender, Urban Culture, and the Making of the Gay Male World, 1890–1940* (New York: Basic Books, 1994), 113–114.

61. Beverley Nichols, *The Star Spangled Manner* (London: Jonathan Cape, 1928), 16–17.

62. Jack Gibson to Richard Halliburton, March 14, 1927, box 25, folder 23, Richard Halliburton Papers.

63. Richard Halliburton to David Laurance Chambers, November 27, 1927, box 25, folder 2, Richard Halliburton Papers.

64. Richard Halliburton to parents, February 6, 1928, box 19, folder 1a, Richard Halliburton Papers.

65. Ibid.

66. Richard Halliburton to parents, January 4, 1927, box 19a, folder 3, Richard Halliburton Papers.

67. Richard Halliburton to parents, January 24, 1928, box 19, folder 1a, Richard Halliburton Papers.

68. Richard Halliburton to parents, January 28, 1927, box 19a, folder 3, Richard Halliburton Papers.

69. Richard Halliburton to parents, January 21, 1928, box 19, folder 1a, Richard Halliburton Papers.

70. Richard Halliburton to David Laurance Chambers, July 20, 1927, box 25, folder 3, Richard Halliburton Papers.

71. Richard Halliburton to parents, February 6, 1928, box 19, folder 1a, Richard Halliburton Papers.

72. Richard Halliburton to parents, February 26, 1928, box 19, folder 1a, Richard Halliburton Papers.

5. Glorious Panama

1. Richard Halliburton to parents, March 30, 1928, box 19, folder 1a, and David Laurance Chambers to Richard Halliburton, January 5, 1928, box 25, folder 21, Richard Halliburton Papers, Manuscripts Division, Department of Rare Books and Special Collections, Princeton University Library, Princeton, NJ.

2. David Laurance Chambers to Richard Halliburton, May 31, 1927, box 25, folder 21, Richard Halliburton Papers.

3. George Weller, "The Passing of the Last Playboy," *Esquire Magazine*, April 1940, 58–111.

4. Thomas B. Kellogg to American Diplomatic and Consular Officers, March 29, 1928, box 25, folder 22, Richard Halliburton Papers.

5. Richard Halliburton to parents, May 1928, box 19, folder 1a, Richard Halliburton Papers.

6. Richard Halliburton to Nelle Nance Halliburton, May 1928, box 19, folder 1a, Richard Halliburton Papers.

7. Richard Halliburton to Nelle Nance Halliburton, June 16, 1928, box 19, folder 1a, Richard Halliburton Papers.

8. Richard Halliburton to parents, June 29, 1928, as quoted in Richard Halliburton, *Richard Halliburton: His Story of His Life's Adventure, as Told in Letters to His Mother and Father* (New York: Garden City Publishing, 1940), 287.

9. David Laurance Chambers to Wesley Halliburton Sr., July 11, 1928, box 25, folder 21, Richard Halliburton Papers.

10. Richard Halliburton to Nelle Nance Halliburton, July 2, 1928, as quoted in Halliburton, *Richard Halliburton*, 287.

11. Richard Halliburton to parents, July 9, 1928, box 19, folder 1a, Richard Halliburton Papers.

12. Richard Halliburton to parents, February 10, 1929, box 19, folder 2, Richard Halliburton Papers.

13. Richard Halliburton, *New Worlds to Conquer* (Indianapolis: Bobbs-Merrill, 1929), 49–50.

14. Richard Halliburton to parents, July 21, 1928, box 19, folder 1a, Richard Halliburton Papers.

15. Halliburton, *New Worlds*, 59.

16. Richard Halliburton to parents, July 6, 1928, box 19, folder 1a, Richard Halliburton Papers.

17. Richard Halliburton to parents, August 7, 1928, as quoted in Halliburton, *Richard Halliburton*, 290. The Sing Sing Correctional Facility is a maximum security prison in Ossining, NY. Its name was changed to Ossining Correctional Facility in 1970.

18. Charles Lindbergh, "To Bogota and Back By Air: Narrative of a 9,500-Mile Flight from Washington, over Thirteen Latin-American Countries and Return, in the Single-Seater Airplane 'Spirit of St. Louis,'" *National Geographic*, May 1928, 530–601.

19. David McCullough, *The Path Between the Seas: The Creation of the Panama Canal, 1870–1914* (New York: Touchstone Books, 1977), 140–141. Precise casualty figures are impossible to calculate, since the company kept only records of whites.

20. M. L. Walker to Richard Halliburton, August 13, 1928, courtesy of the Halliburton Archives, Barrett Library, Rhodes College, Memphis, TN.

21. "Halliburton to Swim the Panama Canal: Plans Start This Week—Governor Warns Him Against Alligators and Typhoid," *New York Times*, August 14, 1928.

22. By 1938 the largest toll collected for a commercial vessel was $18,985 for the *Empress of Britain*; the battleship *Renown* was $22,500.

23. "The Press: Last Adventure," *Time*, June 19, 1939, http://content.time.com/time /magazine/article/0,9171,761535,00.html.

24. "Halliburton to Swim the Panama Canal," *New York Times*.

25. Thomas Wright to Richard Halliburton, January 3, 1929, box 25, folder 22, Richard Halliburton Papers.

26. "Halliburton Starts Panama Canal Swim: Writer Makes Less Than Four Miles in First Effort—Faces Alligators Today," *New York Times*, August 15, 1928.

27. Ibid.

28. Lindbergh, "To Bogota and Back," 573.

29. "Open Gatun Locks Just for Halliburton: Officials Use Same Power to Lift Swimmer as for 44,799 Ton Battleship," *New York Times*, August 17, 1928.

30. McCullough, *Path*, 591.

31. Ibid., 602.

32. Fred C. Cole, "The Partial-Payment Swim," *New Yorker*, January 4, 1930, 62.

33. Ibid.

34. "Big Canal Radio Station: Its Communication Field Will Cover Thousands of Miles," *New York Times*, August 10, 1913.

35. Richard Halliburton to Wesley Halliburton Sr., August 24, 1928, box 19, folder 1a, Richard Halliburton Papers.

36. Richard Halliburton to parents, August 25, 1928, box 19, folder 1a, Richard Halliburton Papers.

37. John Nicholls Booth, video interview, February 15–16, 1986, courtesy of the Halliburton Archives.

38. Ibid.

39. Ibid.

40. Richard Halliburton to David Laurance Chambers, March 14, 1928, box 25, folder 4, Richard Halliburton Papers.

41. "Names Peak for Balboa: Halliburton Says He Found Pacific Discoverer's Hill," *New York Times*, September 7, 1928.

42. Ibid.

43. Ibid.

44. David Laurance Chambers to Richard Halliburton, October 26, 1928, box 25, folder 21, Richard Halliburton Papers.

45. Richard Halliburton to parents, October 1, 1928, box 19, folder 1a, Richard Halliburton Papers.

46. Richard Halliburton to parents, October 24, 1928, as quoted in Halliburton, *Richard Halliburton*, 294.

47. Richard Halliburton to parents, October 24, 1928, box 19, folder 1a, Richard Halliburton Papers.

48. Al E. Ruger to Richard Halliburton, October 3, 1929, box 25, folder 22, Richard Halliburton Papers.

49. Sean Dennis Cashman, *America in the Twenties and Thirties: The Olympian Age of Franklin Delano Roosevelt* (New York: New York University Press, 1989), 527.

50. Richard Halliburton to parents, January 14, 1929, box 19, folder 2, Richard Halliburton Papers.

51. Halliburton, *New Worlds*, 266.

6. Hollywood Lights

1. Lucy Moore, *Anything Goes: A Biography of the Roaring Twenties* (New York: Overlook Press, 2010), 315.

2. Ibid., 329.

3. Richard Halliburton to parents, January 23, 1929, box 19, folder 2, Richard Halliburton Papers, Manuscripts Division, Department of Rare Books and Special Collections, Princeton University Library, Princeton, NJ.

4. Richard Halliburton to parents, February 8, 1929, as quoted in Richard Halliburton, *Richard Halliburton: His Story of His Life's Adventure, as Told in Letters to His Mother and Father* (New York: Garden City Publishing, 1940), 298.

5. "Mr. Halliburton Plays Robinson Crusoe," *New York Times*, December 15, 1929.

6. Richard Halliburton to parents, April 1930, as quoted in Halliburton, *Richard Halliburton*, 304.

7. Corey C. Ford, "The Adventure Racket," *Vanity Fair*, July 1929, 35.

8. Richard Halliburton to David Laurance Chambers, April 10, 1930, box 25, folder 6, Richard Halliburton Papers.

9. Richard Halliburton to parents, October 22, 1929, as quoted in Halliburton, *Richard Halliburton*, 304.

10. Richard Halliburton, writing in guestbook of Stan Hywet Hall, March 10, 1929, courtesy of Harriet D. Chapman.

11. Margaret DeVault, e-mail correspondence with author, December 5, 2014.

12. Ibid.

13. Moore, *Anything Goes*, 14.

14. Richard Halliburton to parents and Mary Hutchison, January 13, 1930, and Richard Halliburton to parents, January 27, 1930, box 19, folder 3, Richard Halliburton Papers.

15. Richard B. Jewell, *The Golden Age of Cinema: Hollywood, 1929–1945* (Malden, MA: Blackwell Publishing, 2007), 206–207.

16. Sean Dennis Cashman, *America in the Twenties and Thirties: The Olympian Age of Franklin Delano Roosevelt* (New York: New York University Press, 1989), 339.

17. Richard Halliburton to parents, Easter Sunday, 1930, box 19, folder 3, Richard Halliburton Papers.

18. Richard Halliburton to parents, January 13, 1927, box 19a, folder 3, Richard Halliburton Papers.

19. George Weller, "The Passing of the Last Playboy," *Esquire Magazine*, April 1940, 58.

20. Richard Halliburton to parents, May 5, 1930, box 19, folder 3, Richard Halliburton Papers.

21. Richard Halliburton to parents, May 27, 1930, box 19, folder 3, Richard Halliburton Papers.

22. Richard Halliburton to parents, May 14, 1930, box 19, folder 3, Richard Halliburton Papers.

23. Jewell, *Golden Age*, 69.

24. Richard Halliburton to parents, October 18, 1932, box 20, folder 1, Richard Halliburton Papers.

25. Mordaunt Hall, review of *India Speaks*, directed by Walter Futter, *New York Times*, May 8, 1933.

26. Available for viewing at the Halliburton Archives, Barrett Library, Rhodes College, Memphis, TN.

27. Richard Halliburton to parents, November 12, 1933, box 20, folder 2, Richard Halliburton Papers.

28. Lauren Kessler, *The Happy Bottom Riding Club: The Life and Times of Pancho Barnes* (New York: Random House, 2000), 80, 82.

29. Ibid., 59.

30. Ibid., 61.

31. Ibid., 62.

32. Moore, *Anything Goes*, 87.

33. Jeanine Basinger, *Silent Stars* (New York: Alfred A. Knopf, 1999), 104.

34. Moore, *Anything Goes*, 87.

35. Basinger, *Silent Stars*, 52, 53, 56.

36. William J. Mann, *Behind the Screen: How Gays and Lesbians Shaped Hollywood, 1910–1969* (New York: Penguin Books, 2001), 91, 97, 99.

37. Allan R. Ellenberger, *Ramon Novarro: A Biography of the Silent Film Idol, 1899–1968* (Jefferson, NC: McFarland, 1999), 142; Mann, *Behind the Screen*, xiv.

38. As quoted in Jonathan Root, *Halliburton: The Magnificent Myth* (New York: Coward-McCann, 1965), 165.

39. Moye W. Stephens Jr., interview by Michael Blankenship, September 20, 1986, courtesy of the Michael E. Blankenship Collection of the Halliburton Archives.

40. Richard Halliburton to parents, May 14, 1930, box 19, folder 3, Richard Halliburton Papers.

41. "On the Screen Horizon: Richard Halliburton's Book, 'The Royal Road to Romance,' Will Be Made into a Film by Fox," *New York Times*, July 27, 1930.

42. Talk of the Town, *New Yorker*, November 8, 1930, 17–18.

43. "We Nominate for Oblivion," *Vanity Fair*, June 1930, box 26, folder 10, Richard Halliburton Papers.

44. Richard Halliburton to parents, May 27, 1930, box 19, folder 3, Richard Halliburton Papers.

45. Loren Daniel Glass, *Authors Inc.: Literary Celebrity in the Modern United States, 1880–1980* (New York: NYU Press, 2004), 154.

46. Greg Daugherty, "The Last Adventure of Richard Halliburton, the Forgotten Hero of 1930s America," Smithsonian.com, March 25, 2014, www.smithsonianmag.com/history /last-adventure-richard-halliburton-forgotten-hero-1930s-america-180950164/.

47. Weller, "Passing," 112.

48. Ibid.

49. Richard Halliburton to parents, June 5, 1930, as quoted in Halliburton, *Richard Halliburton*, 306.

50. Irvine O. Hockaday Jr., telephone interview with author, October 30, 2014.

51. Richard Halliburton to Wesley Halliburton Sr., May 30, 1927, box 9a, folder 3, Richard Halliburton Papers.

52. Tom D. Crouch, *Wings-A History of Aviation from Kites to the Space Age* (Washington, DC: Smithsonian National Air & Space Museum/W. W. Norton, 2003), 122, 123.

53. Ibid., 9.

54. "All Roads Lead to Romance, Richard Halliburton Finds," *Cumberland Evening Times*, January 2, 1930.

7. The *Flying Carpet*

1. As quoted in Barbara Hunter Shultz, *Flying Carpets, Flying Wings: The Biography of Moye W. Stephens* (Lancaster, CA: Little Buttes Publishing, 2010), 123–129.

2. Ibid., 123–129.

3. Ibid., 25.

4. Ronald Gilliam, "Around the World in the Flying Carpet," *Aviation History* 14, no. 5 (May 2004): 22, 60.

5. Loring A. Schuler to Wesley Halliburton Sr., October 4, 1930, box 25, folder 22, Richard Halliburton Papers, Manuscripts Division, Department of Rare Books and Special Collections, Princeton University Library, Princeton, NJ.

6. "Left Home with $5; Returns as a Millionaire," *Memphis Commercial Appeal*, July 16, 1932.

7. William Short, interview with author, Rhodes College, Memphis, TN, September 14–15, 2015.

8. Richard Halliburton to David Laurance Chambers, November 4, 1930, box 25, folder 6, Richard Halliburton Papers.

9. Richard Halliburton to Nelle Nance Halliburton, November 7, 1930, box 19, folder 3, Richard Halliburton Papers.

10. Richard Halliburton to David Laurance Chambers, November 30, 1930, box 25, folder 6, Richard Halliburton Papers.

11. Richard Halliburton to parents, November 19, 1930, box 19, folder 3, Richard Halliburton Papers.

12. Gilliam, "Around the World."

13. Shultz, *Flying Carpets*, 313.

14. Ibid., 151.

15. Richard Halliburton to parents, October 6, 1930, box 19, folder 3, Richard Halliburton Papers.

16. Richard Halliburton to parents, January 14, 1931, box 19, folder 4, Richard Halliburton Papers.

17. Richard Halliburton to parents, January 14, 1931, box 19, folder 4, Richard Halliburton Papers.

18. Shultz, *Flying Carpets*, 144–145.

19. Richard Halliburton to home, February 5, 1931, box 19, folder 4, Richard Halliburton Papers.

20. Richard Halliburton to parents, January 28, 1931, box 19, folder 4, Richard Halliburton Papers.

21. Richard Halliburton to parents, January 30, 1931, box 19, folder 4, Richard Halliburton Papers.

22. Richard Halliburton to parents, February 5, 1931, box 19, folder 4, Richard Halliburton Papers.

23. Richard Halliburton to parents, January 30, 1931, box 19, folder 4, Richard Halliburton Papers.

24. Richard Halliburton to parents, February 5, 1931, box 19, folder 4, Richard Halliburton Papers.

25. Richard Halliburton to parents, February 21, 1931, box 19, folder 4, Richard Halliburton Papers.

26. Ibid.

27. Ibid.

28. Richard Halliburton to parents, March 20, 1931, box 19, folder 4, Richard Halliburton Papers.

29. Richard Halliburton to parents, March 31, 1931, box 19, folder 4, Richard Halliburton Papers.

30. Moye W. Stephens Jr., interview by Michael Blankenship, September 20, 1986, courtesy of the Michael E. Blankenship Collection of the Halliburton Archives, Barrett Library, Rhodes College, Memphis, TN.

31. Richard Halliburton to parents, April 25, 1931, box 19, folder 4, Richard Halliburton Papers.

32. Richard Halliburton to parents, April 4, 1931, box 19, folder 4, Richard Halliburton Papers.

33. Stephens, interview by Blankenship.

34. Gilliam, "Around the World."

35. Richard Halliburton to parents, April 25, 1931, box 19, folder 4, Richard Halliburton Papers.

36. Richard Halliburton to parents, April 4, 1931, box 19, folder 4, Richard Halliburton Papers; Gilliam, "Around the World."

37. Richard Halliburton to parents, April 25, 1931, box 19, folder 4, Richard Halliburton Papers; Stephens, interview by Blankenship.

38. Ibid.

39. Richard Halliburton to parents, May 11, 1931, box 19, folder 4, Richard Halliburton Papers.

40. Michael E. Blankenship, e-mail correspondence with author, December 7, 2014.

41. Stephens, interview by Blankenship.

42. Richard Halliburton to parents, May 11, 1931, box 19, folder 4, Richard Halliburton Papers.

43. Don Brown, "Richard Halliburton Finds Human Slavery in French Africa—but It Doesn't Work," *Chicago Daily Tribune*.

44. Stephens, interview by Blankenship.

45. Richard Halliburton to David Laurance Chambers, September 29, 1926, box 25, folder 2, Richard Halliburton Papers.

46. Richard Halliburton to parents, August 17, 1931, box 19, folder 4, Richard Halliburton Papers.

47. Review of *The Flying Carpet* by Richard Halliburton, *New Yorker*, November 12, 1932, 82–83.

48. Richard Halliburton to parents, September 25, 1931, box 19, folder 4, Richard Halliburton Papers.

49. Richard Halliburton to parents, September 9, 1931, box 19, folder 4, Richard Halliburton Papers; Stephens, interview by Blankenship.

50. Richard Halliburton to parents, September 9, 1931, box 19, folder 4, Richard Halliburton Papers.

51. Ibid.

52. Stephens, interview by Blankenship.

53. Ibid.

54. Richard Halliburton to parents, November 10, 1931, box 19, folder 4, Richard Halliburton Papers.

55. Richard Halliburton to parents, December 4, 1931, box 19, folder 4, Richard Halliburton Papers.

56. "Young German Aviatrix Finds Thrills in India: Elly Beinhorn, Flying Around the World, Does Stunts For a Maharajah and Chats with Tagore," *New York Times*, April 3, 1932.

57. Richard Halliburton to Douglas Fairbanks, January 6, 1932, box 25, folder 22, Richard Halliburton Papers.

58. Douglas Fairbanks to Richard Halliburton, February 9, 1932, box 25, folder 22, Richard Halliburton Papers.

59. James Douglas-Hamilton, *Roof of the World: Man's First Flight over Everest* (Edinburgh: Mainstream Publishing, 1983), 17.

60. Stephens, interview by Blankenship.

61. Ronald Gilliam, "Around the World in the Flying Carpet," *Aviation History* 14, no. 5 (May 2004).

62. Ibid.

63. "To Try Everest Flight: Writer Announces He Will Seek to Take Plane over Peak in Fall," *New York Times*, June 16, 1932.

64. Richard Halliburton to parents, January 23, 1932, box 20, folder 1, Richard Halliburton Papers.

65. Ibid.

66. Richard Halliburton to parents, February 4, 1932, March 8, 1931, and March 23, 1931, box 20, folder 1, Richard Halliburton Papers.

67. Stephens, interview by Blankenship.

68. Richard Halliburton to parents, May 10, 1932, box 20, folder 1, Richard Halliburton Papers.

69. Ibid.

70. Ibid.

71. "The Ranee Describes Her Adventure," *Sarawak Gazette*, May 2, 1932.

72. Ibid.

73. "Bizarre Experiences Recounted by Richard Halliburton," *Lethbridge Herald* (Alberta, Canada), June 17, 1932.

74. Stephens, interview by Blankenship.

75. Ibid.

76. As quoted in Gordon Sinclair, *Bright Paths to Adventure* (Toronto: McClelland & Steward, 1945), 88.

77. Ibid., 86.

78. Richard Halliburton to parents, May 10, 1932, box 20, folder 1, Richard Halliburton Papers.

8. Interview with an Assassin

1. Richard Halliburton to parents, May 31, 1932, box 20, folder 1, Richard Halliburton Papers, Manuscripts Division, Department of Rare Books and Special Collections, Princeton University Library, Princeton, NJ.

2. Richard Halliburton to parents, July 16, 1932, box 20, folder 1, Richard Halliburton Papers.

3. Richard Halliburton to parents, September 15, 1932, box 20, folder 1, Richard Halliburton Papers.

4. Richard Halliburton to parents, November 13, 1932, box 20, folder 1, Richard Halliburton Papers.

5. Richard Halliburton to parents, October 18, 1932, box 20, folder 1, Richard Halliburton Papers.

6. Richard Halliburton to parents, May 31, 1932, box 20, folder 1, Richard Halliburton Papers.

7. "Catholic Actors Meet: 450 Persons Present at Monthly Session at Astor," *New York Times*, January 21, 1933.

8. John W. Jarrell, "No Barber Shops Open," *State Journal* (Topeka, KS), November 5, 1932.

9. Herbert Waggoner, "Teachers Take a Flying Trip," *Hutchinson News*, November 4, 1932.

10. Richard Halliburton to parents, November 30, 1932, box 20, folder 1, Richard Halliburton Papers.

11. Frank Nelson Doubleday to Richard Halliburton, January 12, 1933, box 25, folder 22, Richard Halliburton Papers.

12. Margaret DeVault, e-mail correspondence with author, December 5, 2014.

13. "Halliburton's Wanderings," *New York Times*, December 4, 1932.

14. "Books: Fair-Haired Carpeteer," *Time*, November 14, 1932, http://content.time.com/time/magazine/article/0,9171,847103,00.html.

15. Richard Halliburton, *Richard Halliburton: His Story of His Life's Adventure, as Told in Letters to His Mother and Father* (New York: Garden City Publishing, 1940), 344;

Charles E. Morris III, "Richard Halliburton's Bearded Tales," *Quarterly Journal of Speech* 95, no. 2 (May 2009).

16. Corey Ford to Richard Halliburton, January 18, 1933, box 25, folder 22, Richard Halliburton Papers.

17. Ibid.

18. John Nicholls Booth, video interview, February 15–16, 1996, courtesy of the Halliburton Archives, Barrett Library, Rhodes College, Memphis, TN.

19. Ibid.

20. Ibid.

21. "More New Yorkers Will Toast with Hoffman Pale Dry Than Any Other Ginger Ale in the World" (advertisement), December 31, 1932, *New Yorker*, 23.

22. The watch is on display at the Halliburton Archives.

23. Christine Sadler, "Memphian Wants to Stop," *Nashville Banner*, February 15, 1933.

24. Richard Halliburton to parents, January 4, 1934, as quoted in Halliburton, *Richard Halliburton*, 349.

25. Richard Halliburton to parents, June 29, 1934, box 20, folder 3, Richard Halliburton Papers.

26. Richard Halliburton to parents, July 13, 1934, box 20, folder 3, Richard Halliburton Papers.

27. Richard Halliburton, *Seven League Boots* (Indianapolis: Bobbs-Merrill, 1935), 22.

28. Mrs. Albert S. Glover to Richard Halliburton, April 22, 1936, box 25, folder 22, Richard Halliburton Papers.

29. Richard Halliburton to parents, August 16, 1934, box 20, folder 3, Richard Halliburton Papers.

30. Halliburton, *Seven League Boots*, 60.

31. Ibid., 71.

32. Richard Halliburton to parents, August 23, 1934, box 20, folder 3, Richard Halliburton Papers.

33. Richard Halliburton to parents, September 11, 1934, box 20, folder 3, Richard Halliburton Papers.

34. Richard Halliburton to parents, October 13, 1934, box 20, folder 3, Richard Halliburton Papers.

35. Ibid.

36. Ibid.

37. Richard Halliburton to parents, October 24, 1934, box 20, folder 3, Richard Halliburton Papers.

38. Ibid.

39. Richard Halliburton to parents, November 7, 1934, box 20, folder 3, Richard Halliburton Papers.

40. Richard Halliburton to parents, September 30, 1934, box 20, folder 3, Richard Halliburton Papers.

41. Richard Halliburton to parents, November 7, 1934, box 20, folder 3, Richard Halliburton Papers.

42. Ibid.

43. *El Paso Herald Post*, June 12, 1935.

44. Richard Halliburton to parents, November 7, 1934, box 20, folder 3, Richard Halliburton Papers.

45. Richard Halliburton to parents, November 7, 1934, box 20, folder 3, Richard Halliburton Papers.

46. Richard Halliburton to parents, January 2, 1935, box 2, folder 4, Richard Halliburton Papers.

47. Ibid.

48. Halliburton, *Seven League Boots*, 108.

49. Richard Halliburton to parents, December 2, 1934, box 20, folder 3, Richard Halliburton Papers.

50. Ibid.

51. Halliburton, *Seven League Boots*, 193.

52. Ibid.

53. "Halliburton on Russia," *Independent* (Helena, MT), January 1, 1935.

54. Richard Halliburton to parents, January 2, 1935, box 20, folder 4, Richard Halliburton Papers.

55. Richard Halliburton to David Laurance Chambers, January 10, 1935, box 25, folder 11, Richard Halliburton Papers.

56. "Says Russia Ousted Him: Halliburton Declares He Talked to Czar's Executioner," *New York Times*, January 13, 1935.

57. Richard Halliburton to parents, January 2, 1935, box 20, folder 4, Richard Halliburton Papers.

58. Ibid.

59. Richard Halliburton to parents and Mary Hutchison, February 12, 1935, box 20, folder 4, Richard Halliburton Papers.

60. Richard Halliburton to parents, February 26, 1935, box 20, folder 4, Richard Halliburton Papers.

61. Donald Ostrowski, "A Reconsideration of Richard Halliburton's Interview with P.Z. Ermakov as Evidence for the Murder of the Romanovs," *Russian History/Histoire Russe* 25, no. 3 (1999).

62. Ibid.

63. Richard Halliburton to parents, February 26, 1935, box 20, folder 4, Richard Halliburton Papers.

64. David Laurance Chambers to Richard Halliburton, April 1, 1935, Lilly Library, courtesy of the Halliburton Archives.

65. David Laurance Chambers to Halliburton, April 26, 1935, Lilly Library, courtesy of the Halliburton Archives.

66. Paul Mooney to William Alexander Levy, May 25, 1935, courtesy of the Halliburton Archives.

67. Michael E. Blankenship, e-mail to author, December 7, 2014.

68. Richard Halliburton to parents, April 25, 1935, as quoted in Halliburton, *Richard Halliburton*, 366.

69. Richard Halliburton to parents, May 8, 1935, box 20, folder 4, Richard Halliburton Papers.

70. Ibid.

71. Richard Halliburton to parents, July 6, 1935, box 20, folder 4, Richard Halliburton Papers.

72. "Halliburton's Elephant Finds Troubles in Alps," *New York Times*, July 22, 1935.

73. David Laurance Chambers to Richard Halliburton, April 26, 1935, Lilly Library, Courtesy of the Halliburton Archives.

74. Richard B. Jewell, *The Golden Age of Cinema: Hollywood, 1929–1945* (Malden, MA: Blackwell Publishing, 2007), 41.

9. Hangover House

1. Richard Halliburton to parents, January 5, 1936, box 21, folder 1, Richard Halliburton Papers, Manuscripts Division, Department of Rare Books and Special Collections, Princeton University Library, Princeton, NJ.

2. Advertisement for yeast tablets, circa 1930s, posted to Etsy by "PhotosandBacon," accessed November 20, 2015, www.etsy.com/listing/189349182/too-skinny-ironized -yeast-tablets-c1930s.

3. "Halliburton Talk to Feature Many Travels," *Covina Argus Citizen*, March 17, 1937.

4. Richard Halliburton to parents, January 5, 1936, and January 20, 1936, box 21, folder 1, Richard Halliburton Papers.

5. "Richard Halliburton, Famous Adventurer Says," *San Bernardo County Sun* (San Bernardo, CA), July 26, 1936.

6. Review of *Seven League Boots*, *Times* (San Mateo, CA), July 25, 1936.

7. Virginia Reese, telephone interview with author, February 25, 2015.

8. Moye W. Stephens Jr., interview by Michael Blankenship, September 20, 1986, courtesy of the Michael E. Blankenship Collection of the Halliburton Archives, Barrett Library, Rhodes College, Memphis, TN.

9. Richard Halliburton, "Richard Halliburton Answers His Critics," *Five Star Weekly*, October 1936.

10. Ibid.

11. Suzanne Thompson, "A Learning Legacy," *Memphis Daily News*, September 3, 1999.

12. John Maize, telephone interview with author, September 25, 2014.

13. Ibid.

14. Ibid.

15. Stuart Heaver, "Richard Halliburton: The Hero Time Forgot," *South China Morning Post*, March 22, 2014, www.scmp.com/magazines/post-magazine/article/1453193/richard -halliburton-hero-time-forgot.

16. Richard Halliburton to Nelle Nance Halliburton, June 7, 1936, box 21, folder 1, Richard Halliburton Papers.

17. Ibid.

18. Richard Halliburton to parents, May 20, 1936, box 21, folder 1, Richard Halliburton Papers.

19. As quoted in Richard Halliburton, *Richard Halliburton: His Story of His Life's Adventure, as Told in Letters to His Mother and Father* (New York: Garden City Publishing, 1940), 378.

20. David Laurance Chambers to Richard Halliburton, July 20, 1936, courtesy of the Halliburton Archives.

21. Richard Halliburton to parents, July 28, 1936, box 21, folder 1, Richard Halliburton Papers.

22. Ibid.

23. Photograph of Halliburton in Yosemite, box 26, Richard Halliburton Papers.

24. Richard Halliburton to parents, July 1, 1936, and July 28, 1936, as quoted in Halliburton, *Richard Halliburton*, 381.

25. Beth Kleid, "Philanthropist William Alexander Receives by Giving," *Los Angeles Times*, December 29, 1989.

26. Stephens, interview by Blankenship.

27. Ibid.

28. Ione Lee Mooney to William Alexander Levy and Paul Mooney, April 10, 1938, courtesy of the Michael E. Blankenship Collection of the Halliburton Archives.

29. Scott Sebastian, "The Halliburton House," *South Laguna Civic Association Bulletin* (South Laguna, CA), Fall 2010, 1.

30. Richard Halliburton to Nelle Nance Halliburton, October 15, 1936, box 21, folder 1, Richard Halliburton Papers.

31. Ibid.

32. Richard Halliburton to parents, November 3–4, 1936, box 21, folder 1, Richard Halliburton Papers.

33. Richard Halliburton to parents, May 2, 1937, box 21, folder 2, Richard Halliburton Papers.

34. Kleid, "Philanthropist."

35. Richard Halliburton to parents, November 3–4, 1936, box 21, folder 1, Richard Halliburton Papers.

36. Jim Carlton, "South Laguna's Forgotten Giant: 50 Years After His Death at Sea, Adventurer Halliburton's Exploits Are as Obscured as His Mansion," *Los Angeles Times*, September 3, 1989.

37. Sebastian, "Halliburton House."

38. Halliburton to parents, November 3–4, 1936, box 21, folder 1, Richard Halliburton Papers.

39. Richard Halliburton to Nelle Nance Halliburton, October 13, 1935, as quoted in Halliburton, *Richard Halliburton*, 383.

40. Richard Halliburton to Nelle Nance Halliburton, November 27, 1936, box 21, folder 1, Richard Halliburton Papers.

41. Richard Halliburton to Wesley Halliburton Sr., November 27, 1936, box 21, folder 1, Richard Halliburton Papers.

42. Ibid.

43. William Alexander Levy to Richard Halliburton, January 27, 1937, courtesy of the Michael E. Blankenship Collection of the Halliburton Archives.

44. Richard Halliburton to William Alexander Levy, February 1, 1937, courtesy of the Michael E. Blankenship Collection of the Halliburton Archives.

45. William Alexander Levy to unknown recipient, February 1937, courtesy of the Michael E. Blankenship Collection of the Halliburton Archives.

46. Richard Halliburton to William Alexander, April 4, 1938, courtesy of the Halliburton Archives.

47. Richard Halliburton to parents, April 27, 1937, box 21, folder 2, Richard Halliburton Papers.

48. Ibid.

49. Richard Halliburton to parents, April 18, 1937, box 21, folder 2, and aerial photo of the house, box 37, folder 4, Richard Halliburton Papers.

50. Photos of Hangover House, box 37, folder 4, Richard Halliburton Papers.

51. Richard Halliburton to William Alexander Levy, February 1937, courtesy of the Michael E. Blankenship Collection of the Halliburton Archives.

52. Richard Halliburton to parents, January 23, 1937, box 21, folder 2, Richard Halliburton Papers.

53. Marilyn Fais, e-mail correspondence with author, May 20, 2015.

54. Ibid.

55. Anne Precht to Richard Halliburton, May 2, 1937, box 25, folder 13, Richard Halliburton Papers.

56. Richard Halliburton to Frances Singer, June 13, 1937, box 25, folder 16, Richard Halliburton Papers.

57. Richard Halliburton to William Alexander Levy, July 13, 1937, courtesy of the Michael E. Blankenship Collection of the Halliburton Archives.

58. Richard Halliburton to William Alexander Levy, August 21, 1937, courtesy of the Michael E. Blankenship Collection of the Halliburton Archives.

59. Paul Mooney to William Alexander Levy, September 1937, courtesy of the Michael E. Blankenship Collection of the Halliburton Archives.

60. Paul Mooney to William Alexander, September 8, 1937, courtesy of the Michael E. Blankenship Collection of the Halliburton Archives.

61. Frank Mickadeit, "Laguna Halts Another Historical Home Remodel," *Orange County Register*, April 18, 2012.

62. William Alexander Levy to Richard Halliburton, March 30, 1938, courtesy of the Michael E. Blankenship Collection of the Halliburton Archives.

63. Richard Halliburton to William Alexander Levy, April 4, 1938, courtesy of the Michael E. Blankenship Collection of the Halliburton Archives.

64. "Hangover: Owner Was Lost at Sea Shortly After Home was Built," *Orange County Register*, March 13, 2011.

65. Claire Marie Vogel, *Laguna Beach*, Images of America (Chicago: Arcadia Publishing, 2009), 64.

10. A New Inspiration

1. Art Linkletter and Dean Jennings, *Confessions of a Happy Man: The Heartwarming Story of a Fabulous Showman* (New York: Giant Cardinal, 1960), 109–110.

2. Ibid.

3. Ibid.

4. James R. Smith, "Golden Gate International Exposition: SFs Final World's Fair—Part II," *Guidelines: Newsletter for San Francisco City Guides and Sponsors*, accessed November 20, 2015, www.sfcityguides.org/public_guidelines.html?article=861&submitted=TRUE.

5. Federal Writers' Project, *Almanac for Thirty-Niners* (Stanford, CA: James Ladd Delkin, 1938), 113.

6. Linkletter, *Confessions*, 109–110.

7. Richard Halliburton to parents, May 2, 1937, box 21, folder 2, Richard Halliburton Papers, Manuscripts Division, Department of Rare Books and Special Collections, Princeton University Library, Princeton, NJ.

8. Richard Halliburton to Wesley Halliburton Sr., May 2, 1937, box 21, folder 2, Richard Halliburton Papers.

9. Helen Rick, review of *Second Book of Marvels*, *Jefferson City Post Tribune*, December 5, 1938.

10. Quoted in Susan Lehman, "Books That Triggered Writers' Wanderlust," *New York Times*, May 14, 2006.

11. R. W. Apple Jr., "An Oasis Between Two Civilizations," *New York Times*, November 8, 1984.

12. Richard Halliburton to parents, June 15, 1938, box 21, folder 3, Richard Halliburton Papers.

13. Halliburton to parents, February 21, 1938, box 21, folder 3, Richard Halliburton Papers.

14. Richard Halliburton to parents, April 12, 1938, box 21, folder 3, Richard Halliburton Papers.

15. Richard Halliburton to parents, May 9, 1938, box 21, folder 3, Richard Halliburton Papers.

16. Ibid.

17. John Nicholls Booth, video interview, February 15–16, 1996, courtesy of the Halliburton Archives, Barrett Library, Rhodes College, Memphis, TN.

18. Ibid.

19. Ibid.

20. Richard Halliburton to parents, May 28, 1938, box 21, folder 3, Richard Halliburton Papers.

21. Richard Halliburton to parents, June 13, 1938, box 21, folder 3, Richard Halliburton Papers.

22. Richard Halliburton to parents, July 6, 1938, box 21, folder 3, Richard Halliburton Papers.

23. "In Town and Out," Tables for Two, *New Yorker*, July 9, 1938, 40.

24. Dale E. Collins, "The Royal Road Across the Pacific," *US Naval Institute Proceedings* 66, no. 446 (April 1940): 501.

25. Richard Halliburton to parents, November 20, 1938, box 21, folder 4, Richard Halliburton Papers.

26. Gordon Torrey to Michael Blankenship, June 22, 1987, courtesy of the Michael E. Blankenship Collection of the Halliburton Archives.

27. Ibid.

28. James Zug, "Sea of Dreams," *Dartmouth Alumni Magazine*, July–August 2014.

29. Gordon Torrey to Michael Blankenship, June 22, 1987, courtesy of the Michael E. Blankenship Collection of the Halliburton Archives.

30. Ibid.

31. "Potter '38 Sails Pacific in Junk with Richard Halliburton, Famed Adventurer," *Dartmouth*, November 29, 1938; Gordon Torrey to Michael Blankenship, November 19, 1987, courtesy of the Michael E. Blankenship Collection of the Halliburton Archives.

32. Richard Halliburton to Vida Halliburton, September 23, 1938, courtesy of the Halliburton Archives.

33. Ibid.

34. Richard Halliburton to parents, September 10, 1938, box 21, folder 3, Richard Halliburton Papers.

35. Richard Halliburton to parents, October 6, 1937, box 21, folder 2, Richard Halliburton Papers.

36. Richard Halliburton to Wesley Halliburton Sr., September 10, 1938, box 21, folder 3, Richard Halliburton Papers.

37. "The President Opens the Golden Gate Exposition in San Francisco from Key West, Florida," February 18, 1939, in *Public Papers of the Presidents of the US: F. D. Roosevelt*, vol. 8 (Best Books, 1941), 300.

38. "It's Here! Bay Area's World's Fair Opens Gates; Oakland Revelers Jam City Streets, Halt Parade," *Oakland Tribune*, February 18, 1938.

39. Ibid.

40. Richard Halliburton to Nelle Nance Halliburton, June 15, 1938, box 21, folder 3, Richard Halliburton Papers.

41. Don C. Skemer, e-mail to author, May 6, 2015.

42. Irvine O. Hockaday Jr., telephone interview with author, October 30, 2014.

43. Richard Halliburton to parents, August 31, 1938, box 21, folder 3, Richard Halliburton Papers.

44. Richard Halliburton to parents, September 10, 1938, box 21, folder 3, Richard Halliburton Papers.

45. Ibid.

46. Richard Halliburton to parents, September 28, 1938, box 21, folder 3, Richard Halliburton Papers.

47. Richard Halliburton to parents, June 17, 1938, box 21, folder 3, Richard Halliburton Papers.

48. Richard Halliburton to D. D. Stetson, September 28, 1938, box 25, folder 19, Richard Halliburton Papers; Western Union telegram sent from San Francisco to Los Angeles, September 23, 1939, to Mrs. Erle Halliburton, courtesy of the Halliburton Archives.

11. The *Sea Dragon*

1. Richard Halliburton to parents, September 28, 1938, as quoted in Richard Halliburton, *Richard Halliburton: His Story of His Life's Adventure, as Told in Letters to His Mother and Father* (New York: Garden City Publishing, 1940), 401.

2. Michael E. Blankenship, e-mail to author, December 7, 2014.

3. Richard Halliburton to parents, August 1, 1938, box 21, folder 3, Richard Halliburton Papers, Manuscripts Division, Department of Rare Books and Special Collections, Princeton University Library, Princeton, NJ.

4. Dale E. Collins, "The Royal Road Across the Pacific," *US Naval Institute Proceedings* 66, no. 446 (April 1940): 501.

5. Ibid.

6. Ibid.

7. Halliburton to parents, October 7, 1938, box 21, folder 3, Richard Halliburton Papers.

8. From the Halliburton Trans-Pacific Junk Sailing Expedition, November 20, 1938, box 25, folder 117, Richard Halliburton Papers.

9. Ibid.

10. Ibid.

11. Richard Halliburton to parents, October 7, 1937, as quoted in Halliburton, *Richard Halliburton*, 408.

12. Richard Halliburton to parents, November 20, 1938, box 21, folder 4, Richard Halliburton Papers.

13. Richard Halliburton to parents, October 7, 1937, as quoted in Halliburton, *Richard Halliburton*, 408.

14. Collins, "Royal Road," 502.

15. Richard Halliburton to parents, January 19, 1938, box 21, folder 4, Richard Halliburton Papers.

16. Richard Halliburton to parents, October 7, 1938, box 21, folder 4, Richard Halliburton Papers.

17. From the Halliburton Trans-Pacific Junk Sailing Expedition, January 18, 1939, Hong Kong, box 25, folder 117, Richard Halliburton Papers.

18. From the Halliburton Trans-Pacific Junk Sailing Expedition, November 20, 1938, box 25, folder 117, Richard Halliburton Papers.

19. Ibid.

20. Gordon Torrey to Michael Blankenship, August 15, 1987, courtesy of the Michael E. Blankenship Collection of the Halliburton Archives, Barrett Library, Rhodes College, Memphis, TN.

21. Philip Snow, *The Fall of Hong Kong: Britain, China and the Japanese Occupation* (New Haven, CT: Yale University Press, 2003), 28, 32; David J. Goldberg, *Discontented America: The United States in the 1920s* (Baltimore: Johns Hopkins University Press, 1999), 29.

22. Richard Halliburton to parents, November 2, 1938, box 21, folder 3, Richard Halliburton Papers.

23. Richard Halliburton to parents, November 10, 1938, box 21, folder 3, Richard Halliburton Papers.

24. Richard Halliburton to parents, January 1, 1939, box 21, folder 4, Richard Halliburton Papers.

25. From the Halliburton Trans-Pacific Junk Sailing Expedition, January 18, 1939, Hong Kong, box 25, folder 117, Richard Halliburton Papers.

26. I .G. Edmonds, "The Mystery of the Hong Kong Sea Dragon," *Pacific Stars and Stripes*, March 23, 1956, 15.

27. From the Halliburton Trans-Pacific Junk Sailing Expedition, January 18, 1939, Hong Kong, box 25, folder 117, Richard Halliburton Papers.

28. Richard Halliburton to parents, January 1, 1939, box 21, folder 4, Richard Halliburton Papers.

29. From the Halliburton Trans-Pacific Junk Sailing Expedition, January 18, 1939, box 25, folder 117, Richard Halliburton Papers.

30. From the Halliburton Trans-Pacific Junk Sailing Expedition, January 1, 1939, box 21, folder 4, Richard Halliburton Papers.

31. Richard Halliburton to parents, November 21, 1938, box 2, folder 3, Richard Halliburton Papers.

32. Richard Halliburton to parents, January 23, 1939, box 21, folder 4, Richard Halliburton Papers.

33. From the Halliburton Trans-Pacific Junk Sailing Expedition, November 20, 1938, box 25, folder 117, Richard Halliburton Papers.

34. Gordon Torrey to Michael Blankenship, September 20, 1988, courtesy of the Michael E. Blankenship Collection of the Halliburton Archives.

35. Halliburton to parents, September 28, 1938, box 21, folder 3, Richard Halliburton Papers.

36. Gordon Torrey to Michael Blankenship, October 11, 1989, courtesy of the Michael E. Blankenship Collection of the Halliburton Archives.

37. Wesley Halliburton Sr. to Roma Borst Hoff, February 9, 1962, courtesy of the Halliburton Archives.

38. Michael E. Blankenship, e-mail to author, December 7, 2014.

39. Halliburton to parents, November 21, 1938, box 21, folder 3, Richard Halliburton Papers.

40. Collins, "Royal Road," 505.

41. From the Halliburton Trans-Pacific Junk Sailing Expedition, January 18, 1939, box 21, folder 4, Richard Halliburton Papers.

42. Gordon Torrey to Michael Blankenship, June 22, 1987, courtesy of the Michael E. Blankenship Collection of the Halliburton Archives.

43. Ibid.

44. William Short, interview with author, Rhodes College, Memphis, TN, October 2014.

45. Photos of Davis and her children, courtesy of the Michael E. Blankenship Collection of the Halliburton Archives.

46. Torrey to Blankenship, June 22, 1987.

47. Ibid.

48. Richard Halliburton to parents, November 21, 1938, box 21, folder 3, Richard Halliburton Papers.

49. Richard Halliburton to parents, January 1, 1939, box 21, folder 4, Richard Halliburton Papers.

50. Richard Halliburton to parents, November 21, 1938, box 21, folder 3, Richard Halliburton Papers.

51. Charles Jokstad, *The Captain and the Sea* (New York: Vantage Press, 1967), 187.

52. As quoted in Jokstad, *Captain*, 187.

53. Ibid.

54. Ibid., 188–189.

55. As quoted in Collins, "Royal Road," 504.

56. From the Halliburton Trans-Pacific Junk Sailing Expedition, November 20, 1938, box 25, folder 117, Richard Halliburton Papers.

57. From the Halliburton Trans-Pacific Junk Sailing Expedition, January 18, 1939, box 21, folder 117, Richard Halliburton Papers.

58. Dick H. Wells to Richard Halliburton, May 25, 1938, box 25, folder 22, Richard Halliburton Papers.

12. So Good-bye Again

1. From the Halliburton Trans-Pacific Junk Sailing Expedition, January 27, 1939, box 25, folder 117, Richard Halliburton Papers, Manuscripts Division, Department of Rare Books and Special Collections, Princeton University Library, Princeton, NJ.

2. Ibid.

3. From the Halliburton Trans-Pacific Junk Sailing Expedition, November 20, 1930, box 25, folder 117, Richard Halliburton Papers.

4. From the Halliburton Trans-Pacific Junk Sailing Expedition, January 27, 1939, box 25, folder 117, Richard Halliburton Papers.

5. Richard Halliburton to parents, January 23, 1939, box 21, folder 4, Richard Halliburton Papers.

6. From the Halliburton Trans-Pacific Junk Sailing Expedition, January 27, 1939, box 25, folder 117, Canton, Richard Halliburton Papers.

7. Richard Halliburton to parents, January 23, 1939, as quoted in Richard Halliburton, *Richard Halliburton: His Story of His Life's Adventure, as Told in Letters to His Mother and Father* (New York: Garden City Publishing, 1940), 422.

8. From the Halliburton Trans-Pacific Junk Sailing Expedition, January 27, 1939, box 25, folder 117, Richard Halliburton Papers.

9. From the Halliburton Trans-Pacific Junk Sailing Expedition, January 1, 1939, box 21, folder 4, Richard Halliburton Papers.

10. Gordon Torrey to Michael Blankenship, June 22, 1987, courtesy of the Michael E. Blankenship Collection of the Halliburton Archives, Barrett Library, Rhodes College, Memphis, TN.

11. Ibid.

12. Ibid.

13. Promotional bill, circa 1935, box 26, folder 12, Richard Halliburton Papers.

14. Richard Halliburton to parents, January 23, 1939, box 21, folder 4, and January 27, 1939, box 22, folder 4, Richard Halliburton Papers.

15. From the Halliburton Trans-Pacific Junk Sailing Expedition, January 27, 1939, box 25, folder 117, Richard Halliburton Papers.

16. James Zug, "Sea of Dreams," *Dartmouth Alumni Magazine*, July–August 2014.

17. As quoted in ibid.

18. Richard Halliburton to parents, January 1, 1939, box 21, folder 4, Richard Halliburton Papers.

19. Richard Halliburton to parents, January 23, 1939, box 21, folder 4, Richard Halliburton Papers.

20. From the Halliburton Trans-Pacific Junk Sailing Expedition, January 18, 1939, box 25, folder 117, Richard Halliburton Papers.

21. Don Skemer, "A New View of Richard Halliburton's Sea Dragon," RBSC Manuscripts Division News, March 17, 2014, https://blogs.princeton.edu/manuscripts/2014/03/17/a-new-view-of-richard-halliburtons-sea-dragon/.

22. Richard Halliburton to parents, February 4, 1939, as quoted in Halliburton, *Richard Halliburton*, 424.

23. Richard Halliburton to parents, February 10, 1939, as quoted in Halliburton, *Richard Halliburton*, 426.

24. Ibid.

25. Ibid., 427.

26. Dale E. Collins, "The Royal Road Across the Pacific," *US Naval Institute Proceedings* 66, no. 446 (April 1940): 502.

27. As quoted in Halliburton, *Richard Halliburton*, 425.

28. Richard Halliburton to parents, February 10, 1939, as quoted in Halliburton, *Richard Halliburton*, 427.

29. From the Halliburton Trans-Pacific Junk Sailing Expedition, February 16, 1939, box 25, folder 117, Richard Halliburton Papers.

30. From the Halliburton Trans-Pacific Junk Sailing Expedition, February 10, 1939, box 21, folder 4, Richard Halliburton Papers.

31. John R. Potter to Edward Howell, January 15, 1946, courtesy of the Michael E. Blankenship Collection of the Halliburton Archives.

32. Richard Halliburton to parents, February 10, 1939, as quoted in Halliburton, *Richard Halliburton*, 427.

33. John R. Potter to Edward Howell, January 15, 1946, courtesy of the Michael E. Blankenship Collection of the Halliburton Archives.

34. Halliburton Trans-Pacific Chinese Junk Sailing Expedition, February 16, 1939, box 25, folder 117, Richard Halliburton Papers.

35. Richard Halliburton to parents, February 10, 1939, as quoted in Halliburton, *Richard Halliburton*, 427.

36. Zug, "Sea of Dreams."

37. John R. Potter to Edward Howell, January 15, 1946, courtesy of the Michael E. Blankenship Collection of the Halliburton Archives.

38. From the Halliburton Trans-Pacific Junk Sailing Expedition, February 10, 1939, *Sea Dragon*, box 21, folder 4, Richard Halliburton Papers.

39. Collins, "Royal Road," 501.

40. Richard Halliburton to parents, February 10, 1939, as quoted in Halliburton, *Richard Halliburton*, 427.

41. Gordon Sinclair, *Bright Paths to Adventure* (Toronto: McClelland & Steward, 1945), 93.

42. As quoted in ibid., 92.

43. Ibid., 97.

44. Richard Halliburton to parents, March 1939, box 21, folder 4, Richard Halliburton Papers.

45. Horace Brock, *Flying the Oceans: A Pilot's Story of Pan Am, 1935–1955* (New York: Jason Aronson, 1978), 110.

46. As quoted in Sinclair, *Bright Paths*, 85, 86.

47. Ibid., 98.

48. Richard Halliburton to parents, March 3, 1939, box 21, folder 4, Richard Halliburton Papers.

49. Sinclair, *Bright Paths*, 86.

50. Edward T. Howell Jr. to Michael C. Blankenship, May 2, 1946, courtesy of the Michael E. Blankenship Collection of the Halliburton Archives.

51. Collins, "Royal Road," 505.

52. Ibid.

53. Ibid., 505.

54. Ibid.

55. Ibid., 506.

13. No Trace

1. "No Trace of Halliburton: Writer and Crew of Ten on Chinese Junk Still Unreported," *New York Times*, April 4, 1939.

2. Joe David Brown, "A Rich Blend of Romance and Reality," *Sports Illustrated*, September 9, 1963.

3. Tennessee Williams to Rosina Otte Dakin, as quoted in *The Selected Letters of Tennessee Williams*, vol. 1, *1920–1945* (New York: New Directions, 2002), 173.

4. "An Odysseus Lost in the Mists," *New Castle News*, April 20, 1939.

5. Marilyn Fais, e-mail to author, May 20, 2015.

6. Bobbs-Merrill Company press release, courtesy of the Halliburton Archives, Barrett Library, Rhodes College, Memphis, TN.

7. Wilfred Crowell, "Author Lost: Richard Halliburton Missing 5 Days," *Nevada State Journal*, March 30, 1939.

8. Wilfred Crowell, "Report Concerning Halliburton Trans-Pacific Chinese Junk Expedition Issued by Manager of Expedition," *Nevada State Journal,* April 17, 1939.

9. "Noted Author Still Is Lost in China Junk: Richard Halliburton Sought by Ships in Pacific," *Nevada State Journal,* March 31, 1939.

10. "No Trace," *New York Times.*

11. Donna Roberts, NOAA's Office of Response and Restoration, Emergency Response Division, e-mail to author, March 13, 2015.

12. "Press Halliburton Plea: Friends Want U.S. Cruiser to Hunt for Missing Craft," *New York Times,* April 8, 1939.

13. Ibid.

14. R. K. Turner, Admiral United States Navy, to Edward Howell Jr., May 2, 1946, courtesy of the Michael E. Blankenship Collection of the Halliburton Archives.

15. Gay Beaman to William Alexander Levy, May 2, 1939, courtesy of the Michael E. Blankenship Collection of the Halliburton Archives.

16. Helene Philibert, Head, Special Research Projects, Executive Office of the Secretary Office of Public Information, Navy Department, to Edward T. Howell Jr., September 20, 1946, courtesy of the Halliburton Archives.

17. Crowell, "Report Concerning Halliburton."

18. "Will Seek Halliburton: Navy to Renew Search for the Author Missing in Pacific," *New York Times,* May 16, 1939.

19. Grace K. Ebright, obituary for Richard Halliburton, *Altoona Mirror,* May 6, 1939.

20. Dale E. Collins, "The Royal Road Across the Pacific," *US Naval Institute Proceedings* 66, no. 446 (April 1940): 506.

21. Ibid.

22. "The Press: Last Adventure," *Time,* June 19, 1939, http://content.time.com/time /magazine/article/0,9171,761535,00.html.

23. Bobbs-Merrill Company to editors, courtesy of the Halliburton Archives; "No Trace," *New York Times.*

24. Ibid.

25. Alicia Mooney to William Alexander Levy, May 2, 1939, courtesy of the Michael E. Blankenship Collection of the Halliburton Archives.

26. Ione Mooney to William Alexander Levy, March 14, 1940, courtesy of the Michael E. Blankenship Collection of the Halliburton Archives.

27. "Gordon Torrey Delayed in Hong Kong by Illness," *Bar Harbor Times,* April 20, 1939.

28. Gordon Torrey to Michael Blankenship, August 15, 1987, courtesy of the Michael E. Blankenship Collection of the Halliburton Archives.

29. Gordon Torrey to Michael Blankenship, June 22, 1987, courtesy of the Michael E. Blankenship Collection of the Halliburton Archives.

30. Sarah Betts Alley, e-mail correspondence with author, September 18, 2014.

31. "Halliburton Dead, Court Declares," *New York Times*, October 5, 1939; First National Bank of Memphis et al v. Jefferson Standard Life Insurance Company et al., no. 43735 RD final decree, in the Chancery Court of Shelby County, TN; "Halliburton Left $100,000," *New York Times*, October 13, 1939.

32. "Father Gives Up Hope for Halliburton Sailor," *New York Times*, October 5, 1939.

33. "Halliburton Lost, Skipper of Junk Says upon Rescue," *Kingston Daily Freeman*, October 10, 1939; "Jurors Decide Roaming Writer Is Legally Dead," *Racine Journal Times*, October 5, 1939.

34. William Alexander to Wesley Halliburton, September 26, 1939, courtesy of the Halliburton Archives.

35. Ione Lee Mooney to William Alexander Levy, November 24, 1939, courtesy of the Halliburton Archives.

36. Ibid.

37. Michael E. Blankenship, e-mail to author, December 7, 2014.

38. David Dempsey, In and Out of Books, *New York Times*, May 7, 1950.

39. Wesley Halliburton Sr. to Rev. George Lapp, December 8, 1939, box 45, folder 1a, Richard Halliburton Papers, Manuscripts Division, Department of Rare Books and Special Collections, Princeton University Library, Princeton, NJ.

40. Wesley Halliburton Sr. to Roma Borst Hoff, December 18, 1941, courtesy of the Halliburton Archives.

41. Wesley Halliburton Sr. to Roma Borst Hoff, September 17, 1941, courtesy of the Halliburton Archives.

42. Wesley Halliburton Sr. to Roma Borst Hoff, December 3, 1950, courtesy of the Halliburton Archives.

43. As quoted in Charles Jokstad, *The Captain and the Sea* (New York: Vantage Press, 1967), 187–188.

44. "The Sea's Memento of Halliburton?" *American Weekly*, May 13, 1945; "Halliburton Six Years," *Indiana Gazette*, March 17, 1990.

45. Dale E. Collins, United States Navy Reserves, to Edward Howell Jr., courtesy of the Halliburton Archives.

46. "Sea's Memento," *American Weekly*; "Halliburton Six Years," *Indiana Gazette*, March 17, 1990.

47. John Maize, telephone interview with author, September 24, 2014.

48. Ibid.

49. Juliet Halliburton Davis to William Short, Curator, Halliburton Archives, January 28, 1987, courtesy of the Halliburton Archives.

50. Richard Halliburton to Wesley Halliburton, August 30, 1937, box 21, folder 2, Richard Halliburton Papers.

51. Contract between Nelle Nance Halliburton and Wesley Halliburton and the Bobbs-Merrill Company, 1940, box 26, folder 3, Richard Halliburton Papers.

52. "Richard Halliburton's Life of Adventure: His Letters to his Father and Mother Are Both Engaging and Revealing," *New York Times*, June 30, 1940.

53. Mary Chapman, e-mail correspondence with author, October 28, 2014.

54. J. Penfield Seiberling, as quoted in Halliburton Bell Tower dedication brochure, courtesy of the Halliburton Archives.

55. Richard Halliburton, interview with author, May 14, 2015.

56. Greg Daugherty, "The Last Adventure of Richard Halliburton, the Forgotten Hero of 1930s America," Smithsonian.com, March 25, 2014, www.smithsonianmag.com/history /last-adventure-richard-halliburton-forgotten-hero-1930s-america-180950164/.

57. Susan Sontag, "Homage to Halliburton," *Oxford American*, March/April 2001.

58. Paul Theroux, letter to author, May 20, 2014.

59. John Nicholls Booth, video interview, February 15–16, 1996, courtesy of the Halliburton Archives.

60. "Innocent Abroad," Books, *Time*, July 8, 1940, http://content.time.com/time/magazine /article/0,9171,795086,00.html.

61. Eleanor Kunitz, United States Maritime Commission, to Wesley Halliburton, September 23, 1944, courtesy of the Halliburton Archives.

62. Brown, "A Rich Blend."

63. George Weller, "The Passing of the Last Playboy," *Esquire Magazine*, April 1940, 58.

Bibliography

Published Sources

Adelson, Andrea. "Buyer Emerges for Neglected Modern Masterpiece." *Laguna Beach Independent*, December 11, 2011.

Air Travel News 3, no. 12 (December 1929).

Alexander, William B. "House for Writer Affords Privacy and Spectacular View." *Architectural Record*, October 1938.

Allan, Tony. *The Glamour Years: Paris, 1919–1940*. New York: Gallery Books, 1977.

American Weekly. "The Sea's Memento of Halliburton?" May 13, 1945.

Architectural Forum, eds. *The Book of Small Houses*. New York: Simon & Schuster, 1936.

Axtell, James. *The Making of Princeton University: From Woodrow Wilson to the Present*. Princeton, NJ: Princeton University Press, 2006.

Bakersfield Californian. "Halliburton Fans Get New Life of Their Hero." December 25, 1965.

Bar Harbor Times. "Gordon Torrey Delayed in Hong Kong by Illness," April 20, 1939.

———. "Gordon Torrey Sailed for Home." January 26, 1939.

Barth, John. *The Last Voyage of Somebody the Sailor*. Boston: Little, Brown, 1991.

Basinger, Jeanine. *Silent Stars*. New York: Alfred A. Knopf, 1999.

Beebe, William. "Adventures in Exploration at the World's End." *Mentor*, April 1925, 3–22.

Beinhorn, Elly. *Flying Girl*. London: Geoffrey Bles, 1935.

Benedict, Burton, et al. *The Anthropology of World's Fairs: San Francisco's Panama Pacific International Exposition of 1915*. London: Lowrie Museum of Anthropology and Scholar Press, 1983.

Besinger, Curtis. *Working with Mr. Wright: What It Was Like*. Cambridge: Cambridge University Press, 1997.

Blankenship, Michael E. "A Fellow Traveler." *Advocate*, July 18, 1989.

Bly, Nellie. *Nellie Bly's Book: Around the World in 72 Days*. Edited by Ira Peck. Brookfield, CT: Twenty-First Century Books, 1998.

Boston Post. "Believe Wreck Sighted Is Junk Sea Dragon." January 6, 1940.

Brainerd Daily Dispatch. "Feats Replete in Halliburton 18 Years' Saga." June 22, 1939.

Brandt, Anthony. "The 100 Greatest Adventure Books of All Time." *National Geographic,* July 2001.

Breashears, David, and Audrey Salkeld. *Last Climb: The Legendary Everest Expeditions of George Mallory.* Washington, DC: National Geographic Society, 1999.

Brock, Horace. *Flying the Oceans: A Pilot's Story of Pan Am, 1935–1955.* New York: Jason Aronson, 1978.

Bronski, Michael. *A Queer History of the United States.* Boston: Beacon Press, 2011.

Brooke, Lady Margaret. *My Life in Sarawak.* London: Methuen, 1913.

Brooke, Rupert. *Letters from America.* Preface by Henry James. New York: Charles Scribner's Sons, 1916.

———. *The Poetical Works.* Edited by Geoffrey Keynes. London & Boston: Faber & Faber, 1985.

Brown, Don. "Richard Halliburton Finds Human Slavery in French Africa—but It Doesn't Work." *Chicago Daily Tribune,* n.d. Box 25, folder 7, Richard Halliburton Papers, Manuscripts Division, Department of Rare Books and Special Collections, Princeton University Library, Princeton, NJ.

Brown, Joe David. "A Rich Blend of Romance and Reality." *Sports Illustrated,* September 9, 1963.

Bruccoli, Matthew J. *Some Sort of Epic Grandeur: The Life of F. Scott Fitzgerald.* 2nd rev. ed. Columbia, SC: University of South Carolina Press, 2002.

Burlingame, Margaret R. "The Laguna Beach Group." *American Magazine of Art* 24, no. 4 (1932): 259–66.

Cameron, May. "Letters of Richard Halliburton Show He Was Eternal Youth." *New York Post,* July 3, 1940.

Carlton, Jim. "South Laguna's Forgotten Giant: 50 Years After His Death at Sea, Adventurer Halliburton's Exploits Are as Obscured as His Mansion." *Los Angeles Times,* September 3, 1989.

Cart, Michael. "The Romance of Travel." *Booklist,* September 15, 2009.

Cashman, Sean Dennis. *America in the Twenties and Thirties: The Olympian Age of Franklin Delano Roosevelt.* New York: New York University Press, 1989.

Chalmer, Dionne. "Rhodes' Halliburton Tower Turns 50." *Commercial Appeal* (Memphis, TN), December 12, 2012.

Champney, Lizzie W. *Three Vassar Girls Abroad: Rambles of Three College Girls on a Vacation Trip Through France and Spain for Amusement and Instruction with Their Haps and Mishaps.* Boston: Estes & Lauriat, 1883.

Chauncey, George. *Gay New York: Gender, Urban Culture, and the Making of the Gay Male World, 1890–1940.* New York: Basic Books, 1994.

Christian Science Monitor. "The Return of the 'Horizon Chaser': Another Generation Can Now Enjoy a Classic Travel Tale from Explorer Richard Halliburton." October 31, 2000.

Churchill, Allen. *The Literary Decade: A Panorama of the Writers, Publishers, and Litterateurs of the 1920s.* Englewood Cliffs, NJ: Prentice-Hall, 1971.

Clymer, Adam. "Yucatan's Chichen Itza: A Halliburton 'Marvel.'" *New York Times,* March 13, 1983.

Coben, Stanley. *Rebellion Against Victorianism: The Impetus for Cultural Change in 1920s America.* New York: Oxford University Press, 1991.

Cole, Fred C. "The Partial-Payment Swim." *New Yorker,* January 4, 1930.

Collins, Dale E. "The Royal Road Across the Pacific." *US Naval Institute Proceedings* 66, no. 446 (April 1940).

Conaway, Dan. "A Memphis Marvel." *Daily News,* June 3, 2011.

Conaway, James. *The Smithsonian: 150 Years of Adventure, Discovery, and Wonder.* New York: Alfred A. Knopf, 1995.

Cortese, James. *Richard Halliburton's Royal Road.* Memphis: White Rose Press, 1989.

Crouch, Tom D. *Wings: A History of Aviation from Kites to the Space Age.* Washington, DC: Smithsonian National Air & Space Museum/W. W. Norton, 2003.

Crowell, Wilfred. "Author Lost: Richard Halliburton Missing 5 Days." *Nevada State Journal,* March 30, 1939.

———. "Report Concerning Halliburton Trans-Pacific Chinese Junk Expedition Issued by Manager of Expedition." *Nevada State Journal,* April 17, 1939.

Dartmouth. "Potter '38 Sails Pacific in Junk with Richard Halliburton, Famed Adventurer." November 29, 1938.

Daugherty, Greg. "The Last Adventure of Richard Halliburton, the Forgotten Hero of 1930s America." Smithsonian.com, March 25, 2014. www.smithsonianmag.com/history/last-adventure-richard-halliburton-forgotten-hero-1930s-america-180950164/.

Davies, Richard. "The Mysterious and Strange End of Richard Halliburton: What Happened to the Most Famous Man in America?" Yahoo! Voices, April 3, 2010. http://voices.yahoo.com/the-mysterious-strange-end-richard-halliburton-5771006.html. Site discontinued.

Dayton, Dorothy. "Richard Halliburton, 'Prince of Lovers,' Talks about Women and Love." *Illustrated Love Magazine,* March 1930.

DeFaa, Chip. "On the Trail of Richard Halliburton '21: A Young Alumnus Searches for the Man Behind the Legend." *Princeton Alumni Weekly,* May 13, 1973.

Delany, Paul. *The Neo-Pagans-Rupert Brooke and the Ordeal of Youth.* New York: Free Press, 1987.

Dempsey, David. In and Out of Books. *New York Times,* May 7, 1950.

Diamond, Barbara. "Work on the Halliburton House Will Resume." *Laguna Beach Coastline Pilot,* April 26, 2012.

Doubleday, F. N. *The Memoirs of a Publisher*. New York: Doubleday, 1927.

Douglas-Hamilton, James. *Roof of the World: Man's First Flight over Everest*. Edinburgh: Mainstream Publishing, 1983.

Eade, Philip. *Sylvia: Queen of the Headhunters*. London: Phoenix, 2008.

Edmonds, I. G. "The Mystery of the Hong Kong Sea Dragon." *Pacific Stars and Stripes*, March 23, 1956.

Edwards, Justin D. *Exotic Journeys: Exploring the Erotics of U.S. Travel Literature, 1840–1930*. Hanover, NH: University Press of New England, 2001.

Ellenberger, Allan R. *Ramon Novarro: A Biography of the Silent Film Idol, 1899–1968*. Jefferson, NC: McFarland, 1999.

Fairbanks, Douglas, Jr. *The Fairbanks Album, Drawn from the Family Archives*. New York: NY Graphic Society, 1975.

First National Bank of Memphis et al. v. Jefferson Standard Life Insurance Company et al. No. 43735 RD final decree. In the Chancery Court of Shelby County, TN.

Fitzgerald, F. Scott. *Correspondence of F. Scott Fitzgerald*. Edited by Matthew J. Bruccoli and Margaret M. Duggan. NY: Random House, 1980.

Fone, Byrne. *Homophobia: A History*. New York: Metropolitan Books, 2000.

Ford, Corey C. "The Adventure Racket." *Vanity Fair*, July 1929.

Fox, Jim. "Cruise Offers Chance for Dip in Panama Canal." *Winnipeg Free Press*, May 25, 2001.

Franck, Harry A. *Sky Roaming Above Two Continents: An Aerial Cruise, with Many Landings in the Countries and Islands That Circle the Caribbean*. New York: Grosset & Dunlap, 1938.

———. *Vagabonding Down the Andes: Being the Narrative of a Journey, Chiefly Afoot, from Panama to Buenos Aires*. Garden City, NY: Garden City Publishing, 1917.

———. *A Vagabond in Sovietland: America's Perennial Rambler Goes Tourist*. New York: Grosset & Dunlap, 1935.

———. *Zone Policeman 88: A Close Range Study of the Panama Canal and Its Workers*. New York: Century, 1913.

Franklin, Mortimer. "Who Said 'No More Thrills?' Halliburton's 'Royal Road to Romance' Leads Him to Hollywood!" *Screenland*, April–October 1933. Internet Archive. https://archive.org/stream/screenland2627unse/screenland2627unse_djvu.txt.

Fussell, Paul. *Abroad: British Literary Traveling Between the Wars*. New York: Oxford University Press, 1980.

Futter, Walter. *India Speaks, with Richard Halliburton, Author of "The Royal Road to Romance," Etc*. New York: Grosset & Dunlap, 1933.

Gelernter, David. *1939: The Lost World of the Fair*. New York: Free Press, 1995.

Giliam, Ronald. "Around the World in the Flying Carpet." *Aviation History* 14 (May 5, 2004).

———. "Moye Stephens Piloted More than 100 Types of Aircraft and Flew Around the World in the Flying Carpet." *Aviation History* 9, no. 6 (July 1999).

Glass, Loren Daniel. *Authors Inc: Literary Celebrity in the Modern United States, 1880–1980.* New York: NYU Press, 2004.

Goldberg, David J. *Discontented America: The United States in the 1920s.* Baltimore: Johns Hopkins University Press, 1999.

Graham, Stephen. *The Gentle Art of Tramping.* London: Robert Holden, 1927. Reprinted by Holmes Press, 2011.

Grant, R. G. *Flight: 100 Years of Aviation.* New York: Dorling Kinderseley Publishing, 2002.

Greene, Graham. *Journey Without Maps.* New York: Penguin Group, 2006.

Guillermoprieto, Alma. "Secrets of the Maya Otherworld." *National Geographic*, August 2013.

Hall, Mordaunt. Review of *India Speaks*, directed by Walter Futter. *New York Times*, May 8, 1933.

Halliburton, Richard. *The Complete Book of Marvels.* Indianapolis: Bobbs-Merrill, 1937.

———. *The Flying Carpet.* Indianapolis: Bobbs-Merrill, 1934.

———. *The Glorious Adventure.* Indianapolis: Bobbs-Merrill, 1927.

———. "Half a Mile of History." *Readers Digest* 31 (October 1937).

———. "I've Eaten Christmas Dinner All Around the World." *Cosmopolitan*, January 1936.

———. *New Worlds to Conquer.* Indianapolis: Bobbs-Merrill, 1929.

———. "The Place Where the Sun Is Tied." *Ladies' Home Journal*, June 1929.

———. "Richard Halliburton Answers His Critics." *Five Star Weekly*, October 1936.

———. *Richard Halliburton: His Story of His Life's Adventure, as Told in Letters to His Mother and Father.* New York: Garden City Publishing, 1940.

———. *The Romantic World of Richard Halliburton.* Indianapolis: Bobbs-Merrill, 1961.

———. *The Royal Road to Romance.* Indianapolis: Bobbs-Merrill, 1925.

———. *Seven League Boots.* Indianapolis: Bobbs-Merrill, 1935.

———. "The S.S. Richard Halliburton." *Ladies' Home Journal*, June 1929.

Hamilton, John Maxwell. *Journalism's Roving Eye: A History of American Foreign Reporting.* Baton Rouge: Louisiana State University Press, 2009.

Harrington, Mildred. "Dick Halliburton Has Followed the Royal Road to Romance." *American Women's Magazine*, October 1926.

Hart, Kelli. "Home for Sale of Adventurer Lost at Sea." *Orange County Register*, March 10, 2011.

Haskin, Frederic Jennings. *The Panama Canal.* New York: Doubleday, 1914.

Heaver, Stuart. "Richard Halliburton: The Hero Time Forgot." *South China Morning Post*, March 22, 2014. www.scmp.com/magazines/post-magazine/article/1453193/richard -halliburton-hero-time-forgot.

Hemingway, Ernest. *Ernest Hemingway: Selected Letters, 1917–1961.* Edited by Carlos Baker. New York: Charles Scribner's Sons, 1981.

Herald Statesman (Yonkers, NY). "W.B. Feakins, Lecture Bureau Manager Dies." March 26, 1956.

Hoffman, Frederick J. *The 20s: American Writing in the Postwar Decade*. New York: Free Press, 1965.

Horwitz, Tony, ed. *The Devil May Care: 50 Intrepid Americans and Their Quest for the Unknown*. Oxford: Oxford University Press, 2003.

Independent (Helena, MT). "Halliburton on Russia." January 2, 1935.

Jackson, Nancy Beth. "Memory of Lincoln's Assassination Lingers About Island Fortress." *New York Times*, October 4, 1970.

Jarrell, John W. "No Barber Shops Open." *State Journal* (Topeka, KS), November 5, 1932.

Jessen, Gene Nora. *The Powder Puff Derby of 1929: The True Story of the First Women's Cross-Country Air Race*. Naperville, IL: Sourcebooks, 2002.

Jewell, Richard B. *The Golden Age of Cinema: Hollywood, 1929–1945*. Malden, MA: Blackwell Publishing, 2007.

Jokstad, Charles. *The Captain and the Sea*. New York: Vantage Press, 1967.

Kelly, Gretchen. "Richard Halliburton—in Search of Adventure." *Metrosource*, Spring 1998.

Kennedy, David M. *Freedom from Fear: The American People in Depression and War, 1929–1945*. Oxford: Oxford University Press, 2001.

Kessler, Lauren. *The Happy Bottom Riding Club: The Life and Times of Pancho Barnes*. New York: Random House, 2000.

Ketchum, Richard M. *Will Rogers: The Man and His Times*. New York: American Heritage Books, 1973.

Kleid, Beth. "Philanthropist William Alexander Receives by Giving." *Los Angeles Times*, December 29, 1989.

Landsburg, Alan. *In Search of Missing Persons*. New York: Alfred A. Knopf, 1927.

Lethbridge Herald (Alberta, Canada). "Bizarre Experiences Recounted by Richard Halliburton." June 17, 1932.

Lindbergh, Charles. "To Bogota and Back by Air: Narrative of a 9,500-Mile Flight from Washington, over Thirteen Latin-American Countries and Return, in the Single-Seater Airplane 'Spirit of St. Louis.'" *National Geographic*, May 1928.

Linkletter, Art, and Dean Jennings. *Confessions of a Happy Man: The Heartwarming Story of a Fabulous Showman*. New York: Giant Cardinal, 1960.

Lipsyte, Robert. "The Masculinity Chart." *Horn Book Magazine*, September–October 2007.

Lock Haven Express. "Notable Lecturer Coming to School: Richard Halliburton Will Speak at High School Early Next April." December 22, 1927.

Lollar, Michael. "TV Execs Shrug at Richard Halliburton's Reality." *Commercial Appeal*, February 1, 2010.

Los Angeles Times. "Halliburton: Adventurer's Legend, Mansion Are All but (Forgotten)." September 3, 1989.

Lylburn, Margaret. "Richard On-the-Go Halliburton Writing in Weston; Tosses Off His World Records to Interviewer." *Bridgeport (CT) Post*, June 29, 1932.

Mann, William J. *Behind the Screen: How Gays and Lesbians Shaped Hollywood, 1910–1969*. New York: Penguin Books, 2001.

Matthews, Herbert L. "The Road that Leads from Devil's Island." *New York Times*, November 5, 1933.

Max, Gerry. *Horizon Chasers: The Lives and Adventures of Richard Halliburton and Paul Mooney*. Jefferson, NC: McFarland, 2007.

———. "Richard Halliburton and Thomas Wolfe: When Youth Kept Open House." *North Carolina Literary Review* 5 (1996).

McClure, Hal. "Hangover House Really Haunted? Villagers Report Flashing Lights at Fabulous Home." *Cedar Rapids Gazette*, January 20, 1957.

McConnell, Curt. *Coast to Coast by Automobile: The Pioneering Trips, 1899–1908*. Stanford, CA: Stanford University Press, 2000.

McCullough, David. *The Path Between the Seas: The Creation of the Panama Canal, 1870–1914*. New York: Touchstone Books, 1977.

Memphis Commercial Appeal. "Left Home with $5; Returns as a Millionaire." July 16, 1932.

Mickadeit, Frank. "Laguna Halts Another Historical Home Remodel." *Orange County Register*, April 18, 2012.

Moore, Lucy. *Anything Goes: A Biography of the Roaring Twenties*. New York: Overlook Press, 2010.

Morris, Charles E., III. "Richard Halliburton's Bearded Tales." *Quarterly Journal of Speech* 95, no. 2 (May 2009): 123–147.

National Geographic. "Underwater Secrets of the Maya." August 2013. http://ngm.nationalgeographic.com/2013/08/sacred-cenotes/nicklen-schwarz-photography#/11-snorkeler-floats-las-calaveras-cenote-670.jpg.

Nevada State Journal. "Noted Author Still Is Lost in China Junk: Richard Halliburton Sought by Ships in Pacific." March 31, 1939.

New Castle News. "An Odysseus Lost in the Mists." April 20, 1939.

New York Times. "An American Swims the Hellespont." September 27, 1925.

———. "Big Canal Radio Station: Its Communication Field Will Cover Thousands of Miles." August 10, 1913.

———. "Catholic Actors Meet: 450 Persons Present at Monthly Session at Astor." January 21, 1933.

———. "Chinese Pirates Seize Vessel, but Lose Fight." November 1922.

———. "Colombia Waits Word of German Girl Flier." June 5, 1932.

———. "Father Gives Up Hope for Halliburton Sailor." October 5, 1939.

———. "Fear Halliburton Died in Turkish Sea: Letter Tells of Attempt of Princeton Graduate to Swim the Hellespont." September 6, 1925.

———. "Finds Halliburton Safe: Father Gets Letter Telling of Author's Swim in Hellespont." September 7, 1925.

———. "Halliburton and His Pilot Fail In Effort to Fly over Everest." January 12, 1939.

———. "Halliburton Dead, Court Declares." October 5, 1939.

———. "Halliburton Left $100,000." October 13, 1939.

———. "Halliburton Meets Alligator in Canal: Writer on Panama Swim Climbs Into Launch and Rifleman Kills Saurian." April 21, 1928.

———. "Halliburton Starts Panama Canal Swim: Writer Makes Less Than Four Miles in First Effort—Faces Alligators Today." August 15, 1928.

———. "Halliburton to Sail Junk Across Pacific: Author and Three Companions Will Start from Hong Kong." October 8, 1938.

———. "Halliburton to Swim the Panama Canal: Plans Start This Week—Governor Warns Him Against Alligators and Typhoid." August 14, 1928.

———. "Halliburton's Elephant Finds Troubles in Alps." July 22, 1935.

———. "Halliburton's Gift Will Aid Princeton." October 16, 1966.

———. "Halliburton's Wanderings." December 4, 1932.

———. "Mr. Halliburton Borrows an Elephant from a Zoo." December 8, 1935.

———. "Mr. Halliburton Plays Robinson Crusoe." December 15, 1929.

———. "Names Peak for Balboa: Halliburton Says He Found Pacific Discoverer's Hill." September 7, 1928.

———. "No Trace of Halliburton: Writer and Crew of Ten on Chinese Junk Still Unreported." April 4, 1939.

———. "On the Screen Horizon: Richard Halliburton's Book, 'The Royal Road to Romance,' Will Be Made into a Film by Fox." July 27, 1930.

———. "Open Gatun Locks Just for Halliburton: Officials Use Same Power to Lift Swimmer as for 44,799 Ton Battleship." August 17, 1928.

———. "Press Halliburton Plea: Friends Want U.S. Cruiser to Hunt for Missing Craft." April 8, 1939.

———. "Princeton to Found Halliburton Library: Writer Willed Estate to Buy Geographical Material." October 16, 1939.

———. "Richard Halliburton's Life of Adventure: His Letters to his Father and Mother Are Both Engaging and Revealing." June 30, 1940.

———. "Says Russia Ousted Him: Halliburton Declares He Talked to Czar's Executioner." January 13, 1935.

———. "Tells of Swimming the Hellespont: Richard Halliburton, Author and Explorer, Returns After Romantic Wandering." December 20, 1925.

———. "3 Alligators Miss Halliburton in Canal: Are Shot in Gaillard Cut and Swimmer Reaches Pedro Miguel Locks." August 23, 1928.

———. "To Try Everest Flight: Writer Announces He Will Seek to Take Plane over Peak in Fall." June 16, 1932.

———. "Will Seek Halliburton: Navy to Renew Search for the Author Missing in Pacific." May 16, 1939.

———. "Wireless Now Open with Canal Zone: First Daylight and Unrelayed Message from New Government Station Reaches Arlington." May 4, 1915.

———. "Young German Aviatrix Finds Thrills in India: Elly Beinhorn, Flying Around the World, Does Stunts for a Maharajah and Chats with Tagore." April 3, 1992.

New Yorker. "In Town and Out." Tables for Two, July 9, 1938.

———. Review of *The Flying Carpet.* November 12, 1932.

———. The Talk of the Town. November 8, 1930.

Newport News. "Books on Russia in Demand Since Roosevelt Recognized Land of Soviets and Caviar." November 26, 1933.

Nichols, Beverley. *The Star Spangled Manner.* London: Jonathan Cape, 1928.

Oakland Tribune. "It's Here! Bay Area's World's Fair Opens Gates; Oakland Revelers Jam City Streets, Halt Parade." February 18, 1938.

Orange County Register. "Hangover: Owner Was Lost at Sea Shortly After Home Was Built." March 13, 2011.

Ostrowski, Donald. "A Reconsideration of Richard Halliburton's Interview with P.Z. Ermakov as Evidence for the Murder of the Romanovs." *Russian History/Histoire Russe* 25, no. 3 (1999): 301–328.

Panama Canal Record: Official Publication of the Panama Canal. Vol. 12.

Parsons, Dana. "He Found No Treasure, but the Quest Was Well Worth It." *Los Angeles Times,* April 16, 1997.

Retired Trans World Airline Pilot's Magazine. "Moye W. Stephens, Richard Halliburton and the Flying Carpet." April 1996.

Rick, Helen. Review of *Second Book of Marvels. Jefferson City Post Tribune,* December 5, 1938.

Rogers, Betty. *Will Rogers: The Story of His Life.* Garden City, NY: Garden City Publishing, 1941.

Root, Jonathan. *Halliburton: The Magnificent Myth.* New York: Coward-McCann, 1965.

Sarawak Gazette. "The Ranee Describes Her Adventure." May 2, 1932.

Schillinger, Liesl. "Walk, Don't Run: Travel by Foot Leaves an Imprint on the Memory, and Slows Down Time for a Precious Moment." *New York Times Style Magazine,* May 11, 2014.

Schlossberg, Linda. "Introduction: Rites of Passing." In *Passing: Identity and Interpretation in Sexuality, Race, and Religion,* edited by Maria Carla Sánchez and Linda Schlossberg. New York: New York University Press, 2001.

Schultz, Barbara Hunter. *Pancho: The Biography of Florence Lowe Barnes.* Lancaster, CA: Little Buttes Publishing, 1996.

Schwartz, David M. "On the Royal Road to Adventure with 'Daring Dick.'" *Smithsonian,* March 1989.

Sebastian, Scott. "The Halliburton House." *South Laguna Civic Association Bulletin* (South Laguna, CA), Fall 2010.

Shariatmadari, David. Review of *Seven League Boots* by Richard Halliburton. *Guardian,* February 1, 2013.

Shultz, Barbara Hunter. *Flying Carpets, Flying Wings: The Biography of Moye W. Stephens.* Lancaster, CA: Little Buttes Publishing, 2010.

Sinclair, Gordon. *Bright Paths to Adventure*. Toronto: McClelland & Steward, 1945.

Skemer, Don. "A New View of Richard Halliburton's Sea Dragon." RBSC Manuscripts Division News, March 17, 2014, https://blogs.princeton.edu/manuscripts/2014/03/17/a-new-view-of-richard-halliburtons-sea-dragon/.

Smith, James R. "Golden Gate International Exposition: SFs Final World's Fair—Part II." *Guidelines: Newsletter for San Francisco City Guides and Sponsors*, accessed November 20, 2015. www.sfcityguides.org/public_guidelines.html?article=861&submitted=TRUE.

Snow, Philip. *The Fall of Hong Kong: Britain, China and the Japanese Occupation*. New Haven, CT: Yale University Press, 2003.

Sonnichsen, Augusta, "Ripley Rival: 7 League Boots." *El Paso Herald Post*, December 6, 1935.

Sontag, Susan. "Homage to Halliburton." *Oxford American*, March/April 2001.

Sullivan, Andrew. *Virtually Normal: An Argument About Homosexuality*. New York: Alfred A. Knopf, 1995.

Syracuse Herald. "Enter a New Ulysses." March 4, 1928.

Tafel, Edgar. *About Wright: An Album of Recollections by Those Who Knew Frank Lloyd Wright*. New York: John Wiley & Sons, 1993.

Tamagne, Florence. *A History of Homosexuality in Europe: Berlin, London, Paris, 1919–1939*. Vol. 1. New York: Algora Publishing, 2004.

Thomasville Times-Enterprise. "Alligators and Sharks Menace Author Now on Atlantic-Pacific Swim." August 22, 1928.

Thompson, J. Eric S. *Maya Archaeologist*. Norman, OK: University of Oklahoma Press, 1963.

Thompson, Ralph. Books of the Times. *New York Times*, July 3, 1930.

Time. "Fair-Haired Carpeteer." Books, November 14, 1932. http://content.time.com/time/magazine/article/0,9171,847103,00.html.

———. "Innocent Abroad." Books, July 8, 1940. http://content.time.com/time/magazine/article/0,9171,795086,00.html.

———. "The Press: Last Adventure." June 19, 1939. http://content.time.com/time/magazine/article/0,9171,761535,00.html.

Titusville Herald. "Vivid Travel Story Told at Woman's Club: Richard Halliburton Entertains with Accounts of His Adventures to Lands of Romance; Gives Holiday Dinner Dance." December 12, 1927.

Townsend, Guy. "Richard Halliburton: The Forgotten Myth—a Brief, Endless Journey on the Road to Romance." *Memphis Magazine*, August 1977.

Tucson Daily Citizen. "Halliburton Wreck Story Is Discounted: Parents of Famed Explorer Visiting in City Say Junk Not Right One." February 10, 1945.

Vogel, Claire Marie. *Laguna Beach*. Images of America. Chicago: Arcadia Publishing, 2009.

Weller, George. "The Passing of the Last Playboy." *Esquire*, April 1940.

Winslow, Anne Goodwin. *The Dwelling Place*. New York: Alfred A. Knopf, 1943.

Unpublished Sources

Alexander, William B. "Meanderings, or The Many Faces of William Alexander." Unpublished manuscript. Author's collection.

Booth, John Nicholls. Video interview, February 14–15, 1996. Courtesy of the Halliburton Archives, Barrett Library, Rhodes College, Memphis, TN.

Conran, Thomas R. Thomas R. Conran to Richard Halliburton, Bobbs-Merrill, April 24, 1925. Courtesy of the Halliburton Archives, Barrett Library, Rhodes College, Memphis, TN.

Davis, Juliet Halliburton. Juliet Halliburton Davis to William Short, Curator, Halliburton Archives, June 28, 1987. Courtesy of the Halliburton Archives, Barrett Library, Rhodes College, Memphis, TN.

Halliburton, Wesley, Sr. and Dr. Roma Borst Hoff. Correspondence. Courtesy of the Halliburton Archives, Barrett Library, Rhodes College, Memphis, TN.

Link, Harold B. Harold B. Link, Manager of the Breakfast Club, Hollywood Roosevelt Hotel, to Richard Halliburton, March 13, 1933. Courtesy of the Halliburton Archives, Barrett Library, Rhodes College, Memphis, TN.

Philibert, Helene. Helene Philibert, Head of Special Research Projects, Executive Office of the Secretary Office of Public Information, Navy Department, to Edward T. Howell Jr., September 20, 1946. Courtesy of the Halliburton Archives, Barrett Library, Rhodes College, Memphis, TN.

Richard Halliburton Memorial Tower Dedication Program. October 17, 1962. Courtesy of the Halliburton Archives, Barrett Library, Rhodes College, Memphis, TN.

"The Richard Halliburton Memorial Tower. Southwestern Memphis. MCMLXII" (brochure). 1963. Courtesy of the Halliburton Archives, Barrett Library, Rhodes College, Memphis, TN.

Stephens, Moye W., Jr. Interview by Michael Blankenship, September 20, 1986. Courtesy of the Michael E. Blankenship Collection of the Halliburton Archives, Barrett Library, Rhodes College, Memphis, TN.

Author Interviews & Correspondence

Sarah Betts Alley

Michael E. Blankenship

Harriet D. Chapman

Mary Chapman

Margaret Devault

Jennifer Fais

Marilyn Fais

Richard Halliburton

Irvine O. Hockaday Jr.

John Maize
Wayne Moran
Cathy Pond
Virginia Reese
Donna Roberts
William Short
Don C. Skemer
Paul Theroux

Archives and Historical Societies

Bar Harbor Historical Society, Mount Desert Island, ME.
Halliburton Archives, Barrett Library, Rhodes College, Memphis, TN.
Mount Desert Island Historical Society, Mount Desert Island, ME.
North East Harbor Library, Mount Desert Island, ME.
Rauner Special Collections Library, Dartmouth University, Hancock, MA.
Richard Halliburton Papers, Manuscripts Division, Department of Rare Books and Special
    Collections, Princeton University Library, Princeton, NJ.
St. Louis Park Historical Society, St. Louis Park, MN.

Index